GOVERNORS STATE UNIVERSITY

W9-AAM-123

3 1611 00090 1758

Early Care and Education for Children in Poverty

SUNY Series, Youth Social Services, Schooling, and Public Policy
    Barry M. Franklin and José R. Rosario, editors
SUNY Series, Early Childhood Education: Inquiries and Insights
    Mary A. Jensen, editor

Edited by
W. STEVEN BARNETT
SARANE SPENCE BOOCOCK

Early Care and Education for Children in Poverty

*Promises, Programs, and
Long-Term Results*

GOVERNORS STATE UNIVERSITY
UNIVERSITY PARK
IL 60466

STATE UNIVERSITY OF NEW YORK PRESS

LC 4091 .E24 1998

Early care and education for
children in poverty

Published by
State University of New York Press, Albany

© 1998 State University of New York

All rights reserved

Printed in the United States of America

No part of this book may be used or reproduced in any manner
whatsoever without written permission. No part of this book may be
stored in a retrieval system or transmitted in any form by any means
including electronic, electrostatic, magnetic tape, mechanical,
photocopying, recording, or otherwise without the prior permission in
writing of the publisher.

For information, address the State University of New York Press,
State University Plaza, Albany, NY 12246

Production design by David Ford
Marketing by Anne M. Valentine

Library of Congress Cataloging-in-Publication Data

Early care and education for children in poverty : promises, programs,
    and long-term results / edited by W. Steven Barnett, Sarane Spence
    Boocock.
        p.   cm. — (SUNY series, youth, social services, schooling,
    and public policy) (SUNY series, early childhood education)
      Includes bibliographical references (p. 273) and index.
      ISBN 0-7914-3619-5 (HC : acid free). — ISBN 0-7914-3620-9 (PB :
    acid free)
        1. Poor children—Education (Early childhood)—United States.
    2. Poor children—Services for—United States.   3. Child care—
    United States.   I. Barnett, W. Steven.   II. Boocock, Sarane
    Spence.   III. Series.   IV. Series: SUNY series, early childhood
    education.
    LC4091.E24   1998
    371.93'08694—dc21   97-17192
                                                                    CIP

10 9 8 7 6 5 4 3 2 1

Contents

Introduction

Much of the world is in the midst of a revolution in the care and education of young children. In the United States prior to 1960, few children under age five attended education programs and it was rare for them to be cared for outside their homes for more than a few hours a day. Thirty years later, most children under age five receive substantial care and education outside the home, and over 80 percent experience some nonparental care and education (West, Hausken, & Collins, 1993). In some other industrial nations, the percentage receiving early care and education (ECE) outside the home is even higher, and strong trends toward more nonparental ECE are apparent in many preindustrial nations, as well.

There is no single force behind this social revolution. Long-term changes in income, family structure, the nature of work, and social norms regarding the appropriate roles of men and women have combined to vastly increase the demand for nonparental early care and education worldwide (Barnett, 1993; Hernandez, 1993). Although the rise in maternal employment is an important factor, increased demand for ECE is only partially due to the increased number of children whose mothers work outside the home. Increased demand for ECE for children whose mothers are not employed outside the home has resulted from increased incomes and shifts toward producing higher-quality (better educated) children as the number of children per family falls. All of the relevant trends seem likely to continue for some time so that further increases in the demand for ECE are projected, and it seems likely that ECE will become a nearly universal experience in industrial countries in the near future with the rest of the world not far behind.

This revolution in the care and education of young children poses serious challenges, not the least of which is how to take advantage of the opportunities it offers. We have chosen to focus this book on the opportunities for ECE to improve the lives of poor children and their families. For decades ECE has been viewed as a promising approach to improving the lives of children in poverty, not just immediately, but permanently. The hope has been that providing higher-quality ECE than parents could offer on their own would lead to persistent improvements in child development. In addition, it has been argued that subsidized child care would increase maternal employment and earnings thereby raising family income and improving the child's home environment. After thirty years of research much remains to be learned about these promises, but the research presented in this book firmly establishes that ECE can fulfill some important promises. However, well-designed and well-implemented policies and programs are required to keep those promises.

This book also provides some insights into what it means for policies and programs to be well designed and well implemented, how much might be gained from improvements in quality, and where increased research is urgently needed to provide information for policy makers. For example, the evidence indicates that Head Start is adequate in providing substantial long-term benefits for children, but it seems likely that much larger benefits could be produced if Head Start had the resources to improve its quality. How much of an increase in employment and earnings would occur if there were large subsidies for high-quality child care available to all parents or some subset of parents is unknown; it has yet to be studied by methods that permit strong inferences. International comparisons suggest that a well-established system of early care and education can improve children's school success and that effective early-education initiatives are feasible even in nations with relatively low per-capita incomes. Analysis of such policies must be informed by an understanding of the complex social system in which they are embedded. For example, child-care programs can have substantial effects on employment and earnings, but these effects are likely to be quite different from country to country.

Many early-childhood educators and children's advocates consider the long-term positive effects of ECE for children in poverty to have been well established years ago. Yet, even a cursory survey of recent publications, public opinion, and politics reveals much disagreement. Confusion and uncertainty regarding the long-term effects of ECE on the disadvantaged have impeded the development of wise ECE policies in public education, Head Start, child care, and welfare reform. This book was developed to help move the field forward by clarifying what is known, contributing new knowledge, and identifying directions for future research that will support the development of better ECE policy.

Support from The David and Lucile Packard Foundation and the Graduate School of Education at Rutgers—The State University of New Jersey allowed us to solicit new research papers and to bring the authors together to discuss their work at the Ninth Annual Rutgers Invitational Symposium on Education (RISE). Although many critical issues regarding long-term benefits of ECE for children in poverty cross disciplinary and professional boundaries, communication across these boundaries is rare. Thus, one of our major objectives was to involve researchers from a wide range of disciplines—education, economics, demography, sociology, psychology, and family and human development—who share an interest in the long-term effects of ECE on poor children and their families.

The book begins with a series of reviews that provide general overviews of research on the long-term effects of ECE. In the first chapter, Steve Barnett (an economist) surveys research on the long-term effects of early-childhood programs on child development and school success. He devotes considerable attention to identifying common methodological difficulties, design flaws, and other limitations that should be taken into account in evaluating the results of research and deriving policy conclusions. Barnett's review indicates that the evidence displays a consistent pattern of long-term effects on disadvantaged children's academic achievement and school success.

This pattern does not extend to IQ. Some evidence suggests that long-term effects on IQ for children in poverty may be produced through early education only if it begins in infancy and continues to school entry. Barnett examines separately the effects of model programs and large-scale public programs operated by Head Start and the public schools. He finds that both have substantial effects on school success, but model programs appear to have larger effects on at least one measure of school success—special-education placement.

The second chapter is a review by Sarane Boocock of sixteen studies of early-childhood programs conducted in fourteen nations outside the United States during the last two decades, chosen particularly for the policy significance of their findings. Boocock, a sociologist, argues that some of the changes in the lives of American children (as described in the later chapter by Hernandez) are the result of social and political changes that are global phenomena. Her investigation indicates that many of the positive findings reported in Barnett's review of American programs are confirmed in the international research. For example, the French and German preschool education systems have been found to reduce the rate of grade repetition. At the same time, review of the international literature reveals some important differences among nations in commonly held values about children and families, as well as in definitions of what constitutes a quality early-childhood program and perceptions of the appropriate role of governments in ensuring program quality.

Next are two reviews of research that focus on more specific aspects of process and outcomes. Ellen Frede (a developmental psychologist and teacher educator) reexamines the long-term studies of preschool program effectiveness, as well as more recent studies of program quality for information on what constitutes program quality. She investigates the influences of curriculum with attention to the structural elements of program quality needed to sustain an approach, in addition to the differences among pedagogical approaches in content and method. From a sociocultural perspective, Frede argues that the most effective curricula are those in which teachers create scaffolds for children's learning that engage children as active learners and that provide experiences that dovetail with the practices and content that children encounter when they enter school. Practices that enhance communication between home and preschool and that encourage teachers to reflect on and improve their teaching are also identified as critical elements in quality programs.

Robert St. Pierre, Jean Layzer, and Helen Barnes (all educational researchers) analyze two-generation programs designed to use direct and indirect pathways simultaneously to benefit children and their parents. Educational services for the children promote their cognitive development, while activities for parents attempt both to support parenting and to encourage the parents' own development and learning. These multistrategy programs are relatively new additions to the broad array of programs designed to serve children and their families, and this review of six two-generation programs reveals considerable variability in content and costs, and mixed results in promoting the development of children and at the same time improving parenting skills and economic self-sufficiency. They present evidence that two-generational programs tend to have weak effects on child development because they do not provide intensive, direct early education to children and instead emphasize family support and service coordination.

Next we move from reviews of research to assessments of specific interventions or programs. Three studies examine very different models of care and education created by some of the pioneers in the field and exemplify very different approaches to the evaluation of innovative programs. Larry Aber, Jeanne Brooks-Gunn, and Rebecca Maynard (two developmental psychologists and an economist) analyze an important example of two-generation programs developed in the context of welfare reform. The Teenage Parent Welfare Demonstration (TPWD), initiated in 1986 by the U.S. Department of Health and Human Services, was a major experiment designed to test the impact of a welfare-to-work program. Aber, Brooks-Gunn, and Maynard examine the policy context in which the TPWD was designed and implemented, and describe how participation in the "enhanced services" group affected teen mothers and their children.

The Carolina Abecedarian Project is a longitudinal experiment in which economically disadvantaged children in the treatment group received a highly intensive and enduring intervention. They were provided with a high-quality, full-day, child-care program for the first five years of life, and follow-up results have now been reported through age fifteen. Frances Campbell, Ronald Helms, Joseph Sparling, and Craig Ramey (developmental psychologists) use these data to investigate longitudinal predictors of academic achievement. Their findings provide insights into the processes through which intervention effects were sustained across ten years of school, and indicate the strength of associations between achievement in high school and other measures such as maternal IQ, home environment scales, and earlier child assessments.

The High/Scope Perry Preschool study is a longitudinal experiment with twenty-five years of follow-up data on the effects of quality preschool education on poor children. It provides detailed data on many dimensions of development, school and adult success, and home and school environments. Steve Barnett, John Young (an educational psychologist), and Larry Schweinhart (an educational researcher) use this rich data set to compare alternative models of the process through which a preschool education programs' effects were produced and sustained. These models represent the major alternative theoretical explanations for preschool program's long-term effects. One model emphasizes effects on cognitive development, another emphasizes socialization and motivation, and the third emphasizes effects on parent involvement. The model emphasizing the importance of initial cognitive effects is supported by the analysis; the other models, and the view that there are no real long-term effects, are rejected.

The last three chapters address issues involved in formulating and implementing public policy regarding early-childhood care and education at the state and national level. The rapidly changing social, economic, and demographic context in which such decisions must be made is reviewed by Donald Hernandez (Chief, Marriage and Family Statistics Branch, U.S. Bureau of the Census). Hernandez shows how these trends affect the needs of children and their families and shape the demand for programs to complement family efforts to educate and care for their children. The author argues that the nation is experiencing a child-care revolution and that public funding for early-childhood programs—like funding for public schools—is justified by the value ECE programs have for the broader society.

Government policies relating to the provision and use of ECE emerge from the complex interactions of such economic and social factors as the demand for women workers in the labor market; the expectations people have for the roles of government, family, business, and other private sector institutions; the politics of population growth; and the value placed on maintaining traditional family structure with a breadwinner, a homemaker, and children. In their chapter, Siv Gustafsson and Frank Stafford (both economists) examine the evolution of public policies toward maternal employment and ECE in the United States, Sweden, and the Netherlands—three highly industrialized countries that differ sharply in the extent and types of government involvement in ECE and in the emphasis government leaders place on promoting or discouraging maternal employment. Their analysis lays out different equity/efficiency trade offs that governments and parents face in allocating resources to children and shows how ECE and related policies affect the labor-market participation and other activities of women with young children.

The book concludes with a chapter on the problems involved in translating research findings into large-scale public programs and policies, by an educational researcher who launched a center dedicated to interdisciplinary policy research, training, and technical assistance, and has worked for many years in partnership with policy makers to improve the lives of young children. As Anna Maria Zervigon-Hakes (an early-childhood educator and policy analyst) makes clear, policy makers and researchers have very different constituencies, styles, and interests. Also, what works in a small-scale research program or even in a large-scale national research or demonstration program may be difficult to replicate on a statewide or national scale. It is not always a straightforward matter to move from research findings to the design of policies and large-scale programs that will produce the desired results. Zervigon-Hakes reviews her own experience during years in which Florida's policy makers wrestled with the decision to entitle infants and toddlers with disabilities and developmental delays to early-intervention services.

When we chose the subtitle for this book, we had two types of "promises" in mind: promise of early care and education to improve child development and school success and maternal success in the labor market, and promise within each child that may be revealed only if they are well cared for and educated. As the book developed, we came to realize that a third type of promise is relevant, the promise of equal opportunity that is a fundamental principle of public policy in the United States. Today, government is having an especially difficult time keeping this promise. The gap between rich and poor is widening and interethnic tensions about fair treatment and economic opportunity run high. Ensuring that families in poverty have access to free or highly subsidized, quality ECE would not by itself produce equality of opportunity, but it would make a significant contribution toward increasing it.

Ironically, the United States—the nation that has invested the most in rigorous research on ECE for children in poverty—has one of the world's most fragmented and incoherent ECE systems (Barnett, 1993). With both a high average income and a high poverty rate, the United States is the industrialized nation that is most able to afford and has the most to gain from a system of high-quality ECE for children in poverty. Yet, the vast majority of poor children and their families do not have access to quality ECE. Head Start's supporters must fight vigorously just to maintain funding levels that allow it to serve less than half of the eligible children in part-day programs. Welfare reform moves ahead to put mothers to work with little consideration for the potential of high-quality ECE programs to enhance child development as well as maternal employment. When thought is given to the need for child care in welfare reform, more often than not proposals are made for the least expensive forms of custodial care. Instead of expanding Head Start into full-day, full-year care when this is needed, Head Start is to be supplemented with wrap-around custodial care without thought to the potential impact on the child. The research presented in this book makes it clear that such public policies are foolish and wasteful. It is not the cost of providing quality early care and education that is high, but the cost of failing to provide it.

Several clear policy recommendations emerge from the research presented in this book. First, government should immediately fund at least one year, and preferrably two years, of preschool education for every poor child. In the United States, the simplest way to achieve this goal would be to increase funding for Head Start. Second, government should immediately increase funding (directly or through tax credits and other subsidies) to improve the quality of early care and education received by all children, but especially poor children. In addition, all new parents could be provided with information about the importance of quality care and education when their child leaves the hospital for home. As part of welfare reform the government should provide or substantially subsidize quality early care and education for the children of low-income working parents. Third, government should gradually increase funding for Head Start and other early-childhood programs so that all poor children can be served at younger ages, first moving to serve all at age three and then moving to serve infants and toddlers with mothers who work outside the home. These three steps can be the beginning of a rational, cost-effective, early-care and education policy in the United States if they are implemented in conjunction with systematic research and evaluation on their impact on children and families.

Recommendations for research in support of public policy that emerge from the following chapters begin with the development of a better understanding of how early care and education affects child development and school success and how positive effects on these can be sustained. Such information would enable policy makers to make better use of scarce resources and to develop more cost-effective programs. Promising new models—including popular parent education and two-generational approaches—need to be tested rigorously. Identifying the essential elements of program quality and the costs and benefits of initiating programs at various ages can be done most directly through experimental studies using random assignment to carefully specified alternatives. Nonexperimental evaluations of early-childhood programs may be biased by high degrees of self-selection (family income, education, child-rearing attitudes and practices, and other family characteristics affect both parental choices and access to alternative programs) when "natural" assignment to various kinds of early care and education occurs.

Several chapters provide evidence of effects of early-childhood programs on families as well as children, but in the absence of more rigorous research specifying the relationships between early care and education and parental employment and earnings, family relationships, and family stability, it is difficult to assess the potential benefits of various policy alternatives. For example, should public resources be concentrated on programs for the most economically disadvantaged children so that they receive more intensive services? Or, should public resources be spread more widely by providing services or subsidies to families who are above the poverty line, but who still have such modest incomes that it is difficult for them to afford quality early-childhood programs? Yet, another alternative would be to make free or highly subsidized quality child care available to all families. Although the economic benefits from improvements in child development seem likely to decline with family income, the benefits from increased maternal productivity and earnings might increase with family income.

Despite the uncertainties that remain, we believe that the following chapters provide ample evidence of the potential public and private benefits of a coherent system of publicly financed quality early care and education for children in poverty. These chapters also identify the changes in public policy that would enable society to construct such a system and the kinds of additional knowledge needed to develop the most economical and effective policies and programs. We hope that the book will strengthen the knowledge base and the will to keep America's promises to its children.

1

W. S. Barnett

Long-Term Effects on Cognitive Development and School Success

Persistent Effects on Cognitive Development and School Success

The contribution of early care and education (ECE) to the cognitive development and school success of children who are economically and socially disadvantaged has become a vital public issue. Experts generally agree that ECE programs can produce short-term gains in disadvantaged children's performance on standardized tests of

Adapted from Barnett, W. S. (1995). Long-term effects of early childhood programs on cognitive and school outcomes. *The Future of Children* (Winter) 5(3):25–50, by permission of Center for the Future of Children, The David and Lucile Packard Foundation.

intelligence and academic ability and that some preschool programs have reduced later grade retention and special-education placement. However, there is a great deal of disagreement about the true nature of these effects, whether they persist, what other effects might be produced, and what is required to produce meaningful long-term effects (e.g., Zigler & Muenchow, 1992; Locurto, 1991; Seitz, 1990; Barnett, 1992; Schweinhart, Barnes, Weikart, Barnett, & Epstein, 1993; Consortium for Longitudinal Studies, 1983; Haskins, 1989; Spitz, 1986, 1991; Datta, 1983). These disagreements are so severe that they make it difficult to develop research-based ECE policy recommendations, and uncertainty and skepticism regarding long-term effects undermines support for existing public programs like Head Start.

This chapter seeks to resolve at least some of the disagreements and provide a stronger knowledge base for policy making through a critical review of research on the effects of ECE on children from low-income families. Results of the review are used to address the following questions: (1) Can ECE programs produce meaningful long-term effects on the cognitive development and school success of economically disadvantaged children? (2) How do the effects of large-scale government programs such as Head Start and public school preschool education compare to those of model programs? (3) Do persistent effects require or benefit from continuation of intervention beyond the preschool years?

Research on Short-Term Effects

Hundreds of studies have examined the immediate and short-term effects of ECE programs. These studies are found in two largely separate streams of research: one on the effects of ordinary child care on children from all backgrounds and the other on the effects of ECE interventions specially designed to improve the cognitive development of economically disadvantaged children. These two research streams have tended to be conducted from different perspectives. Initially, research on child care focused on possible negative effects on the mother-child relationship and social development with distinctly less attention to possible effects on cognitive development. More recently, child-care research has become more nuanced and begun to examine the effects on cognitive development of variations in the quality of care and possible interactions with the child's home environment and family circumstances. Research on interventions for disadvantaged children initially emphasized the potential for positive effects on cognitive development, especially as measured by IQ. Over time, interest grew in the effects of interventions on other aspects of cognitive development, on school success, and on socialization.

Child-care research presents no consistent evidence that child care per se is harmful to child development regardless of the age at which a child begins out-of-home care (Lamb & Sternberg, 1990; Zaslow, 1991). Variations in the quality of child care appear to be important determinants of the impact of child care, though the effects of quality seem to vary with child and family characteristics. Higher-quality child care has been found to be associated with better cognitive and social development contemporaneously and into the first few years of school (Lamb & Sternberg, 1990; Phillips, McCartney, & Scarr, 1987; Zaslow, 1991; Helburn & Culkin, 1995). A new large-scale study of infant child care conducted by the NICHD Early Child Care Research Network (1996) found evidence that the frequency of insecure attachment was increased by poor quality care, increased hours of care, and instability of care arrangements, *but only when* the child's mother was rated as "insensitive" in her interactions with the child.

Another recent investigation found that age at entry or years of experience and type of care (child's own home, other home, or center) during the preschool years influenced the reading and math achievement of children at ages five and six (Caughy, DiPietro, & Strobino, 1994). Effects were positive for children from impoverished homes. For these children, earlier entry/more years produced a larger effect on reading scores, and center-based care had a larger effect on math scores. Conversely, effects were negative for children in the highest income families. The interaction appears to be due to differences in the quality of home environments rather than to income per se: children whose home environments were relatively poor (as measured by Caldwell's HOME) gained the most, while children whose home environments were very highly supportive of cognitive development and socialization had lower scores if they had been in other care. This study of effects on achievement is especially interesting because two other studies failed to find positive effects of ordinary child care on IQ (the PPVT) for four-year-old children (Baydar & Brooks-Gunn, 1991; Desai, Chase-Lansdale, & Michael, 1989).

From the intervention research, it appears that programs designed for disadvantaged children, including large-scale public programs, can produce immediate effect sizes for IQ and achievement of about 0.5 standard deviations, equivalent to about 8 IQ points (White & Casto, 1985; McKey et al., 1985; Ramey, Bryant, & Suarez, 1985). Somewhat smaller average effect sizes were found for immediate effects on socioemotional outcomes such as self-esteem, academic motivation, and social behavior. On average, these estimated effects declined over time and were negligible several years after children exit the programs. However, some programs produced sizeable gains that persisted into the school years for IQ, achievement, grade retention, and special-education placement. A variety of different approaches produced positive effects, but the magnitude of initial effects appears to be roughly related to a program's intensity, breadth, and amount of involvement with children and their families (Ramey, Bryant, & Suarez, 1985).

One difficulty in interpreting the research results is that most studies relied on natural variation in participation in ECE, making it difficult to separate the effects of ECE from the effects of family characteristics that influence ECE enrollment decisions (e.g., parents' income, socioeconomic status, education, and attitudes toward education and child rearing). Experiments in which children are randomly assigned to specially designed ECE programs are extremely valuable because they make it easier to separate program effects from family background effects. Thus, short-term results from relatively new randomized experiments are worth summarizing briefly.

The CARE study randomly assigned children (N=57) to three conditions: a high-quality, full-day, year-round ECE program and home visits for parent education from shortly after birth to age five, home visits alone, and a control group (Roberts et al., 1989; Wasik et al., 1990). At age five, the ECE plus home visits group had higher IQs and better language skills (but did no better on a reading test) than the other two groups despite substantial participation of the others in community child care. No effects were found on parenting.

The Infant Health and Development Program (IDHP) study is an eight-site randomized trial (N=985) of ECE from birth to age three for low-birth-weight infants primarily, but not entirely, from low-income families (IHDP, 1990; Brooks-Gunn et al., 1994). The program consisted of weekly home visits for the first year directed at both parents' and children's needs, followed by biweekly home visits and full-day ECE for the child from age one to age three. By age three, the program had increased children's IQs by thirteen points and improved child behavior slightly as measured by the Child Behavior Checklist. Small effects were found on maternal employment (one month more), but not on maternal education or fertility. Effects on the children were no longer apparent for the full sample at age five and age eight follow-up. However, modest effects on IQ and achievement remained at ages five and eight for children above 2,000 grams birth weight (McCarton et al., 1997).

The Comprehensive Child Development Program (CCDP) sought to increase and improve social, health, and education services for families with young children through home visitors who served as case managers (St. Pierre and Lopez, 1994). Families (N=4,411, 21 sites) had a child under one year of age at study entry and were to be visited twice monthly. The CCDP substantially increased mother's participation in parenting education, mental-health services, and education, slightly increased children's use of health services, and substantially increased children's participation in formal ECE. After several years, only extremely small effects were found for mothers and children.

Even Start provided parenting education, adult education, and early-childhood education plus a variety of supporting services (St. Pierre et al., 1993). Extent and duration of services varied widely across families, though nearly all children received some early-childhood education. Experiments at five sites with three- and four-year-old children (N=164) found small positive effects on a measure of school readiness skills two and one half years after program entry. Small effects also were found on one aspect of home environment (reading materials) and on parents' expectations for children's academic success.

In sum, ECE has important impacts on cognitive development and abilities associated with school success immediately and in the short term. Effects appear to depend on program quality and the child's home environment and are larger for well-designed, intensive ECE interventions than for ordinary child care or programs focused on increasing families' use of existing health, social, and educational services. Some, but not all, studies report that effects decline after children leave the ECE program.

Research on Long-Term Effects

Studies were selected for review of research on long-term effects if they met four criteria: (1) children entered the program before age five, except for Head Start, which mostly serves three and four year olds but serves five year olds under some circumstances, such as when public kindergarten is not available; (2) the program served economically disadvantaged children; (3) at least one measure of cognitive development, school progress, or socialization was collected at or beyond age eight (third grade); and (4) the research design provided a no-treatment comparison to a comparable group or adjusted for socioeconomic differences. These criteria excluded studies of children who were not economically disadvantaged, studies of kindergarten, case studies of individual children, simple before-and-after comparisons of children in ECE, and studies that compared disadvantaged children to more advantaged children without any statistical adjustments for differences in family background. The requirement for follow-up to at least third grade allowed sufficient time to observe fade-out in effects (Caldwell, 1987). Thirty-eight studies were identified that met the review criteria. This is a larger number of long-term studies than in previous reviews including the well-known quantitative syntheses (White & Casto, 1985; McKey et al., 1985).

Program and Study Characteristics

The thirty-eight studies were divided into two categories for review based on the nature of the ECE program and the research design. In fifteen studies, researchers developed their own ECE programs to study the effects of exemplary programs. Some of these model programs might be characterized as family-support programs in today's terminology; most, if not all, of them worked with parents in some way. In twenty-three other studies, researchers investigated the effects of ongoing, large-scale, public ECE programs; twelve studied Head Start programs, seven examined public-school programs, and four studied a mix of Head Start and public-school programs.

Model-Program Studies

The fifteen studies of model programs are described in Table 1-1. Generally, the model ECE programs are likely to have been of higher quality than the large-scale public programs. Reasons for this include: (1) the close supervision and direction of experts, (2) highly qualified staff, and (3) low child-staff ratios and small group size. These advantages were made possible by higher levels of funding per child than are available to Head Start and public-school programs. In all but one study the majority of children were African American. The Houston Parent Child Development Center (PCDC) served Hispanic American families. The average level of mother's education was under twelve years in all studies, and under ten years in five studies. Three model-program studies limited their target populations in ways that could have affected their results. The Harlem Training Project served only boys. The Perry Preschool study selected children based on low IQ scores, and its sample had substantially lower IQs at age three than children in other studies. The Milwaukee study selected children whose mothers had low IQs (below 75).

As can be seen from Table 1-1, the model programs varied in entrance age, duration, services provided, and historical context (1962 to 1980). Most of the comparison children began formal education at kindergarten, but, especially in the later studies, it is likely that significant percentages of the comparison groups attended a preschool or child-care program (as this became more common and Head Start and public school preschool programs grew). For example, in the Abecedarian study, which enrolled newborns between 1972 and 1980, two thirds of the control group attended an ECE program for twelve months or more by age five (Burchinal, Lee, & Ramey, 1989). Clearly, this could lead to some underestimation of the effects of ECE programs.

Head Start and Public School Programs

The twenty-three studies of Head Start and public school ECE programs are identified and described in Table 1-2. None of these programs took children before age three, and most served children part-day for one school year at age four. Class size and child-teacher ratio tended to be higher than in model programs. Head Start programs had broader missions than most public school programs; their goals included improving health and nutrition, and providing services to parents and the community (Zigler & Styfco, 1993). The programs studied seem generally representative of public programs for poor children over the past several decades. In three studies, ECE program participation was associated with differential school-age programs. In the Cincinnati Title I study most full-day kindergarten students had attended preschool and most half-day kindergarten students had not. In the two Child Parent Center (CPC) studies, services began in preschool and continued as enriched education through third grade.

Research Design

Three key aspects of research design are described in Tables 1-1 and 1-2 for model-program and Head Start and public school program studies. These are: (1) the ways in which the comparison groups were formed, (2) initial and follow-up sample sizes, and (3) length of follow-up. Each of these has important implications for the validity and interpretation of study findings.

Table 1-1.
Model Early Childhood Programs

Program Name (Years of Operation) (Sources)	Program Description	Ages of Participation	Research Design/ Methodological Concerns
1. Carolina Abecedarian (1972–1985) (Campbell & Ramey, 1993, 1994; Campbell, 1994)	Preschool-age: full-day child care School-age: parent program	Entry: 6 weeks to 3 months Exit: 5 to 8 years	Randomized.
2. Houston Parent Child Development Center (1970–1980) (Andrews et al., 1982; Johnson & Walker, 1991)	Home visits Full-day child care Center-based program for parents	Entry: 1 to 3 years Exit: 3 to 5 years	Randomized High attrition.[c]
3. Florida Parent Education Project (1966–1970) (Jester & Guinagh, 1983)	Home visits Twice weekly part-day preschool (ages 2 to 3 years)	Entry: 3 to 24 months Exit: 3 years	Initially randomized with one group, and additional control group members added at 24 months. Not randomized.[d] High attrition. School-administered tests.[e]
4. Milwaukee Project (1968–1978) (Garber, 1988)	Full-day child care Job and academic training for mothers	Entry: 3 to 6 months Exit: 3 years	Groups of 3 to 4 children assigned alternately to E and C groups. Small sample.
5. Syracuse Family Research Program (1969–1975) (Lally, Mangione, & Honig, 1988)	Home visits Full-day child care	Entry: 6 months Exit: 5 years	Matched comparison group selected at 36 months. Not randomized.
6. Yale Child Welfare Research Program (1968–1974) (Seitz, Rosenbaum, & Apfel, 1985; Seitz & Apfel, 1994)	Home visits Full-day child care Pediatric care Developmental screenings	Entry: Prenatal Exit: 30 months	Two comparison groups for same neighborhoods for first follow-up. Matched comparison group selected from follow-up at 30 months. Not randomized. School-administered tests.
7. Verbal Interaction Project (1967–1972) (Levenstein, O'Hara, & Madden, 1983)	Home visits	Entry: 2 to 3 years Exit: 4 years	Six groups with three matched comparison groups. Not randomized.

Initial Sample Size[a]	Follow-up Sample Size	Time of Follow-up	IQ[a,b]	School Outcomes[a]

E = 57
 C = 54
	Age 8
	 E = 48
	 C = 42
	 Age 15
	 E = 48
	 C = 44
		8, 12, and 15 years	Age 12; E > C
			 E = 93.7
			 C = 88.4
				Achievement test: E > C at age 15
				 Special education: E < C at age 15:
				   E = 24%, C = 48%
				 Grade retention: E < C at age 15:
				   E = 39%, C = 59%

E = 97
 C = 119
	School date
	 E = 50
	 C = 87
	 IQ data
	 E = 39
	 C = 78
		Grades 2 to 5	Not measured	Achievement tests: E = C, but positive trend
				 Grades: E = C
				 Bilingual education: E < C
				   E = 16%, c = 36%
				 Special education: E = C, grades 2 to 5
				   E = 27%, C = 31%
				 Grade retention: E = C, grades 2 to 5
				   E = 16%, C = 29%

E = 288
 C = 109
	E = 83
	 C = 24
		Grades 4 to 7	E = C (grades 4 to 7)
			 E = 83.1
			 C = 79.8
				Math achievement: E > C
				 Reading achievement: E = C
				 Special education: E < C, grade 7
				   E = 23%, C = 54%
				 Grade retention: E = C, grade 7
				   E = 28%, C = 29%

E = 20
 C = 20
	E = 17
	 C = 24
		Grade 4
		 Grade 8
			Grade 8: E > C
			 E = 101
			 C = 91
				Achievement tests: E = C, but positive trend
				 Grades: E = C
				 Special education: E = C, grade 4
				   E = 41%, C = 89%
				 Grade retention: E = C, grade 4
				   E = 29%, C = 56%

E = 82 C = 72	Parents E = 52 C = 42 Children E = 49 C = 39	Grades 7 to 8	E = C, age 5 on Stanford-Binet	Teacher ratings: E > C, but for girls only Grades: E > C, but for girls only Attendance: E > C, but for girls only
E = 18 C = 18	Age 7 to 8 E = 17 C1 = 33 C2 = 31 Age 10 E = 16 C = 16	Age 7 to 8 and age 10	E = C at age 10	Achievement tests: E = C Attendance: E > C Teacher ratings: E = C, but positive trend for boys only Special education: E = C E = 25%, C = 50%

E = 111
 C = 51
	E = 79
	 C = 49
		Grades 3	E>C at grade 3
			 E = 101.9
			 C = 93.6
				Achievement test: E > C
				 Special education: E < C, grade 7
				   E = 14%, C = 39%
				 Grade retention: E = C, grade 7
				   E = 13%, C = 19%

Table 1-1. (*continued*)
Model Early Childhood Programs

Program Name (Years of Operation) (Sources)	Program Description	Ages of Participation	Research Design/ Methodological Concerns
8. Early Training Project (1962–1967) (Gray, Ramsey, & Klaus, 1982, 1983)	Home visits Summer part-day preschool program	Entry: 4 to 5 years Exit: 6 years	Randomized. School-administered tests.
9. Experimental Variation of Head Start (1968–1969) (Karnes, Schwedel, & Williams, 1983)	Part-day preschool program	Entry: 4 years Exit: 5 years	Post hoc comparison group from same communities. Not randomized. High attrition. School-administered tests.
10. Halem Training Project (1966–1967) (Palmer, 1983)	One-to-one tutoring or child-directed play	Entry: 2 to 3 years Exit: 4 years	Comparison group recruited from children born 1 to 2 months later.
11. High/Scope Perry Preschool Project (1962–1967) (Weikart, Bond, & McNeil, 1978; Schweinhart et al., 1993; Barnett, Young, & Schweinhart, this volume)	Home visits Part-day preschool program	Entry: 3 to 4 years Exit: 5 years	Randomized.
12. Howard University Project (1964–1966) (Herzog, Newcomb, & Cisin, 1974)	Part-day preschool program	Entry: 3 years Exit: 5 years	Comparison group from neighboring tracts. Not randomized.
13. Institute for Developmental Studies (1963–1967) (Deutsch, Deutsch, Jordan, & Grallo, 1983)	Home visits Part-day preschool program Parent center school (K–3)	Entry: 3 years Exit: 9 years	Randomized. High attrition. School-administered tests.
14. Philadelphia Project (1963–1964) (Beller, 1983)	Home visits Part-day preschool program	Entry: 4 years Exit: 5 years	Matched comparison group from same kindergarten classes. Not randomized. School-administered tests.
15. Curriculum Comparison Study (1965–1967) (Miller & Bizzell, 1983, 1984)	Part-day preschool program Kindergarten program	Entry: 4 years Exit: 5 or 6 years	Post hoc comparison group from original pool. Not randomized. School-administered tests.

a. Throughout Table 1-1, E refers to the experimental or intervention group, and C refers to the control or comparison group. Outcomes listed as E>C or E<C were statistically significant at the p<.05 level.
b. IQs were measured using the WISC or WISC-R, unless otherwise noted.
c. Results may be biased because of high attrition rates.

Initial Sample Size[a]	Follow-up Sample Size	Time of Follow-up	IQ[a,b]	School Outcomes[a]

E=44 C=21	E=36 C=16	Post-high school	E=C age 17 E=78.7 C=76.4	Achievement tests: E=C
				Special education: E<C, grade 12
				  E=5%, C=29%
				Grade retention: E=C
				  E=58%, C=61%
				High school graduation: E=C
				  E=68%, C=52%

E=116 C=24	E=102 C=19	Post-high school	E<C at age 13 E=85.0 C=91.0	Achievement tests: E=C, but positive trend
				Special education: E=C, grade 7
				  E=13%, C=15%
				Grade retention: E=C, grade 7
				  E=10%, C=16%

E=244 C=68	E=168 C=51	Grade 7	E=C at age 12 E=92.1 C=88.9	Math achievement: E>C Reading achievement: E<C Grade retention: E<C, grade 7 E=30%, C=52%

E=58 C=65	E=58 C=65	Post-high school	E=C at age 14 E=81.0 C=81.0	Achievement tests: E>C
				Grades: E>C
				Special education: E=C, grade 12
				  E=37%, C=50%
				Grade retention: E=C, grade 12
				  E=15%, C=20%
				High school graduation: E>C
				  E=67%, C=49%

E=38 C=69	E=30 C=69	Grade 4	Not measured	Grade retention: E=C E=33%, C=47%

E=312 C=191	E=63 C=34	Grade 7	Not measured	Special education: E=C
				  E=0%, C=13%
				Grade retention: E=C
				  E=23%, C=43%

E=60 C=53	E=44 C=37	Post-high school	E>C at age 10 on Stanford-Binet E=98.4 C=91.7	Achievement test: E=C, but positive trend
				Special education: E=C, grade 12
				  E=5%, C=6%
				Grade retention: E=C, grade 12
				  E=38%, C=53%

E=244 C=68	E=168 C=51	Post-high school	Not measured	Special education: E=C, grade 12
				  E=32%, C=63%
				Grade retention: E=C, grade 12
				  E=26%, C=58%
				High school graduation: E=C
				  E=67%, C=53%

d. Results may be biased because children were not randomly assigned to experimental and control or comparison groups.

e. Results may be biased because school-administered tests were used to measure achievement.

Table 1-2.
Large-Scale Public Early Childhood Programs[a]

Program Name (Years of Operation) (Source)	Ages of Participation	Design	Initial Sample Size[b]
1. Child-Parent Center (1965–1977) (Fuerst & Fuerst, 1993)	Entry: 3 or 4 years Exit: 9 years	Compared former CPC children with non-CPC children from same feeder schools.	E=684 C=304
2. Child-Parent Center II (1983–1985) (Reynolds, 1994a, 1994b, 1993)	Entry: 4 or 5 years Exit: 6 years	Compared former CPC children with several other groups.	Unknown
3. Cincinnati Title I Preschool (1969–1970; 1970–1971) (Nieman & Gastright, 1981)	Entry: 4 or 5 years Exit: 6 years	Compared children who attended full-day kindergarten and mostly had preschool with children who attended half-day kindergarten and mostly had no preschool.	E=688 C=524
4. Maryland Extended Elementary Pre-K (1977–1980) (Eckroade, Salehi, & Carter, 1988; Eckroade, Salehi, & Wode, 1991)	Entry: 4 years Exit: 5 years	Compared attenders to nonattenders, including only children continuously enrolled in school district (kindergarten to grade 5).	Unknown
5. New York State Experimental Prekindergarten (1975–1976) (State Ed. Dept., Univ. of the State of NY, 1982)	Entry: 3 or 4 years Exit: 5 years	Compared attenders with children in same district on waiting list and with children in other districts with no prekindergarten program.	1800[h]
6. Florida Prekindergarten Early Intervention Cohort 1 (King, Cappelini, & Gravens, 1995)	Entry: 4 years Exit: 5 years	Compared Pre-K early-intervention children with children from same schools who qualified for free/reduced lunch.	Unknown
7. Florida Prekindergarten Early Intervention Cohort 2 (King, Cappelini, & Rohani, 1995)	Entry: 4 years Exit: 5 years	Compared Pre-K early-intervention children with children from same schools who qualified for free/reduced lunch.	Unknown
8. Florida Chapter I (King, Rohani, & Cappelini, 1995)	Entry: 4 years Exit: 5 years	Compared children screened into with those screened out of Chapter I Pre-K based on a test (DIAL-R).	E=103 C=121
9. Detroit Head Start and Title I Preschool (1972–1973) (Clark, 1979)	Entry: 4 years Exit: 5 years	Compared children who had attended Head Start or Title I preschool with children who were eligible but did not attend.	Unknown
10. D.C. Public Schools and Head Start (1986–1987) (Marcon, 1990, 1993)	Entry: 4 years Exit: 5 years	Compared children who had attended public school or Head Start with children in same kindergartens who had not.	E=372 C=89
11. Philadelphia School District Get Set and Head Start (1969–1970; 1970–1971) (Copple, Cline, & Smith, 1987)	Entry: 4 years Exit: 5 years	Compared children in enriched K-3 program (follow-through) who had and had not attended preschool.	E=1,082 C=1,615
12. Seattle DISTAR and Head Start (1970–1971) (Evans, 1985)	Entry: 4 years Exit: 5 years	Compared children who had attended Head Start and DISTAR with matched children from same school and grades.	E=92 C=unknown

Follow-up Sample Size	Time of Last Follow-up	School Outcomes[b]	Methodological Concerns

E=513
C=244
	Post-high school	Achievement test: E>C at grade 2,
		  E=C at grade 8
		High school graduation: E>C
		  E=62%, C=49%
			Not randomized.[c] No pretest.[d]
			School-administered tests.[e]

E=757 C=130	Grade 7	Achievement tests: E>C for grades K to 7 Special education: E<C, E=12%, C=22% Grade retention: E<C, E=24%, C=34%	Not randomized. No pretest. School-administered tests.

E=410
C=141
	Grade 8	Achievement tests: E>C for grades 1, 5, 8
		Special education: E=C, grade 8
		  E=5%, C=11%
		Grade retention: E=C, grade 8
		  E=9%, C=12%
			Not randomized. No pretest.
			School-administered tests.

E=356
C=306
	Grade 8	Achievement tests: E>C for grades 3, 5, 8
		Special education: E<C, grade 8
		  E=15%, C=22%
		Grade retention: E<C, grade 8
		  E=31%, C=45%
			Not randomized. No pretest.
			High attrition.[f]
			School-administered tests.

E=1,348 C=258	Grade 3	Achievement tests: E>C in kindergarten E=C in grade 1 Special education: E=C, E=2%, C=5% Grade retention: E<C, E=16%, C=21%	Not randomized. High attrition.
E=350 C=352	Grades 3 and 4	Achievement tests: E>C in kindergarten E=C in grades 1 to 3, E<C in grade 4 Special education: E=C, E=25%, C=25% Grade retention: E=C, E=3%, C=3% Disciplined: E<C, E=11%, C=32%	Not randomized. No pretest. High attrition. School-administered tests. Pre-K E children attended schools in poorer communities. First year of program operation.
E=983 C=1,054	Grades 3 and 4	Achievement tests: E>C in kindergarten E=C in grades 1 to 4 Special education: E=C, E=17%, C=15% Grade retention: E<C, E=9%, C=13%	Not randomized. No pretest. High attrition. School-administered tests.

E=54
C=65
	Grade 8	Achievement tests: E>C in grades 1,2,4,7,8
		  E=C in grades 5,6
		  (no data for grade 3)
			Not randomized.
			High attrition.
			School-administered tests.

Unknown	Grade 4	Achievement tests: E>C in grade 4	Not randomized. No pretest. School-administered tests. Bias toward no effect.[g]

E varies
C varies
	Grades 4 and 5	Achievement tests: E=C in grades 3 to 5
		Special education: E=C, grade 4
		  E=10%, C=9%
		Grade retention: E=C, grade 4
		  E=31%, C=38%
			Not randomized. Bias toward no effect.
			High attrition.

E=688 C=524	Grades 4 to 8, varies by cohort	Achievement test: E=C Grade retention: E<C	Not randomized. No pretest. Bias toward no effect. High attrition. School-administered tests.
E=44 C=20	Grades 6 and 8	Achievement tests: E=C, but positive trend in grades 6 and 8	Not randomized. No pretest. High attrition. School-administered tests.

Table 1-2. (*continued*)
Large-Scale Public Early Childhood Programs[a]

Program Name (Years of Operation) (Source)	Ages of Participation	Design	Initial Sample Size[b]
13. Cincinnati Head Start (1968–1969) (O'Piela, 1976)	Entry: 4 years Exit: 5 years	Compared third graders who had attended Head Start with those who had not.	Unknown
14. Detroit Head Start (1969–1970) (Pinkleton, 1976)	Entry: 4 years Exit: 5 or 6 years	Compared children who had attended Head Start with children in Title I elementary programs.	Unknown
15. ETS Longitudinal Study of Head Start (1969–1970; 1970–1971) (Shipman, 1970, 1976; Lee et al., 1990)	Entry: 4 or 5 years Exit: 5 or 6 years	Compared children who had attended Head Start with siblings who had not, using fixed-effects model and percentile scores.	1,875
16, Hartford Head Start (1965–1966) (Goodstein, 1975)	Entry: 4 years Exit: 5 years	Compared children who had attended Head Start with low-income children who had not.	293
17. Kanawha County, West Virginia Head Start[a] (1973–1974) (Kanawha Bd. of Ed., 1978)	Entry: 4 years Exit: 5 years	Compared children who had attended Head Start with low-income children who had not.	Unknown
18. Montgomery County, Maryland Head Start (1970–1971; 1974–1975; 1978–1979) (Hebbeler, 1985)	Entry: 4 years Exit: 5 years	Compared children who had attended eight or nine months with those who had attended one month or less.	E=1,915 C=619
19. NBER-NLSCM Head Start (1979–1989) (Currie & Thomas, 1995)	Entry: 3 to 5 years Exit: 5 to 6 years	Compared children who had attended Head Start with low-income children who had not, using a fixed-effects model and raw scores.	6,676
20. New Haven Head Start (1968–1969) (Abelson, 1974; Abelson, Zigler, & DeBlasi, 1974)	Entry: 4 years Exit: 5 years	Compared children who had attended Head Start with those who had not.	E=61 C=48
21. Pennsylvania Head Start (1986–1987) (Reedy, 1991)	Entry: 3 to 5 years Exit: 5 to 6 years	Compared children who had attended Head Start with children who had applied but had not been admitted.	E=98 C=unknown
22. Rome, Georgia Head Start (1966) (McDonald & Monroe, 1981)	Entry: 3 to 5 years Exit: 5 to 6 years	Compared children who attended Head Start with all children in first grade in disadvantaged schools in 1966.	E=130 C=88
23. Westinghouse National Evaluation of Head Start (1965–1966) (Westinghouse Learning Corp. & Ohio University, 1969)	Entry: 4 or 5 years Exit: 5 or 6 years	Compared children who attended Head Start with those who did not (matched within grade).	Unknown

a. Programs are grouped such that public-school program studies are listed first, followed by program studies involving both public-school programs and Head Start, and then all Head Start studies.

b. Throughout Table1-2, E refers to the experimental or intervention group, and C refers to the control or comparison group. Outcomes listed as E>C or E<C were statistically significant at the p<.05 level.

c. Results may be biased because children were not randomly assigned to experimental and control or comparison groups.

Follow-up Sample Size	Time of Last Follow-up	School Outcomes[b]	Methodological Concerns
Unknown	Grade 3	Achievement tests: E=C in grade 3	Not randomized.[c] No pretest.[d] Bias toward no effect.[g]
Unknown	Grade 4	Achievement tests: E>C in grade 4	Not randomized. No pretest. School-administered tests.[e] Bias toward no effect.
852	Grade 3	Achievement tests: E>C in grade 1, E=C in grades 2 and 3	Not randomized. High attrition.[f] Bias toward no effect.
E=148 C=50	Grade 6	Achievement tests: E=C in grade 6 Special education: E=C, E=5%, C=10% Grade retention: E<C, E=10%, C=22%	Not randomized. No pretest. High attrition. School-administered tests.
Unknown	Grade 3	Achievement tests: E=C in grade 3	Not randomized. No pretest. High attrition. School-administered tests.
E=186 C=112	Grade 11	Achievement tests: E=C, but negative trend in most grades, C>C in grade 11	Not randomized. No pretest. High attrition. Fixed-effects model assumes no family effects. Used percentile scores that have floor effect for blacks.
762	Grade varies up to 12	Achievement tests: E>C, whites only Grade retention: E<C, whites only	Not randomized. No pretest. High attrition. Fixed-effects model assumes no family effects. Used percentile scores that have floor effect for blacks.
E=35 C=26	Grade 3	Achievement tests: E>C in grade 1, E=C in grade 3 Grade retention: E<C, E=18%, C=35%	Not randomized. No pretest. High attrition. Bias toward no effect.
E=54 C=18	Grade 3	Achievement tests: E=C, but positive trend in grades 2 and 3	Not randomized. No pretest.
E=94 C=60	Post-high school	Achievement tests: E>C in grade 5, E=C in grades 6 and above Special education: E<C, E=11%, C=25% Grade retention: E=C, E=51%, C=63% High school graduation: E>C, E=50%, C=33%	Not randomized. No pretest. School-administered tests.
E=1,988 C=1,992	Grades 1 to 3	Achievement tests: E>C in grade 1, E=C in grades 2 and 3	Not randomized. No pretest. Bias toward no effect.

d. No pretest was given to assess/control for initial differences between groups.
e. Result may be biased because school-administered tests were used to measure achievement.
f. Results may be biased because of high attrition rates.
g. Design flaws bias the estimated effect of the program on children's achievement toward zero.
h. The numbers of children in experimental and comparison groups were not reported separately.

Model-Program Study Designs

Seven model-program studies formed comparison groups by randomly assigning children to experimental and control groups from the same pool of potential participants or by using procedures that approximated random assignment (field studies rarely carry off anything perfectly).[1] This increases confidence that estimated effects in these studies are due to the program rather than to preexisting (though perhaps unmeasured) differences between program and comparison groups. However, the benefits of random assignment can be lost as the result of severe attrition (loss of study participants over time) or small sample size, and small sample size can severely limit the power of a study to detect important effects. Only two of these experimental studies began with sample sizes larger than thirty in each group and had low attrition throughout follow-up—the Abecedarian and Perry Preschool studies. Two other experimental studies (Milwaukee and the Early Training Project) began with extremely small sample sizes, which rendered random assignment less useful and provided these studies with very little power to detect even fairly large effects. The remaining four experimental studies suffered massive attrition that could have invalidated the initial random assignment.[2]

The other eight model-program studies constructed comparison groups, usually at a later date. Some of the approaches to constructing comparison groups seem likely to have created group differences that favored the ECE group. The two curriculum studies formed no-ECE groups after the fact by selecting children who had not attended another ECE program. This eliminated from the potential comparison pool those children whose parents sought out early educational experiences for them and were most comparable to the treatment group families with respect to parental attitudes and behavior regarding education. In the Harlem Training Project, attrition during a waiting period prior to entry at age three may have introduced differences favoring this later entry group as it had a higher IQ prior to treatment than the control group (Lazar et al., 1982). The Yale Child Welfare Research Program study obtained a control group thirty months after it selected the program group using the same clinic records used to identify the program group. However, the program group was invited to receive child care and other services while the comparison group was invited to participate in data collection. There was sufficient rejection of the offer in both cases to significantly influence group composition. Moreover, the passage of time before the comparison group was contacted meant that many who moved were lost from the comparison group. Those moving without leaving a forwarding address might have been the least economically and socially successful. Finally, three times the number of months of clinic records were required to obtain the program group as the comparison group suggesting that the population using the clinic had changed or that methods used to select the two groups differed (Seitz, Rosenbaum, & Apfel, 1985).

Head Start and Public School Research Designs

All of the large-scale, public program studies used quasi-experimental designs. Some constructed comparison groups from waiting lists or other groups of children thought to be similar to program children. Others simply relied on natural variation in program attendance within a sample. Both strategies raise questions about the comparability of the groups due to self-selection and administrative selection. Self-selection occurs when some parents exert more effort to obtain educational opportunities for their children including ECE programs, good neighborhood schools groups, good teachers within schools, and good educational experiences outside of school. The educational success of their children is unlikely to be comparable even without the benefit of preschool. The results of administrative selection are less clear. Programs might seek to enroll the most needy, those easiest to recruit, or those thought most likely to gain from the program. The Head Start and public school program studies are at a distinct disadvantage in dealing with this problem compared to the model-program studies. Not only did they not use random assignment, but because comparison groups were not identified prospectively, there are no pretest measures of children's cognitive abilities to offer as evidence that the groups were initially the same or to use to adjust later measures.[3]

Some of the Head Start and public school program studies used statistical adjustments for variations in family background characteristics to try to eliminate possible biases introduced by differences between program and comparison groups. Several of the most recent studies employed complex statistical procedures that explicitly attempt to remove the effects of selection. However, the extent to which these statistical methods produce more accurate estimates of effects is unclear, and alternative approaches can produce conflicting results (Barnett & Camilli, 1997; Campbell, 1991; Cook, 1991).

Findings of Long-Term Studies

Most long-term research has focused on the effects of ECE on cognitive ability and school success. Results in these domains are reported in Table 1-1 for model programs and Table 1-2 for large-scale programs. Outcome measures included are IQ, achievement, grade retention, special-education placement, and high school graduation. After a review of these findings, results are summarized for the relatively small number of studies reporting results for socialization and parent outcomes.

IQ Effects

All of the model-program studies found that their ECE programs produced IQ gains at some point. In most cases IQ effects were sustained until school entry at age five, at which time ten studies reported effects between 4 and 11 IQ points, the Milwaukee study reported a gain of 25 points, and the Syracuse study reported no effect. Three studies did not measure IQ at school entry. Data on the persistence of IQ effects is provided by Table 1-1 which reports the most distant follow-up comparison of IQs. The two experimental studies that enrolled infants in full-day educational child-care programs reported the largest initial effects (Milwaukee & Abecedarian) and found that some IQ gain persisted at least into adolescence.[4] The other studies that enrolled infants did not find persistent effects, but both were quasi-experimental and one ceased serving children before age three.

None of the large-scale program studies provided IQ data on Stanford-Binet or WISC IQ tests comparable to the data from the model-program studies. A small number of studies provided results on the Peabody Picture Vocabulary Test (PPVT), and the WLC study administered the Illinois Test of Psycholinguistic Abilities (ITPA). Whether these tests should be considered comparable to IQ tests is questionable. With one exception, no effects are found on these measures after school entry.

The exception is a study by Currie and Thomas (1995), which finds that Head Start produced persistent effects on PPVT scores for white but not African American children using data from the National Longitudinal Survey. Their results were challenged by Barnett and Camilli (1997) who found serious limitations in the data and methods employed by Currie and Thomas. Among the most important of these: their methodology relies on questionable assumptions and leads to the selection of a biased sample; the PPVT-R percentile scores analyzed by Currie and Thomas exhibit a number of problems including an extremely strong floor effect that does not lift with age for African Americans; and alternative analyses that are equally plausible produce different results and raise questions about the meaningfulness of any analyses employing the NLS data.

Achievement Effects

Five of eleven model-program studies with achievement test data found statistically significant positive effects beyond grade three. Evidence of effects was strongest in the studies that randomized assignment to program and control groups. The Abecedarian and Perry Preschool studies found achievement effects persisting to ages fourteen and fifteen. The Florida Parent Education study found effects through grade four. The Milwaukee study found that effects were statistically significant only to grade two.[5] The ETP and IDS programs did not find effects on achievement. In contrast to the experimental studies, none of the quasi-experimental model-program studies found persistent effects on achievement, though some found statistically significant initial effects.

The achievement test results of the Head Start and public school studies were as variable as the results of the model-program studies. Of the twenty-four studies reporting achievement-test results, nine found significant positive effects at latest follow-up. The other fifteen studies found no effects or that the effects faded out. Fade-out occurred early in most cases, but was not found until at least sixth grade in three studies. Note that studies finding no effect do not necessarily imply that there were no effects before third grade as several measured achievement only at grade three or later.

A naive interpretation of the results of these studies would be to say that most ECE programs have failed to produce long-lasting gains in achievement for disadvantaged children. Based on this conclusion, one might seek to identify the characteristics of successful programs or to find explanations for fade-out in subsequent school experiences (e.g., the poor schools attended by disadvantaged children especially in the inner cities). However, this conclusion is incorrect, and the subsequent search for sources of fade-out is premature. Instead, the evidence of fade-out in achievement appears to result largely from flaws in research design and very high attrition rates for achievement-test data, which reduced sample size (thereby decreasing the statistical power to detect effects) and biased estimated effects toward zero. Studies that found no effects or fade-out were vulnerable to selective attrition because they obtained their achievement test data from schools' routine testing programs or they suffered from another design flaw that produced a similar problem even though they administered their own achievement tests.

The most common source of achievement test data in these studies was standardized tests routinely administered by schools. Although this strategy provided data at low cost, it had several unfortunate consequences. First, the quality and uniformity of test administration can be expected to be lower when testing is done for entire classes by teachers rather than individually by well-trained testing specialists. Second, some data are lost simply because the tests used vary from school to school and year to year. Third, schools' testing programs administer tests by grade so that children who are retained in grade are not tested with their age cohort. Many studies collected the data by grade and simply lost data on children who had been retained. Even in the rare cases where data on children behind grade level are added later, the scores are not comparable because they are obtained at different ages. Fourth, children expected to perform poorly are systematically excluded from school testing. The use of routine testing to hold schools accountable places pressure on school administrators to remove poor performers from the test pool at each grade level (McGill-Franzen & Allington, 1993). Many schools do not test children in special-education classes. Poor students are more frequently absent and are more likely to miss tests (sometimes because they have been encouraged to miss them).

Studies relying on school-administered tests at best have test scores with lower reliability and smaller sample sizes, both of which would reduce their ability to detect program effects. At worst, they systematically lose the more poorly performing students from year to year as the cumulative percentage of children retained in grade, placed in special education, or otherwise omitted from testing grows. The result is that any differences between program and comparison groups are gradually "erased" as grade level rises and the children for whom achievement tests are available become more similar across the two groups.

Some studies had idiosyncratic flaws that led to similar biases in achievement-test data, even though tests were specially administered for the studies. For example, the New Haven Head Start study individually administered achievement tests, but only to children at expected grade level. As there was significantly less grade retention in the program group over time, this had the effect of gradually equating the tested program and control groups on performance. The ETS Head Start study tested only children in classes where at least 50 percent of the children were study participants, probably in order to save on the costs of testing.[6] This eliminated from testing children who had been retained in grade or placed in special-education classes. Unfortunately, data on grade retention and special education were not collected.

The Westinghouse national evaluation of Head Start formed its comparison group by matching former Head Start children in grades one, two, and three with other children in their grade levels. This automatically equated the two groups on grade level and generated comparison groups that included children from older cohorts who had been retained. Evidence of this is provided by comparisons of the ages of Head Start and comparison groups at each grade. In first grade where an effect on achievement is found, the Head Start and comparison groups are not significantly different in age. In the second and third grade where effects "fade out," the Head Start groups are significantly younger than the comparison groups, and the age gap widens from second to third grade.

For the most part, the studies that found persistent effects did not suffer from these attrition-related problems. The two experimental studies of model programs that provided strong evidence of persistent effects on achievement began with reasonable sample sizes, administered their own achievement tests, and had relatively low rates of attrition. The Child-Parent Center II study obtained and analyzed test scores for children who had been retained in grade even though it relied on school-administered tests. The Cincinnati Title I study had very low rates of grade retention and special education placement that were unlikely to introduce much difference between groups.

Research on the achievement effects of Head Start using the NLSCM deserves special attention because of the use of national data and attention to issues of selection bias in the statistical approaches. Currie and Thomas (1995) found effects on achievement only for white children. Barnett and Camilli's (1997) analyses found evidence of long-term effects on achievement for all ethnic groups. Barnett and Camilli also concluded that the NLSCM data had so many limitations as a basis for estimating Head Start effects that they should not be used for this purpose.

Effects on School Success

School success was primarily measured by rates of grade retention, special education, and high school graduation. Across all studies, the findings were relatively uniform and constitute overwhelming evidence that ECE can produce sizeable improvements in school success. All but one of the model-program studies reported grade retention and special education rates, and in all of these the rates are lower for the program group. The one model-program study that did not report rates (Syracuse) simply reported that there was no statistically significant difference. Despite small sample sizes, statistical significance on one or the other was found in five model-program studies, and the Perry Preschool study found significant effects for number of years of special education placement.

In the Head Start and public school studies, statistically significant effects on grade retention or special education were found in ten of the thirteen studies that collected the relevant data. The Cincinnati Title I study did not find a statistically significant effect on either, but the base rates for retention and special-education placement were relatively low. The Washington, D.C. study suggests a small effect on grade retention (not statistically significant) and no effect on special education placement, but a limitation of this study is that the comparison group is less disadvantaged and these estimates were not adjusted for this difference between the groups (Marcon, 1993).[7] The Florida prekindergarten studies (one finds a difference and one does not) are limited by a lack of comparability between program and comparison groups. The only control for differences was that both groups qualified for free or reduced-price school lunch.

Three model-program studies, one Head Start study, and one public school study provide data on high school graduation. All five produced large estimates of effects on the graduation rate, though only in the three with larger sample sizes were these statistically significant. Further support for positive effects of ECE on high school graduation can be drawn from the many other studies that find effects on achievement, grade retention, and special education placement—all of which are predictive of high school graduation (Natriello et al., 1987; Roderick, 1994).

Are Public Programs as Effective as Model Programs?

A critical issue for ECE policy is the extent to which cognitive development and school success can be enhanced by public programs provided on a large scale and not just by model programs provided to small numbers of children (whose success might be attributed to exceptional leadership, motivation, intensity of services, and staff qualifications). Two types of information can be used to address this issue: cross-study comparisons and within-study comparisons where a single study examines more than one type of program.

Cross-Study Comparisons

To facilitate comparisons, results for model and large-scale public programs were presented separately in the tables and text. Clearly, both types of programs have been found to produce positive effects, but the size of effects produced by the two types of programs may not be the same. Size comparisons are precluded for IQ and achievement-test effects by the lack of IQ measures in Head Start and public school studies and the serious problems with achievement-test data in many studies. However, it is possible to compare the size of effects on school success.

Effects on grade retention, special education, and high school graduation are easily summarized across studies as differences in the cumulative percentages of program and comparison groups ever to experience those outcomes. Table 1-3 presents medians, means, and standard deviations of effects for all three school outcomes by program type. Average effects are substantial for both types of programs, but effects on special education are much larger for model programs—24 percentage points for model programs, 5 percentage points for Head Start and public-school programs. There is no statistically significant difference in effects on grade retention. However, the size of the estimated difference is potentially important. Effects are comparable for high school graduation, but the much smaller number of studies with this outcome measure limits the value of this last comparison.

Potential explanations for the differences in results between the two types of program studies were investigated with regression analyses that controlled for design (randomized or not), length of follow-up, age of entry (prior to age three or not), and the comparison group's rate of grade retention or special-education placement. The comparison group's rate had a significant ($p<.01$) positive effect on the estimated program effect—the higher the comparison group's rate, the larger a program's effect. Moreover, after adjusting for the control group's rate there was no significant difference in effects on grade retention or special education between the two types of programs. The other study characteristics had no statistically significant effects on size of program effects.

One might conclude from these results that Head Start and public school programs are about as effective as model programs when the population served is taken into account, despite the

Table 1-3.
Percentage Point Change in Students Retained in Grade, in Special Education, and Graduating from High School by Type of Program

Outcome Measure	Model Programs				Head Start/Public School			
	Median	Mean	s.d.	N	Median	Mean	s.d.	N
Grade Retention	-14.5	-14.9	9.8	14	-10.0	-9.5	-6.4	11
Special Education	-24.0	-19.6*	14.6	11	-5.0	-4.7*	5.3	9
H.S. Graduation	16.0	16.0	2.0	3	15.0	15.0	2.8	2

Note: The NLSCM data set estimate of Head Start's effect on grade retention was calculated as a weighted average of effects estimated by ethnicity.
*Statistically significant difference, $p < .05$.

differences in the average effects shown in Table 1-3. Model programs may produce larger effects on average because the model programs studied served children who were more likely to be retained in grade or placed in special education because the children were more disadvantaged or the local schools had high rates as a matter of policy. For example, a Head Start program in an area where schools strongly avoid grade retention and special education placements as a matter of policy would be extremely limited in its potential to reduce these outcomes.

However, there are reasons to be wary of accepting the conclusion that the two types of programs are equally effective. Model programs could have larger effects because they are much more careful in targeting services on children who are seriously disadvantaged. More importantly, few studies of the two types of programs overlap in the degree of disadvantage of the children served so that considerable extrapolation is involved. It could be much more difficult to produce gains for the most highly disadvantaged children so that the higher quality of model programs is required to produce their results. Program quality and intensity were represented crudely in the analysis and their true values may highly correlate with the degree of disadvantage of the population served (i.e., better programs take on greater challenges). Results from studies that directly compare model and large-scale public programs serving the same population would be more persuasive.

Within-Study Comparisons

Unfortunately, only one of the studies reported in Tables 1-1 and 1-2 compares a model program to large-scale public programs. The

Abecedarian study investigated the effects of the comparison group's participation in other forms of ECE (Burchinal et al., 1989). Comparison-group children who had attended community ECE programs that met federal guidelines for quality were found to have higher IQ scores than comparison-group children with minimal ECE experience. The estimated effect at school entry was roughly half the size of the effect of the Abecedarian program. As there was self-selection into these higher-quality, community-based programs, this effect probably should be considered an upper-bound estimate. In addition, it should be recognized that the Abecedarian program provided greater quality and quantity of ECE.

Additional information is provided by a study in which four- and five-year-old children from families in poverty were randomly assigned to either a model program or Head Start and Title 1 public school classrooms. Model-program children entered the Learning-to-Learn program at age four (n=22) or five (n=23) and continued in it through first grade. The control group entered Head Start at age four (n=22) or a public school Title 1 classroom at age five (n=23) and continued in Title 1 classrooms through first grade.

Children who attended the model program scored higher on IQ and achievement tests from the end of the preschool year through third grade (Van de Reit & Resnick, 1973). A further follow-up examined grades, grade retention, and special education placement in fourth through sixth grade. The Learning-to-Learn group had higher reading grades in fourth and fifth grade and significantly fewer grade retentions and special education placements through sixth grade. The lack of an effect on grades at sixth grade could easily reflect the difference between groups in grade level and special education placements.[8]

Economic Value of Benefits

A key question for public policy is the extent to which evidence of a positive economic return for ECE can be generalized to the Head Start and public school programs. The only benefit-cost analysis conducted to date is based on data from the High/Scope Perry Preschool study through age twenty-seven (Barnett, 1993, 1996b). The results of that analysis are summarized in Table 1-4. As can be seen, the estimated benefits are quite large. In fact, the rate of return exceeds that on investments in the stock market (Barnett, 1996b).

Although studies of Head Start and public school programs do not provide all of the data needed for a comparable benefit-cost analysis, comparisons can be made on several key outcome measures. The High/Scope Perry Preschool program's effects were five points on grade rentention, thirteen points on special education, and eighteen points on graduation. These are reasonably similar to the median effects estimated for Head Start and public school programs in Table 1-3. As public programs are less expensive than the Perry Preschool model, it seems fair to conclude that public ECE programs are likely to be a sound economic investment.

Must Intervention Continue Beyond Preschool?

The belief that intervention must continue into the elementary school years if the effects of ECE programs on disadvantaged children's achievement and school success are to be sustained grows out of the belief that effects fade out. This review shows that underlying belief about fade-out to be incorrect. Model programs, Head Start programs, and public school programs all have been found to produce long-term effects on achievement and school success *without* school-age intervention. Those who believe that elementary schools do not serve disadvantaged children well may find this puzzling. However, the persistence of effects even when the quality of subsequent education is fairly low is consistent with the widely held view that children play an active role in their own learning in and out of school. Moreover, even poorly run schools (one might say, especially poorly run schools) offer greater learning opportunities for children who begin kindergarten and each subsequent grade with greater abilities (Allington & Walmsley, 1995; Entwisle, 1995).

Two studies explicitly compared the effects of extended elementary programs with the effects of ECE programs alone, though only one employed an experimental design. The Abecedarian study randomly assigned half of the program and control groups to a special school-age program at age five in order to compare the effects of ECE alone, ECE plus an enriched school-age program, the school-age program alone, and no intervention. The schoolage program was provided for the first three years of elementary school and consisted of biweekly home visits by teachers providing individualized supplemental activities in partnership with parents. Supplemental learning activities were developed with the child's classroom teacher. Home visiting teachers provided other social supports for the families and served as advocates with the schools. By adolescence the results were clear. ECE alone produced substantial effects on IQ, achievement, and school progress. The school-age program alone was largely ineffective, and as an add-on it had no effects on IQ and mixed effects on school success and achievement.

Table 1-4.
**Present Value of Costs and Benefits Per Child Discounted
at 3 percent**

Cost or Benefit[a]	Recipients of Costs and Benefits		
	Whole Society	Preschool Participants	General Public
Measured Benefits			
Child care	738	728	0
K–12 education	6,872	0	6872
Adult education	283	0	283
College[b]	–868	0	–868
Earnings[c]	14,498	10,270	4,229
Crime	49,044	0	49,044
Welfare	219	–2,193	2,412
Benefit subtotal	70,786	8,815	61,972
Projected Benefits			
Earning	15,833	11,215	4,618
Crime	21,337	0	21,337
Welfare	46	–460	506
Projected subtotal	37,216	10,755	26,461
Total Benefits	108,002	19,511	88,433
Preschool Cost	–$ 12,356	0	–$ 12,356
Net Benefits	$ 95,646	$19,570	$ 76,077

a. Costs and disbenefits appear as negative numbers.
b. Some small portion of college costs are likely to have been borne by the participants, but these could not be estimated from the available information.
c. The benefits reported under earnings include all costs paid by the employer to hire a participant. Allocation between participants and taxpayers assumes a 25% marginal tax rate, that the value of fringe benefits to the employee equals 10% of salary, and that other costs to the employer equal 10% of salary.
Source: Barnett, 1996b.

By contrast the nonexperimental CPC II study found that enriched elementary school services added substantially to the effects of ECE with the size of the effect increasing directly with the number of years of elementary services. Possibly the CPC II elementary school program was much more effective compared to local regular education than was the Abecedarian elementary program. The CPC II program featured smaller classes, additional classroom and support staff, and an emphasis on parent involvement in the classroom. Alternatively, the CPC II's estimated effect for the elementary program may be biased upward by self-selection. Participation in the CPC program and length of participation in CPC were functions of parent choice. Special analyses were conducted to minimize the effects of selection, and tests for selection bias were negative. However, it is unclear how well such analyses actually perform in correcting and detecting selection bias (Campbell, 1991; Cook, 1991).

A third source of information is research on elementary education of disadvantaged students. Elementary education of disadvantaged children has significant shortcomings, and there is mounting evidence that it could be substantially improved (Allington & Walmsley, 1995; Barnett, 1996a; Haynes & Comer, 1993; Levin, 1987; Purkey & Smith, 1983; Ross, Smith, Casey, & Slavin, 1995). The question that arises is whether improvements in elementary education for disadvantaged children might obviate the need for high-quality ECE. Although the evidence to date is sparse, it appears that ECE and elementary education improvement together produce larger benefits for disadvantaged children than elementary education improvement alone (Slavin, Karweit, & Wasik, 1994).

Summary and Conclusions

For economically disadvantaged children, ECE substantially improves cognitive development during early childhood and produces long-term increases in achievement (learning) and school success. The evidence of long-term effects is provided by thirty-eight studies and generalizes across a wide range of programs and communities. Although many studies fail to find persistent achievement effects this is plausibly explained by flaws in study design and follow-up procedures. Positive effects on grade retention and special education are found in the overwhelming majority of studies, and evidence for positive effects on high school graduation is strong though limited to the small number of studies with very long-term follow-up.

Head Start and public school programs produce the same types of effects as the model programs, but their effects are on average smaller. It is difficult to assess why effects are smaller for public programs because there are several plausible explanations. Overall, model programs began at earlier ages, lasted longer, were more intense, and were better implemented. There is some evidence that all of these program characteristics influence effectiveness. Comparison group rates of grade retention and special education placement were much higher in model-program studies than in Head

Start and public school program studies. This could reflect measurement problems in studies of public programs. Alternatively, it is possible that model programs have tended to target children at much higher risk of school failure. In this case, the results of cross-study comparisons imply that the size of effects varies directly with the degree of risk for school failure of the children served.

When the evidence from short-term studies on child care is added, the issues of program quality and population risk can be seen to intersect. The size of program effects is a function of the distance between the quality of the learning environment provided by ECE and the quality of the learning environment in the home and community. Thus, effects might be increased either by increasing program quality or targeting more severely disadvantaged children and families. The greater effectiveness of model programs would appear to be due to both when the full range of evidence is examined. Unfortunately, ECE programs serving low-income children often fall short of desired levels of quality and do not have the resources required to replicate model-program quality (Phillips, 1987; Lamb & Sternberg, 1990; Zigler & Styfco, 1993).

Continued intervention into the elementary school years is not necessary to prevent a fade-out in effects. Nevertheless, the quality of elementary schools is an important concern in efforts to improve the cognitive development and educational success of children in poverty. Obviously, some schools provide better environments than others for children to develop and learn. Some schools may be so poor as to "hold back" children who received quality ECE. Some schools may devote more resources to children who begin school behind enabling them to "catch up." However, neither seems to occur in the majority of cases, and the educational needs of children in poverty are so great that investments in both quality ECE and quality elementary education are likely to produce large benefits.

In light of the evidence, every child living in poverty in the United States ought to be provided with at least one year of ECE. The only comprehensive benefit-cost analysis conducted to date is based on the High/Scope Perry Preschool. However, a comparison of costs and effects for this model program to the median for public programs is quite favorable to the latter—similar effects and lower costs. This suggests that society would gain greatly by extending current public ECE programs to all disadvantaged children. A conservative strategy would be to increase the quality of public programs to approach the levels of model programs found to be effective in true experiments and to gradually increase the number of years of ECE publicly provided in conjunction with evaluations of the effects.

Expansion of the current Head Start program to serve all eligible children with the addition of funds for quality improvement is the simplest way to pursue this policy goal. However, it is only the first step toward improved ECE policy. Thirty years of rising maternal labor force participation and recent federal welfare reform have made Head Start's half-day preschool approach obsolete for much of the population. New models must be developed and implemented for three and four year olds and for younger children. In 1990, nearly half the children under age three were cared for by someone other than a parent. There are important opportunities here, and benefits are likely to be greatest if policy is supported by research that reduces the uncertainties about ECE and its long-term effects.

Future research must provide policy makers with a better understanding of the effects of program characteristics on child development and school success. Among the program characteristics most deserving attention are entry age, duration, intensity, quality of the learning environment, mode of delivery (home versus center), parent involvement, and family-support services.[9] Cross-study comparisons provide some evidence that birth through age five interventions may yield larger, and with respect to IQ, more persistent effects than later ECE interventions.[10] However, in these comparisons entry age and duration tend to be confounded with intensity. Within-study comparisons reveal little or no effect of entry age, but have examined only small differences for older pre-schoolers. The question of timing and duration is further informed by research indicating that environmental impacts on brain development differ in their consequences for cognitive development depending on the age at which they occur (Chugani et al., 1987; Chugani & Phelps, 1986; Kolb, 1989). One may reasonably conclude that high-quality, full-day, year-round ECE begining in infancy and continuing to school entry is likely to produce the greatest cognitive and academic gains for disadvantaged children.

The weight of the evidence indicates that home visits tend to be ineffective in improving children's cognitive development and school success whether provided alone or in conjunction with center-based ECE (see also Boutte, 1992). However, there are a few exceptions with short-term positive effects in the United States (Olds & Kitzman, 1993), and positive effects into the school years have been found in a Turkish study (Kagitcibasi, 1996; Boocock, this volume). Variations in program design and target population might explain the variations in results. Thus, it might be productive to develop and subject to rigorous long-term evaluation home-visiting models designed (based on what seems to have worked best in the past) to improve disadvantaged children's cognitive development.

The information needed to produce better-informed policy could be produced through experiments in conjunction with the gradual expansion of existing federal and state ECE programs. For example, as Head Start expands to serve infants, grants can be conditioned on participation in experiments using random assignment, and the Early Head Start study is proceeding along these lines. However, care must be exercized to ensure that research leads the way with programs that are realistically designed to produce large effects. Such programs provide children with large quantities of high-quality, center-based ECE rather than focusing on extensive case management and home visits. Whether similar effects can be produced with family home day care in the first three years remains to be investigated. A similar approach could be taken to investigate the potential returns to investing in Head Start quality. The large numbers of unserved children means that it would be possible to study the effects of a $1,000 per child increase in funding (or specified improvements in teacher qualifications, group sizes, or supervision and in-service professional development) using random assignment either within or across Head Start grantees.

Other important issues for future research that can be addressed in experiments with expanded public services include the appropriate target population, direct public provision of services versus public provision of vouchers for privately purchased ECE, and long-term effects on maternal employment and earnings. Some programs could be expanded to serve children up to 150 percent of the poverty level. States might compare the cost, quality, and effectiveness of school-provided ECE with the services parents purchase using vouchers. Head Start or public school programs could be expanded to provide full-day, year-round care. Although effects on maternal employment were not considered in this review, they could be substantial and will be a central issue as welfare reform evolves. These and similar studies would substantially strengthen the research base for ECE policy and could enhance public confidence that ECE policy benefits both disadvantaged children and the nation as a whole.

Notes

1. In some cases departures from perfect adherence to random assignment occurred, but impacts on results were negligible. For example,

in the Perry Preschool study younger siblings of children already in the study were assigned to the same groups as their older siblings to prevent treatment diffusion, and two children whose mothers worked were shifted from the program to the control group. Neither departure from random assignment had a significant effect on the results, and they tended to bias estimates of program effects downward (Schweinhart et al., 1993).

Even the best-designed studies are potentially affected by queuing bias or bandwagon effects and can provide only partial equilibrium estimates of preschool education's effects. Queuing bias is an issue because the treatment is not provided to everyone and may confer advantages on participants at the expense of others. For example, if schools refer a fixed percentage of students to special education, other students replace treatment-group members in special education and there are no cost savings. Bandwagon effects may occur when a program provided on a large scale produces changes in norms or in the social climate.

2. Attrition is important for two reasons. First, it reduces a study's statistical power to detect effects, in some cases to the point that even large effects might not be statistically significant using conventional criteria (e.g., $p<.05$). Second, it reduces confidence that: (a) the final sample is comparable to the initial sample and (b) the final program and comparison groups are comparable to each other. If the final sample differs substantially from the original, the results might not generalize to the original target population. If treatment and comparison groups lose comparability, the results of a comparison can be totally misleading. Studies that have no pretreatment data on both groups are particularly weakened by attrition because they cannot compare final groups to initial groups. The more extensive the attrition the greater the chance that differences large enough to be misleading might occur.

Two types of attrition can occur prior to follow-up: attrition due to refusal to participate in the study and attrition during the service delivery period. Parents who are highly motivated to obtain educational advantages for their children might decline to participate in an experiment for fear of assignment to the control group. Quasi-experimental studies face the opposite problem that the most motivated parents may be the most successful in obtaining entry to a program that is limited in its availability. Attrition during the program period might occur selectively because parents who feel that a program "works" for their child or those who most highly value education may be much more likely to stick with a program, especially if it requires parent participation. Such selective attrition can severely bias the results of a study if outcomes are more heavily influenced by preexisting differences between the follow-up groups than by the preschool program.

The "Initial Ns" reported in Tables 1-1 and 1-2 refer to participants remaining at the end of the service delivery period and so do not reveal the extent of attrition prior to that time. The extent of refusal to participate is not always reported, and it is difficult to judge how much of a problem it might present. Loss of subjects during the intervention period is more commonly reported, and most studies lost only a few participants during the intervention period. Among the model-program studies, only the Houston PCDC study lost most of its sample during the service delivery period, and in follow-up it identified only a small minority of those who completed the program. The Milwaukee study identified fifty-five qualified participants, lost fifteen of these prior to the intervention, and lost five additional participants while delivering services so that those available for follow-up were 64 percent of the original group. The Perry Preschool study began with 128 participants and lost four who moved and one who died between ages three and five so that it remained virtually intact from entry to follow-up (Schweinhart et al., 1993). The Abecedarian study began with 111 participants and lost nine who moved, four who died, and one who was diagnosed as moderately retarded between birth and age five. This left 87 percent of the sample at entry for follow-up. The Institute for Developmental Studies (IDS) and Florida studies lost the overwhelming majority of their study participants in follow-up.

3. Three model-program studies provide information about the biases introduced by quasi-experimental strategies because they included both randomized control groups and quasi-experimental comparison groups. In the IDS study data the quasi-experimental groups scored lower than the control group on the Stanford-Binet IQ test and would have led to larger estimated effects at kindergarten and third grade. In the ETP study the true control group did not differ from the program group on IQ or achievement during the early school years, but the quasi-experimental (called a "distal control" group) scored lower on virtually all measures in all years through age ten. However, at ages seventeen and twenty-one, the quasi-experimental group tended to outperform the controls on a wide range of measures including IQ, achievement, grades, graduation, and desire to seek higher education. In contrast to the quasi-experimental results reviewed in this paper, the VIP study's short-term experimental investigation and an independent experiment in Bermuda found no significant effects on IQ, the PPVT, or any other cognitive measures for the VIP (Levenstein, O'Hara, & Madden, 1983; Scarr & McCartney, 1988).

4. The Harlem study reported a significant effect at age twelve on the performance IQ subscale only. However, this can be explained as the result of preexisting IQ differences between the program and control groups.

5. The reporting of achievement test data for the Milwaukee study leaves a great deal to be desired. The tables reporting results present no sample size information and no standard errors so that it is impossible to verify claims about statistical significance.

6. Data from this study have recently reemerged in a study by Lee and colleagues (1990) which interpreted reductions in the estimated effects of Head Start from kindergarten and first grade as a genuine decline and

suggested that this might be due to the lack of supportive school experiences and home environments.

7. The report does not explain why adjustment was not made for differences in economic disadvantage, though perhaps the only variable available—participation in the subsidized school lunch program—was judged too crude to be of much use.

8. The Learning-to-Learn study was not included in Tables 1-1 and 1-2 because the children who entered at age five attended special programs rather than regular kindergarten. No significant effects were found for age of entry (and estimated effects of preschool alone are not reported). This could be due to the strength of the interventions at ages five and six, but it could also be due to preexisting differences between children entering at ages four and five as age of entry was not determined by random assignment.

9. Most of the programs studied involved parents and some worked so extensively with parents as well as children that they could be characterized as family support programs. It is difficult to compare the extensiveness of parent activities across programs given the information reported on programs, but those with the greatest emphasis on parents do not appear to be most effective.

10. It is unclear why IQ effects fade out and how important it might be if IQ effects persisted. Some equalization of IQs might be expected when children who did not attend ECE enter formal education (Ceci, 1991; Gallagher & Ramey, 1987; Husen & Tuijnman, 1991). For example, in the High/Scope Perry Preschool study (Schweinhart et al., 1993) control group IQs rose after they entered school. However, in this and other studies the primary cause of the fade-out in IQ effects is not increased IQs for the comparison group, but gradual decreases for the ECE group.

Some regard IQ as an extremely narrow and relatively uninteresting measure of cognitive ability (Sternberg & Detterman, 1986; Gardner, 1983). Those who regard IQ as more important emphasize its predictive power. IQ correlates about .50 with grades and number of years of education, explaining about 25 percent of their variance in the general population (Neisser et al., 1995). However, this does not mean that IQ causes 25 percent of the variation in school success. Moreover, if IQ is important primarily because it predicts school success, then IQ's importance diminishes when IQ effects diverge from effects on achievement and school progress.

2

S. S. Boocock and M. B. Larner

Long-Term Outcomes in Other Nations

Although most of the research discussed in this book pertains to early-childhood programs in the United States, increased utilization of nonparental child care and rising preschool enrollments are worldwide trends, precipitated by social and economic changes that are themselves global phenomena. The author of a recent international review of early-childhood education notes, for example, that "The U.S. and many other countries in the world are becoming increasingly similar in family characteristics;

Adapted from Boocock, S. S. (1995). Early childhood programs in other nations: Goals and outcomes. *The Future of Children* (Winter 5(3):94–114, by permission of Center for the Future of Children, The David and Lucile Packard Foundation.

increasing participation of mothers in the labor force, dwindling family size, and disappearing extended-family support are almost worldwide phenomena" (Olmsted, 1989, p. 34).[1] Demand for preschool services has also been fueled by the tremendous growth and broader dissemination of knowledge about human development—in particular, about the crucial importance of the early years of life and the untapped learning potential, as well as the vulnerabilities of infants and young children.

The international interest in early-childhood programs does not mean that preschool facilities and services are evenly distributed, either within or among countries. The overall availability and quality of preschool programs tend to be much higher in rich industrialized nations than in poor developing ones, yet large differences distinguish even nations that are geographically close and at similar levels of economic development. For example, almost 100 percent of all French and Belgian children are enrolled in an educational preschool program by age three, compared to 28 percent of Spanish and Portugese children and less than 6 percent of Swiss children (OECD, 1993). In most nations, access to preschool facilities is much greater in urban centers than in rural areas, and enrollment rates for children from upper- or middle-class homes exceed those for poor children—though again, the size of the gaps, and the extent to which they are closing varies from one nation to another. Finally, government involvement in the provision of preschool services takes different forms, from full funding and direct sponsorship of programs to a more modest role of regulating programs provided by the private sector and paid for by parents.

Only recently has systematic international research begun to document the linkages between national policy, early-childhood programs, and outcomes for children. A number of handbooks and reports describe child and family policies and offer estimates of preschool enrollments in various nations, but only a few discuss research on the effects of the programs they describe.[2] Several projects now underway involve cross-national comparisons of early-childhood services, and some plan assessments of short- and long-term effects of preschool experiences in a later phase of the project.[3] The relationship between research and policy development varies across countries. For the most part, however, early-childhood policies in other nations have evolved independent of the research foundation that has been so important in the development of U.S. early-childhood policy.

A comprehensive cross-cultural review of research on the outcomes of early-childhood programs is not possible in this chapter.[4]

Rather its objective is to complement the reviews of U.S. studies on the long-term outcomes of early-childhood programs provided in other chapters by examining comparable international research. The chapter begins with an overview of the research approaches most commonly used in the international literature on early-childhood programs. Subsequent sections will discuss the aims, designs, and findings of the studies chosen for review, organized by region and by country within region. The chapter will conclude with a brief review of major research results and a consideration of their implications for American policy, practice, and research.

Methodological Concerns in International Research on Early-Childhood Programs

Definitional Issues

There are, of course, formidable difficulties in comparing data collected in different countries. Many problems arise from differences in the way early-childhood services are organized and defined. The programs examined in these studies served children ranging in age from birth to elementary school entry. Some provided child care for children with working parents, others prepared children for school entry, and others offered a broad range of health, developmental, and social services. The outcomes sought by the program designers and, to some extent, measured by researchers range from cognitive development and school success or failure, to emotional development and social skills, to the reduction of inequalities based on racial, ethnic, social class and gender differeces. Most of the effects measured pertain to children, but a few studies also considered impacts on families.

Figure 2-1 offers a schematic view of the different settings and programs that children may experience before entering school. In many but not all countries, a distinction is made between services labeled as child-care services versus preschool or kindergarten, and the two types of programs are likely to be administered by different government ministries or agencies. "Care" usually refers to full-day programs for families with working parents or parents who are otherwise unable to provide care, and it is often available to children of varied ages; "preschool education" usually refers to part-day programs with an educational orientation that are reserved for children three or older. The distinction between preschool and child-care programs will be used in this chapter, though it is important to

Figure 2-1.
**Early Childhood Care and Education Settings
for Children Aged Birth to Five Years**

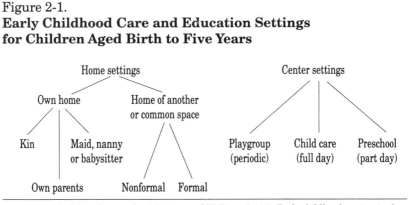

Sources: Modified from diagram by J. Bairrao and W. Tietze (1993). *Early childhood services in the European Community.* A report submitted to the Commission of the European Community Task Force on Human Resources, Education, Training, and Youth. Terminology adapted from P. Moss (1990). Child care in the European Community. *Women of Europe*, Supplement 31. Brussels: European Commission Childcare Network.

remember that the programs in each category vary in the age range of children who participate, the services delivered, and the level of public versus private funding and control. The studies to be reviewed here cover various areas of Figure 2-1. Some *focus* upon a particular type of program or setting; some *compare* the outcomes of two or more programs or settings; one study attempts a comprehensive assessment of all of the major types of early-childhood care and programs available to preschool children in one country (United Kingdom).

Design Issues

In contrast with the U.S. studies reviewed in several of the other chapters in this book (for example, those by Barnett and by St. Pierre et al.), few of the international studies employed an experimental design with random assignment of children to program and control groups. This lack of randomness adds to the difficulty of assessing the validity of the research findings, because effects that are due to self-selection or other factors not under the researchers' control may be erroneously attributed to a preschool program. Other problems arise from variations in the kinds of information collected and modes of record keeping, and these difficulties are compounded when cross-national comparisons are made. Even when a multi-nation study is designed and administered by a single organization with well-trained staff (for example, the United Nations or High/ Scope), it is difficult to ensure the accuracy and comparability of data. Resolution of these problems has been a focus of several international projects or publications and will not be attempted here, but it should be kept in mind that the following discussion will draw from research of varying quality and from data sets that are not always, strictly speaking, comparable.[5]

The studies included in this review fall into three major groups: large-scale surveys, studies comparing children with different child-care or preschool experiences, and evaluations testing the impacts of particular early-childhood programs or program models. These three research approaches will be briefly described below; the designs of several studies exemplifying each approach are outlined in Table 2-1. (The substantive findings of these and other studies will be discussed in the following sections of this chapter.)

Surveys have been used in several nations to investigate whether exposure to preschool programs is associated with positive outcomes for children. The five surveys in Table 2-1 have sample sizes of over one thousand children that were drawn to represent the residents of a nation (or some smaller jurisdiction). Some gathered data on the same children during early childhood and again later. Others focused on older children but included questions about the children's past experiences to contrast groups with different exposure to preschool programs.

Comparative studies of existing programs focus on smaller samples than the surveys and gather more detailed information about children's preschool experiences and later development. The four studies of this type in Table 2-1 (Studies 6–9) took advantage of naturally occurring variations in children's enrollment in early-childhood programs to investigate how attending those typical programs contributed to, or hampered, children's progress in school and other settings.

Finally, a number of the studies examined are *evaluations* of specific program models serving limited numbers of children (Studies 10–16 in Table 2-1). In some cases (for example, the South Korean study), several early-childhood education models are contrasted. In all these studies, comparisons are made with groups that received no early-childhood program, though only in the Columbian study were the children randomly assigned to program or control groups. More often the researchers found comparison groups in neighboring communities or among slightly older children.

All three types of studies can be used to serve policy purposes. For instance, the findings of surveys have helped justify the

Table 2-1.

Illustrative International Research Studies

Country	Purpose of Study	Sample size and design
Large-scale surveys		
1. France	Identify impact of amount of preschool on retention and achievement at grades 1 and 5	20,000+ children National sample of sixth graders in 1980
2. United Kingdom	Identify impact of type of preschool attended (if any) on educational achievement and behavior in school	9,000 children All children born during one week in 1970 Longitudinal follow-ups at ages five and ten
3. Germany	Identify impact of availability of preschool places on promotion rates and placement in special education	203 schools 6% stratified random sample of elementary schools in one state
4. Japan	Identify impact of attendance at preschool, child-care center, or no program, on fifth grade national achievement-test scores	4,000 elementary school graduates, class of 1968, in three prefectures
5. Thailand	Identify impact of attendance at two-year or one-year kindergarten, child-care center, or no program on school achievement	11,442 children National stratified random sample of third graders
Comparative studies of existing programs		
6. Canada	Identify differences in the development of children in three types of child care	105 child-parent-caretaker triads, in one city Families randomly selected from twenty-five child-care centers, twenty-four licensed family day-care homes, twenty-five nonlicensed family day-care homes, recruited though official and informal sources
7. Sweden	Compare school performance and behavior of children who began out-of-home care in first year of life vs. later	128 children, selected randomly from families with three- to four-year-old children, in eight neighborhoods of two cities Longitudinal follow-ups at ages eight (92% retention) and thirteen (89% retention)

Country	Purpose of Study	Sample size and design
8. Singapore	Compare children attending different types of preschool programs on cognitive ability, language skills, and social behavior	2,418 three to six year olds, randomly selected from 10% national random sample of public and private preschools
9. Australia #1	Identify impact of early nonmaternal child care on school readiness and social and emotional problem	Random sample of 8,471 mothers of first graders in three cities

Evaluations of experimental or model programs

10. Ireland	Assess impact of two-year preschool program on disadvantaged children's school and life success	Program: ninety children (all eligible three year olds in one inner-city area) Comparison: 60 eight year olds from same area Longitudinal follow-ups each year to age eight (program group) and at age sixteen (both groups, retention = 83/90 and 53/60)
11. South Korea	Assess impact of four early-education curricula (Montessori, open education, child-centered traditional, academic drill) on cognitive and socioemotional development and school success	Program: 121 children in four urban kindergarten classes Comparison: thirty-one children with no kindergarten experience Non-random assignment Longitudinal follow-ups in forth grade (retention 117/152) and middle school (retention 102)
12. Columbia	Assess impact of multifaceted health, nutrition, and preschool program on malnourished children's health, cogitive ability, and retention in school	Program: 301 children in one city randomly assigned to treatment for one, two, three, or four years Comparison: one impoverished, no treatment group; one higher income group
13. India #1	Assess impact of center-based preschool program on health, cognitive ability, behavior, and school readiness of impoverished rural children	Program: sixty two year olds, sixty five year olds, in six village day-care centers Comparison: sixty two year olds, sixty five year olds, in similar villages with no day-care program
14. India #2	Assess impact of comprehensive nutrition, health, and preschool	Program: 214 children Comparison: 205 children,

Table 2-1. (*continued*)

Country	Purpose of Study	Sample size and design
	program (ICDS) on cognitive ability and school attendance	from randomly selected villages in adjoining area
	Assess impact of ICDS on school success	Program: 1,271 children Comparison: 436 children, from same area
15. Australia #2	Assess impact of five experimental models on disadvantaged children's success in 1st grade	Program: 225 children, in one low-income housing project, nonrandomly assigned to five experimental programs Comparison: thirty-nine children added at preschool stage, sixty-two added in kindergarten year
16. Turkey	Assess impact of educational child care and maternal training on children's cognitive ability, school success, and attitudes, mothers' parenting skills and family status	251 low-income families with three- or five-year-old child Intervention 1: educational child care, custodial care, or home care, non-randomly assigned Intervention 2: HIPPY training for mothers, randomly assigned Longitudinal follow-ups after four, seven, and ten years

Sources: 1. McMahan, 1992; 2. Osborn & Milbank, 1987; 3. Tietze, 1987; 4. Nitta & Nagano, 1975; 5. Raudenbush, Kidchanapanish, & Sang, 1991; 6. Goelman & Pence, 1987; 7. Andersson, 1992; 8. Sim & Kam, 1992; 9. Ochiltree & Edgar, 1990; 10. Kellaghan & Greaney, 1993; 11. Rhee & Lee, 1983, 1987, & 1990; 12. McKay et al., 1978; 13. Zaveri, 1994; 14. Myers, 1992, pp. 103–4, 243–44; 15. Braithwaite, 1983; 16. Kagitcibasi, 1991.

adoption of national policies, such as the French government's investment in universal preschool to prepare children to succeed in public school. Research that documents the quality of diverse early-childhood programs can guide decisions concerning government regulation and financing, as it has in Sweden. Such studies can demonstrate the potential that exemplary early-childhood programs have to improve outcomes for particular groups of children, and provide a background for further testing with a more rigorous research design or with a different population of children.

Research Findings by Geographical Area

The following review is based on studies of early-childhood programs conducted outside the United States during the past two decades, chosen to illustrate and illuminate important issues of early-childhood policy, practice, and research. It should not be viewed as covering all, or even a representative sample of all, relevant international studies.[6]

North America

Canada

Because of its geographical closeness, its similar levels of economic development, and its cultural diversity, Canada's approach to early-childhood care and education seems especially relevant to the United States. While neither country has a comprehensive national early-childhood policy, Canada's social welfare policies and programs are more inclusive and generous than those of the United States, though they are less so than those of most European countries. Systematic research is, however, a relatively recent development in Canada.

In the late 1980s, a major comparative study, the Victoria Day Care Research Project, examined 105 children who were using one of the major types of child care available in Canada: child-care centers, care in the homes of regulated family child-care providers, and care by unregulated home caregivers (Goelman and Pence, 1987; see Study 6 in Table 2-1). The Victoria study compared the experiences of children in these three care settings and found high correlations between family resources, quality of child-care setting, and children's cognitive and social development. Children who attended day-care centers tended to have higher levels of language development and more highly developed play and activity patterns than children in family day care.

The quality of care in family child-care homes was more variable than center care and it was a more potent predictor of children's language development—that is, children in high-quality homes developed well, while those in less adequate homes developed much more poorly. Family day care that was regulated by government authorities tended to be of better quality than that offered in unlicensed homes, even when the regulations were "minimal" and "minimally enforced." Across settings, the quality of care exerted more influence on the development of lower-class than middle-class children. (A study of middle-class Canadian fourth graders, by a different group of researchers, found no differences between children who had attended a Montessori playschool, other pre-schools, or no preschool.)[7] The researchers pointed out that in Canada as in the United States, child care often exacerbates socio-economic inequities rather than reducing them. Many children in the study experienced the "worst of both worlds" in that they came from low-resource families *and* attended low-quality family day care. To date, however, the kinds of longitudinal data needed to assess the long-term effects of early child-care experiences in Canada have not been gathered.

Western Europe

The most highly developed early-childhood systems may be found among the nations comprising the European Community, plus the Nordic nations. Outside of the United States, this is also the area of the world from which information about preschool programs and their effects is most readily available. The opening of national frontiers for trade and travel seems to have been accompanied by an increased sharing of information, joint planning, and collaborative research, although each nation's policies and programs retain distinctive characteristics that reflect historical and cultural differences.

Here five of the most often cited European studies are reviewed, including surveys, comparative studies, and an evaluation. Several studies traced the effects of various types of child care and preschool education for periods up to twelve years.

France

A prime example of how survey research can contribute to policy development is provided by studies conducted by the French Ministry of Education between 1983 and 1990 to gauge the effects of large-scale expansion of the preschool system on later success in school (McMahan, 1992; see Table 2-1, Study 1). The French *ecole maternelle*, or nursery school, is now attended by close to 100 percent of all three to five year olds and a growing number of two year olds. Preschool teachers in France have the same training, civil-service status, and salaries as primary school teachers. The popular full-day programs emphasize academic activities, and group sizes and child/teacher ratios tend to be large by American stan-dards (twenty-five children per class is the mean, though as many as thirty-five may be included).

The impetus for the expansion of the *ecole maternelle* system during the 1970s and 1980s was concern over the large number of children who had to repeat first grade or otherwise fell behind in primary education (see the chapter by Barnett, Young, and Schweinhart for discussion of similar concerns in the United States). To discover whether attending preschool affected retention rates, the government launched a survey of a national sample of twenty thousand students who were sixth graders in 1980, comparing those who had attended preschool for one, two, or three years before entering elementary school.

The survey findings indicated that every year of preschool reduced the likelihood of school failure, especially for children from the most disadvantaged homes. Each year of preschool narrowed the retention rate "gap" between children whose fathers were in the highest occupational category and those with unemployed or unskilled fathers. That gap was 30 percent for children with one year of preschool, 27 percent for those with two years, and 24 percent for those with three years in preschool. (Those differences may seem small, but the very large sample sizes make them quite reliable estimates of truly different experiences.) While children from higher status homes and children in urban areas had the most preschool experience and were more likely to be promoted on schedule, the subsequent expansion of the *ecole maternelle* system is likely to have reduced these disparities still further.

United Kingdom

A similarly massive survey, the Child Health and Education Study (CHES) examines the effects of naturally occurring preschool and child-care programs in the United Kingdom, a nation with a much more diverse system than France. Estimates are that 44 percent of British three and four year olds attend public or private nursery schools, and many children enter public school classes at age four (Curtis, 1992). Public investment in full-day child care is limited; many families rely on individual childminders, who may or may not be registered with the government. Children who have a parent at home during the day often attend organized playgroups several times a week.

The CHES is a longitudinal study that followed the development of all the approximately nine thousand children born during one week in 1970 (Table 2-1, Study 2). Researchers collected data on cognitive functioning, educational achievement, and behavior ratings by mothers and teachers when the children were five and ten years old. Comparisons between children who attended playgroups, private or public nursery schools, or no preschool at all showed that experience in any preschool (including playgroups) contributed to cognitive development and school achievement throughout the period studied. Disadvantaged children gained slightly more from attending preschool than did more advantaged children. Contrary to the researchers' expectations, preschool experience did not affect aspects of children's socioemotional development, such as self-concept, skill in getting along with other children, or their ability to apply themselves to school work.

The researchers concluded that preschool experience per se had more influence on children's subsequent development than the type of preschool attended: "provided the child receives proper care, has interesting activities and other children to play with (which are common elements in the majority of preschool institutions) the actual type of preschool experience matters very little" (Osborn & Milbank, 1987, p. 239).

Germany

A related policy study using different methods was conducted in 1987 in the former West Germany, a country where between 65 percent and 70 percent of children between three and six attend half-day kindergartens that are provided by the government at no cost to parents (Moss, 1990, p. 10). To evaluate whether providing preschool opportunities increases elementary school success, the researchers analyzed statistics routinely collected by schools, including the percent of children retained in grade or assigned to special education in grades one to four, as well as community factors such as population density, socioeconomic status, and the number of preschool places available in the school district (Table 2-1, Study 3). The study combined data from 203 elementary schools in one Western German state, and it produced results very similar to the British and French surveys described above (Tietze, 1987).

Elementary schools in districts with high preschool availability had lower rates of retention in grade and assignment to special education. Indeed, no other factor studied influenced school outcomes as consistently as having some preschool experience. The German researchers concluded, like their French colleagues, that a well-established preschool system can improve children's school readiness and ease the transition into elementary school. Taken together, the large-scale studies of French, British, and German preschool systems provide solid evidence that preschool attendance, under the "normal, everyday conditions of a well-established preschool service," can have strong positive effects on children's school readiness and their subsequent academic performance (Tietze, 1987, p. 151). This seems to be true whether the preschool system is relatively uniform, as in the case of the French *ecole maternelle*, or is characterized by much greater diversity in institutions or programs, as is the case in Germany and Britain.

Sweden

Given that 86% of Swedish mothers with preschool-aged children are employed, it is not surprising that programs offering full-time child care are the centerpiece of the Swedish early-childhood system. Local governments provide carefully supervised child-care through centers and family child care homes to approximately 47 percent of children between birth and school entry at age seven, although many infants are cared for by their parents during paid parental leaves (Gunnarsson, 1993). (For a fuller discussion of Swedish public policy regarding children and their families, see the chapter by Gustafsson and Stafford.)

Systematic studies of Swedish child care have been carried out since the mid-1960s (Lamb, Hwang, & Broberg, 1991). By comparison with the French, British, and German surveys described above, most Swedish studies use small but carefully designed samples, and they collect data that allow detailed comparisons of existing programs. Often researchers treat child care as just one among several environments that affect children's development and well being, and they attempt to examine the influences of in-home and outside-the-home child care simultaneously.

Chosen for this review is a study that followed 128 children born in 1975 from age three to age thirteen, with an 89 percent retention rate (see Table 2-1, Study 7). Information on the children's child-care experiences during infancy was obtained from their mothers. The results show distinct advantages to children of early nonparental child care. Whether they attended centers or family child care, children placed in outside-the-home care before age one had greater verbal facility and were rated as more persistent and independent, less anxious, and more confident than children cared for at home or children placed in day care at a later age. The study's lead investigator concluded that "early entrance into day care tends to predict a creative, socially confident, popular, open, and independent adolescent" (Andersson, 1992, p. 32–33).

Two other Swedish longitudinal studies have yielded similar findings (Broberg, Hwang, Lamb, & Ketterlinus, 1989; Cochran & Gunnarsson, 1985).[8] Together, these studies suggest that nonparental care of adequate quality, even for infants and for long periods of time, need not have adverse effects on children's development and well being, and may in fact benefit children in many ways.

The impressive outcomes reported in these carefully designed studies may be explained by the fact that Sweden has a national policy of providing public child care that is well funded and supported by regulations regarding staff, group size, daily routines, and the design of the child's environment. This does not mean that all centers are identical. Indeed, Swedish child-care environments differ considerably in such characteristics as group composition, atmosphere, and staff experience and working methods. However, government funding and oversight ensure that variations stay within specified limits and do not fall below an agreed-upon threshold of quality (Lamb, Hwang, & Broberg, 1991, p. 117).

Overall, the Swedish studies found the quality of care provided in children's own homes was a better predictor of subsequent development than variations in preschool experience or the more crude measure of family socioeconomic status (SES). These studies used fine-grained measures of the quality of home care, focusing on interactions between parents and children rather than simple measures of whether the mother works.[9] The surprising finding that family SES is relatively unimportant may reflect the fact that in Sweden, differences in family socio-economic status, like differences in the quality of preschool facilities, are relatively small. By contrast, in Canada and the United States, both family SES and program quality vary widely, and research shows that both variables have substantial effects on children's development.

Ireland

The last study from Western Europe differs from the others in examining an experimental program that targeted children living in an impoverished area of Dublin (Study 10). Based upon developmental theory and influenced by U.S. compensatory education programs like those discussed in this book, the Dublin project offered a two-year, half-day preschool program to ninety children who were aged three in 1969. The program aimed to enhance children's cognitive development, learning skills, and personal and social development; it also sought to involve parents in their children's preschool experience through home visits by teachers and social workers.

Measures of cognitive development, school achievement, and parent involvement were collected at ages five, eight, and sixteen on the program participants and a control group of sixty children from the same neighborhood. The participating children showed significant improvements on standardized tests at age five. The greatest benefits appeared among the least able children and among girls rather than boys. At age eight, however, most of these initial gains were not maintained. By secondary school, the preschool participants were more likely than nonparticipants to remain in school, and they were two to three times as likely to take the examinations required for further education. However, there were no differences between the groups in employment or in the percentage who had been in trouble with the police (about 20 percent of each group). These mixed results led the researchers to conclude that "the extent of the problems—social as well as educational—which children experience in a disadvantaged area" limit the power of a single intervention to bring about change (Kellaghan & Greaney, 1993, p. 21).[10]

East Asia and the Pacific Rim

As the results of comparative studies of elementary and secondary students have shown (Bracey, 1996; Stevenson & Stigler, 1994) this area contains some of the world's most highly developed nations, educationally as well as economically. In Hong Kong, Taiwan, Singapore, South Korea, and Japan—nations that share a common heritage of Confucian values in a context of rapid industrial growth—most children attend preschool by age three, and many preschool programs focus on preparing children for the academic demands of school. For example, the participation of over 90 percent of Hong Kong's three to six year olds in preschool has been explained this way:

> This high proportion reflects the value that the Chinese traditionally attach to education, but it also reflects the economic and educational situation. . . . Formal schooling is an important avenue to social and economic mobility, and preschool is perceived as the first step along this avenue. (Opper, 1989, p. 119–20)

The following studies from Japan, Singapore, and South Korea, all nations with high rates of enrollment in formal preschool programs, examine the effects of preschool experience on child outcomes, either by comparing two broad types of early-childhood programs (child care versus academic preschool in Japan), or by comparing a variety of specific preschool models (in the South Korean study).

Japan

In a pattern that resembles many North American and Western European countries, the Japanese system of early-childhood services is broken into two parts: (1) *yochien*, or preschools, under the auspices of the Ministry of Education, are primarily private, part-day programs, based on the European kindergarten model and designed to prepare three to six year old children for elementary school; and (2) *hoiku-en*, or child-care programs, under the auspices of the Ministry of Welfare, are full-day programs for children of all ages from families deemed "in need of care" by government authorities. Currently, more than 90 percent of Japanese children attend one— sometimes both—of these programs before they enter elementary school (Boocock, 1991).

Although Japanese government agencies maintain very accurate records on enrollments, staff, and equipment, and there is a veritable flood of theoretical and philosophical works on child rearing and early-childhood education, virtually no research has been conducted on the effects of different types of preschool programs. In 1975, a retrospective study of four thousand fifth graders addressed the question of whether preschool experience is associated with higher scores on national achievement tests (Nitta and Nagano, 1975; also see Table 2-1, Study 4). The sample included about equal numbers of children who had attended *yochien, hoiku-en*, or neither type of program.

The study found that children with preschool experience of either type had higher test scores than those who attended no preschool, but that relationship was affected by family economic status. Overall, children who attended *yochien* received the highest test scores. However, lower-class children did best if they attended the full-day *hoiku-en*, and the authors speculated that the more academic preschool programs were less suited to the needs of these children than the full-day programs which offered more comprehensive services. This conclusion echoes the Canadian study by stressing the importance of examining the fit between the needs of low-income children and the characteristics of the early-childhood programs they attend.

Singapore

Singapore is a highly urbanized, multiethnic society with a distinctive state ideology that espouses the peaceful coexistence of heterogeneous groups within the framework of the nation state (there are three official languages), equitable distribution of public resources and services among majority and minority groups, and full participation of women in the labor force without sacrificing their roles as mothers and caregivers. The government has sought to mitigate the strains on working women through direct and indirect support for organized child-care services. Between 1982 and 1993, the number of child-care centers increased from 33 centers with

2,023 places to 319 centers with 23,235 places. The majority of all children now attend preschool (more than 70 percent participating in programs offered by the dominant political party), though there are substantial differences among families of Chinese, Indian, and Maylay ethnicity in child-care arrangements and type of preschool experiences as well as in family size and structure and mothers' labor-force participation (Yeoh & Huang, 1995).

In 1983, a nine-year study was launched by the National Institute of Education to produce a developmental profile of the nation's preschool children, compare the outcomes of different types of preschools, and develop a plan for improving preschool curriculum and teacher training (Sim & Kam, 1992; also see Table 2-1, Study 8). A sample of 2,413 three to six year olds, randomly selected from 10 percent of all Singapore preschools (also randomly selected), were observed and tested, on a broad array of cognitive and behavioral measures, at four points over a two-and-a-half-year period. The study's results indicated that preschool experience prepared children to handle the academic demands of elementary school and it improved children's skills at sharing and cooperating—a valued benefit in a society in which most children grow up in one- or two-child families.

Though most Singapore children are not native speakers of English, it is the language used in most Singapore elementary schools, so the study paid special attention to mastery of English. Children who attended private preschools performed better on English-language tasks than their peers in the preschools funded by the dominant political party, perhaps because the children in private preschools were more likely to have well-educated, higher-income parents who spoke English at home. The effects of ethnicity are difficult to assess, because Maylay- and Tamil-speaking children formed such a small proportion of the total sample (reflecting their much lower rates of attendance in child-care centers and kinder-gartens). By age six, however, all the children had begun to learn English, and the language abilities of children from minority groups did not differ markedly from children from majority (i.e., Chinese) families. In sum, the Singapore children studied were distinguished both by their early bilingualism and their high level of proficiency in preliteracy skills, a finding that may be of particular interest to American policy makers concerned with the complex issues of bilingual education.

South Korea

A longitudinal study of kindergartens conducted in South Korea during the mid-1980s explored the effects of different early-childhood educational models on children's development. The study examined 121 children who attended four urban kindergarten classrooms that reflected four different educational approaches (Montessori, open education, child-centered traditional, and academic drill), and compared them with thirty-one children who had no kindergarten experience (Rhee and Lee, 1983, 1987, 1990; also see Table 2-1, Study 11). Data on the children's cognitive and socioemotional development and their school achievement were gathered in kindergarten and at grades four and seven. Although the research design is weakened by the nonrandom assignment to the different classes, the study has an eight-year follow-up period and the retention rate was high.

The study results show that the four curricular approaches yielded different patterns of school readiness during the kindergarten year, but the distinctions between the programs faded by fourth grade and were gone by the seventh grade. However, significant differences distinguished the kindergarten groups from the control group on all the measures except the children's IQ. The study's conclusion that the long-run advantages of any of the preschool programs studied are large relative to the differences between forms of preschool education is consistent with the British and German research discussed earlier.

Australia and New Zealand

The Pacific Rim nations that are closest to the United States racially, linguistically, and culturally—Australia and New Zealand—have both experienced sharply increased demand for early-childhood programs. In New Zealand, 42 percent of children under five attend part-day preschool programs, 16 percent attend full-day child-care programs, and another 23 percent are enrolled in part-time play centers operated by parents (Smith, 1992). In Australia, it is estimated that 32 percent of children aged three to five attend part-day preschool programs and another 20 percent are in child-care centers (McLean et al., 1992). Both countries have also undertaken systemic reforms, propelled by increasing rates of maternal employment and the growing insistence of indigenous peoples and other disadvantaged groups that their preschool needs be met.

The Mt. Druitt Project (Table 2-1, Study 15) was launched in the mid-1970s to serve families living in a low-income public housing project (Braithwaite, 1983). A total of 225 children received a year of preschool services through one of five models (including a home-based approach as well as four center-based models), although assignment to the groups was not randomized. The children were followed by researchers until the end of first grade and compared with thirty-nine control children identified during preschool and another sixty-two control children identified during kindergarten.

Children who attended any of the preschool programs performed better than the comparison groups when they entered public kindergarten, but their superiority dissipated by the end of first grade. An unexpected family-level benefit also emerged: parents who participated in the home-based program established a network to organize other social, educational, and welfare activities independent of the project. The positive but short-lived effects of preschool attendance on children's cognitive development parallel findings of the Dublin Project described earlier. However, the study's outcomes must be interpreted with caution, since assignment to experimental or control groups was not random and the children were not followed past first grade.

A second Australian study, the Australian Early Childhood Study (Table 2-1, Study 9), gathered data from 8,471 urban mothers of first-year elementary school children, focusing on children's social and emotional problems that indicated a lack of readiness for school (Ochiltree & Edgar, 1990). The results indicated that participating in nonmaternal child care, even in the first year of life, did not put children at greater risk of developing these problems. Family background factors, including ethnicity, the family's financial situation, and the mothers' satisfaction with their lives, had greater effects on children's socio-emotional development and school readiness than did maternal employment and the exposure to child care that follows from it.

These findings echo the Swedish child-care research showing that maternal employment and participation in out-of-home child care even during infancy need not harm children and that aspects of the home environment affect children's social and emotional development as much or more than the experiences they have in child care. The AECS also reflects the attention paid in Australia and New Zealand to the effects of child-care availability and quality on women's lives. In both countries, reviews of research on the outcomes associated with children's participation in early-childhood programs have identified a number of benefits for parents as well, including enhanced relationships with children, alleviation of maternal stress, upgrading of education or training credentials, and improved employment status (Wylie, 1994; Podmore, 1993).

Developing Nations in Latin America and Asia

The availability of early-childhood programs in most developing nations remains limited, and until recently there has been little research on their long-term effects. The past two decades have, however, seen a multiplication of efforts to expand preschool services in the developing nations of Latin America, Asia, and Africa, where pre-primary education is sometimes viewed as a strategy for promoting national development. Preschool projects in the developing world are often funded by outside sources (private foundations, the World Bank, or UNESCO and UNICEF), and they are increasingly employing an approach that engages local communities in the design, operation, and evaluation of the programs (see, for example, Philp, 1988).

One of the major barriers to school success for poor children in developing nations is that many suffer from malnutrition and health problems severe enough to impair their cognitive and socio-emotional development. A twenty-five-year longitudinal study in four Guatamalan villages found benefits of a supplementary feeding program on several indicators of cognitive development that lasted over the entire period of the study (Pollitt et al., 1993). Two Jamaican studies documented similar benefits of school breakfast programs (Chandler et al., 1995). A number of projects have attempted to improve children's overall development through pre-school programs that link nutrition supplements and health education with activities offering cognitive and psychosocial stimulation as well.

Columbia

The most systematic intervention and research program combining nutritional and educational enrichment was conducted in Cali, Columbia, a rapidly expanding city of about one million people with a high proportion of impoverished families, many of them headed by women. The Cali intervention is a preschool program integrating nutrition supplementation, health surveillance, child care, and educational components (Table 2-1, Study 12). A sample of 301 malnourished, extremely poor children were randomly assigned to groups who began receiving the program at ages three, four, five, or six years, or not at all. The longitudinal evaluation compared those children with control groups and examined how the duration of the treatment affected physical growth, cognitive development, and retention in grade until the children reached ten years of age (McKay et al., 1978; McKay and McKay, 1983).

All the experimental groups in the Cali Project improved more in cognitive ability than the control group of low-income children, and the size of children's cognitive gains was related to the length of the treatment the child received. Modest IQ gains persisted to age eight, and treatment-group children were somewhat more likely than low-income, control-group children to be promoted throughout the first three grades in school. Children who received nutritional supplements without participating in the preschool activities made significant gains in height and weight, but their cognitive abilities did not improve until they entered the preschool part of the program.

Interpreting these long-term effects is difficult because the children attended ninety-three different elementary schools that varied in curriculum and quality, and many children changed schools, some more than once. A recent secondary analysis of the Cali data on physical development showed that while children exposed at an earlier age and for a longer period of time showed the greatest gains in weight and height during the preschool period, these improvements could no longer be detected three years after the termination of the intervention (Perez-Escamilla & Pollitt, 1995). Still the Cali project provides convincing, if not conclusive, evidence regarding the potential of well-designed preschool interventions for fostering physical, mental, and social growth among chronically deprived children.[11]

India

Two studies from India, based on contrasting approaches, illustrate a basic dilemma facing a populous nation attempting to upgrade its preschool system. Only about 12 percent of India's children are reached by early-childhood services, and only about half of the children enrolled in primary school complete the first year, in part because child labor remains prevalent, and girls often stay home to care for their younger siblings (Kaul, 1992). These stark conditions provide the context into which Indian preschool programs must fit.

The Villege Preschool Study (Table 2-1, Study 13) evaluates the effectiveness of a set of forty-nine relatively high-quality, foundation-funded child-care centers. A two-year longitudinal study compared 120 children in six villages who attended the programs with a matched sample of 120 who did not attend (Zaveri, 1994). The findings showed a general pattern of more favorable results on a variety of developmental measures for the children who attended the centers, though many of the differences were not statistically significant. The results of this demonstration project suggest that early-childhood models originally developed for industrialized,

Western nations can be adapted for countries at different stages of development, but even had the results of the evaluation been more conclusive, the wide dissemination of such a program is highly unlikely in a nation with India's resource constraints.

A clear contrast to the demonstration-program approach is offered by the Indian government's effort to provide services to children in poverty through the massive Integrated Child Development Service (ICDS), started in 1975 (Study 14). Paraprofessional workers gather between twenty and forty children in *anganwadi* (literally, courtyard) centers for several hours each weekday for supplementary feeding, health checkups, and educational activities. This program is the largest of its kind in the world. In 1987–88, there were more than 88,400 centers, reaching 4.6 million children six years old and younger (Kaul, 1992, p. 277).

Studies conducted in 1986 and 1987 gathered information on the health and school performance of a few hundred participants and comparison children. Results suggest that the programs can claim some successes in reducing infant mortality, malnutrition, and morbidity, as well as school repetition or dropout. Still most of the centers operate at "a minimum level of quality," and many of the "teachers" lack any training. Two projects supported by the World Bank are attempting to improve ICDS program consistency, worker training, and the delivery of food and educational supplies (Myers, 1992, pp. 103–4, 243–44; Young, 1996, pp. 73–74).

Turkey

Although free, compulsory primary schooling is provided for Turkish children aged six to fourteen, less than 2 percent of children under six now attend an organized preschool program, and recent government planning documents call for increased investment in preschool programs (Gurkan, 1992).

The Early Enrichment Project (Table 2-1, Study 16) was initiated during the 1980s to assess different approaches to early-childhood care and education, in particular, to test the effects on children and parents of two interventions: (1) participation in existing child care programs offering either educational or only custodial care. versus home care, and (2) an adaptation of HIPPY, a home enrichment program, originally designed for disadvantaged Israeli children, in which paraprofessionals train mothers to work with their preschool-aged children on a series of educational activities (Kagitcibasi, 1991, 1995; for a description of HIPPY and the results of research on its effectiveness, see Lombard, 1994). Assignment to the three child-care settings was not random, though selection of mothers to receive HIPPY training (half of the mothers in each child-care context, beginning in the second year of the project) was random. The longitudinal study included 251 low-income families with children aged three to five years who received different combinations of treatments, and data on the children's cognitive development, social development, and school achievement were gathered four, seven, and ten years later.

Overall, the findings showed that children who attended the educational day-care programs out-performed children in custodial child care and home care on almost all measures of children's cognitive development. Similarly, children whose mothers received the HIPPY training surpassed control groups of children on cognitive development and school achievement. The group that experienced both educational day care and home instruction by mothers had the highest scores on virtually every measure. Thus the effects of child care and mother training appeared to be additive, though the authors of the report believe that there may be a ceiling effect as well as possible interaction effects. For example, the HIPPY program seemed to be especially beneficial for children who did not have access to a quality preschool program. The longitudinal follow-up conducted six years after the completion of the inter-vention program, showed that the children (now young adolescents) whose mothers had received training had more positive attitudes toward school, showed better school performance over the five years of primary school, and were more likely still to be in school at age thirteen to fifteen than those whose mothers had not been trained.

The analysis also found direct effects of the HIPPY training on mothers: "compared with the control group of mothers, trained mothers were found to enjoy a higher status in the family vis-à-vis their greater participation in decision making in the family as well as more role sharing and communication with their spouses. They also had more say in child discipline." The author concludes that their findings offer support for a model of "intersecting needs of women and children" rather than for a model that assumes con-flicting needs (Kagitcibasi, 1991, p. 17).

Of course the results of this study must be interpreted with caution, since the original assignment to groups was not random. It does, however, suggest the benefits of combining developmental child care with activities designed for parents—a conclusion that links the Turkish project with the studies of maternal employment and child care conducted in Australia and Sweden and with the two-generation projects discussed in the chapter by St. Pierre, Layzer, and Barnes.[12] The Turkish Early Enrichment project is also a notable example of effective translation of research findings into large-scale programs and policies (see the chapter by Zervigon-Hakes). The methods developed in the project have been revised and tested with other groups, and a shorter and more cost-effective version of the program is now conducted on a national scale, in cooperation with the Turkish Ministry of Education. There has been collaboration with UNICEF, the World Bank, and various local groups as well (Kagitcibasi, 1996, pp. 17ff).

Thailand

Large-scale survey research on early-childhood services and their effects is rare among developing nations, but the example in Table 2-1 (Study 5) provides evidence of the potential benefits of preschool education as a tool of national development, and like the Turkish Early Enrichment project, underscores the importance of cooperation between researchers and policy makers.

Thailand is a nation that is moving rapidly out of the "developing nation" category, partly as a result of a series of national economic, social, and education development plans implemented during the 1970s and 1980s. Among the studies commissioned by the National Education Commission (NEC) of Thailand was a study of academic achievement, based on a stratified random sample of over 11,000 Thai children who were third graders in 1982. The research reviewed here involved reanalysis of data from this study. Comparisons of the school achievement of children who had attended a two-year kindergarten, a one-year kindergarten, a child-care center, or who had had no preschool experience, showed that children who had attended preschool scored significantly higher on tests of math and language achievement than children who had not attended preschool. Significantly higher achievement was also found among higher SES children and urban children—who were much more likely than poor children and rural children to have attended preschool (Raudenbush, Kidchanapanish, & Sang, 1991).

These findings are consistent with the French, British, and German studies examined earlier. The Thai study provided empirical support for government efforts to expand the preschool system, and the findings on the achievement gaps between advantaged and disadvantaged children and their differential access to quality preprimary education led the NEC to target deprived areas, including remote rural areas, congested slum areas, and localities with a high proportion of residents speaking languages other than Thai. As a result of these policy initiatives, preprimary enrollments for children aged three to six more than tripled between 1979 and

1987. The NEC also made a series of recommendations for improving the quality of preschool institutions and programs, including development of preschool models appropriate to specific local conditions, and upgrading the health and nutrition as well as the cognitive development of disadvantaged children.

Lessons for Americans

In many ways, the findings of the international research reviewed here confirm basic conclusions drawn in the research conducted in the United States on early-childhood programs for disadvantaged children. Maternal employment and participation in out-of-home child care, even during infancy, appear not to harm children and may yield benefits, to children and their families, if the child care is of adequate quality (a condition that is not always met in the United States).[13] Attendance at preschool programs is associated with cognitive gains and improved performance in school throughout the world, and having some preschool experience appears to matter more to children than exposure to any particular curriculum or program model. Preschool experience also appears to be a stronger force in the lives of low-income than more advantaged children, and preschool attendance can narrow the gaps in achievement that separate children from different socioeconomic strata. Though some of the beneficial effects for children in poverty appear to diminish over time, others are impressively long lasting.

This review suggests that much can be gained from examining the outcomes of early-childhood programs in other nations. Decisions about early-childhood policy and programs are, increasingly, made under conditions that are truly international in scope and impact. Intense pressures to economize on preschool services by reducing government support or relaxing standards are being felt worldwide, even in nations like Sweden and France where programs are well established and have wide public support. Learning from each others' experiences may be the only way we can gain the knowledge needed to design preschools that can withstand the social, political, and economic forces that affect children's lives everywhere.

The chapter closes by suggesting how the insights gained from this international review might be applied to three issues regarding early childhood policy, practice, and research in the United States.

What constitutes "quality" in
early-childhood programs?

There is now ample evidence from well-designed studies from a number of different countries that experience in good-quality early-childhood programs does not harm children, even very young ones. This does not mean there there is a global consensus on what constitutes a quality program. One fundamental disagreement contrasts a child-centered or "developmentally appropriate" model of early-childhood education that emphasizes play, with a view of preschool as a downward extension of formal schooling that introduces children to serious learning as early as possible. The child-centered model originated in Western societies and is based upon assumptions about the nature of children and childhood that are not embraced by all cultures. For example, free play is explicitly rejected in New Zealand preschools operated by Maori groups, and by many parents and teachers in industrialized Asian nations. Moreover, there may be little agreement on what constitutes "developmentally appropriate" practice even among teachers who claim to be using it (Clark, 1988, p. 216).

A number of the indicators of quality considered essential by American evaluators are accorded less importance elsewhere. For example, U.S. research on quality routinely includes data on staffing ratios and group sizes and compares existing practices to the standards set by professional organizations (for example, the National Association for the Education of Young Children). Small groups and low child-to-staff ratios are considered hallmarks of quality. In contrast, many high-quality programs in other countries—including the French *ecole maternelle*, most Japanese *yochien*, and the highly regarded preschools in the Italian town of Reggio Emilia—routinely use class sizes and child-to-staff ratios that violate U.S. standards (New, 1990; Edwards, Gandini, & Forman, 1993).

In recent years, parental involvement in early-childhood programs has come to be viewed as an important component of quality. Greater involvment, it is argued, makes parents more knowledgeable about their children's capacities, and better able to provide the kind of home environment that enhances children's development and school readiness (see, for example, Cochran, 1996, p. 52). The few studies in which parents' and teachers' views have been elicited indicate that parents and professionals agree on the need for improved communication between home and preschool but differ on the ways in which parents should be involved. Parents tend to desire a more active role for themselves, for example, as classroom aides or in a decision-making capacity on a preschool board. Professionals tend to prefer a more passive role for parents, as the recipients of professional advice and guidance, or as "volunteers" to raise money or to help out with the more mundane care-taking tasks (Carlson and Stenmalm, 1989; Sharpe, 1991). A review of research commissioned by the Department of Education and Science, United Kingdom, concluded that the extent of parental involvement depends on how one measures involvement, that the majority of parents are not much involved in their children's preschools however it is measured (though this does not necessarily mean that they are not involved with their children or lack interest in their education), and that staff attitudes and mutual distrust between parents and caretakers are difficult to change (Clark, 1988, p. 143). Studies that provide concrete evidence on the outcomes of specific forms of parental involvement, like the Turkish Early Enrichment Project, are scarce.

Conceptions of what constitutes quality in early-childhood programs may also reflect the values that are promoted in different societies. In his review of U.S. studies, Barnett found that outcomes related to children's cognitive development and school achievement were emphasized more heavily than their development of social skills. In 1970, Urie Bronfenbrenner, who observed programs in the United States and the Soviet Union, warned Americans that, "If the Russians have gone too far in subjecting the child and his peer group to conformity to a single set of values imposed by the adult society, perhaps we have reached the point of diminishing returns in allowing excessive autonomy and in failing to utilize the constructive potential of the peer group in developing social responsibility and consideration for others" (Bronfenbrenner, 1970, pp. 165–66).

Similarly, a more recent ethnographic study comparing a single preschool in the United States (Hawaii) with ones in Japan and the People's Republic of China concluded that what set the Asian preschools most apart from the American one was the importance they placed upon group life. Japanese parents, for example, "send their children to preschool not just for child care and not just so the children can learn to modify their behavior to conform to the demands of society but, more profoundly, to facilitate the development of a group-oriented, outward-facing sense of self" (Tobin, Wu, & Davidson, 1989, p. 58). Even taking into account differences in cultural values, evidence from several East Asian nations indicates that it is possible to make children's socialization to group life a central focus of preschool programs without sacrificing later academic success.[14]

*Can early-childhood programs
reduce educational inequities?*

A recent overview of early-childhood programs from an international perspective concluded that since the most disadvantaged groups tend to have the least political power, their needs—including their needs for high-quality early-childhood services—are likely to go unmet:

> Although early intervention programs are part of many nations' plans for social and political reform, in many instances insufficient funding and an inadequate vision result in a system of under-staffed, ill-equipped, and poorly housed programs. . . . [T]he result is often a substandard public system of early education that serves the needs of a few poor children and their families, and a separate usually higher quality private service for the middle and upper class. (Prochner, 1992, p. 13)

This review has identified two quite different strategies with demonstrable potential for reducing the vast inequalities among children from different social and political backgrounds. First, research from nations that vary economically, socially, and politi-cally offers considerable evidence that large-scale national efforts to expand preschool systems at reasonable levels of quality can reduce rates of early school failure among disadvantaged children. (It also suggests the potential costs to societies if large numbers of children receive inadequate care and education during the first years of their lives and if many women are forced to remain at home for lack of child care or to accept inadequate care.) Second, a growing body of evidence from developing nations indicates that well-designed, cost-effective interventions targeted at disadvantaged groups can ameli-orate some of the adverse effects of poverty and discrimination. The interventions included in this review differ in their details, but share certain general characteristics: (1) they are comprehensive, typically providing nutritional and medical services as well as educational enrichment; (2) they provide adequate training for caretakers, whether parents or others; and (3) they begin early in the child's life and continue over sustained periods of time. Given the large and growing numbers of children living in poverty in the United States (as documented in the chapter by Hernandez), some of the models being developed in the Third World may offer solu-tions to American problems as well.

Can research make a difference?

While some distinct patterns regarding the long-term effects of early-childhood programs have emerged from this international review, it is important to keep in mind that the research selected for this review is uneven in quality, and some of the claims made for particular programs or policies rest upon rather weak evidential grounds. As we have seen, studies that are truly longitudinal (rather than cross-sectional), experimental studies with random assignment to experimental and control groups and high rates of retention of subjects, and evaluations of new programs conducted by external reviewers (rather than by the program designers) are still scarce.

This review underscores the value of applying a variety of research approaches as well as the importance of efforts to improve the methods by which data are gathered and analyzed. The French, British, and Thai studies reviewed in this chapter demonstrate how large-scale national surveys can provide empirical support for the expansion and upgrading of national preschool systems. The value of such studies may be even greater if they are supplemented by smaller-scale studies allowing detailed observations that reveal the processes by which long-term effects are produced. For example, a study involving many hours of observation in a few playgroups and nursery schools in one British city (Bruner, 1980) produced a rich body of knowledge about the nature of children's play and adult-child interactions in different preschool settings that could not be obtained from a large national survey like the Child Health and Education Study. The advantages of long-term longitudinal evaluations must be weighed not only against their costs but also against their diminishing relevance over time: what "worked" say for children in the socioeconomic context of the 1970s may be less applicable to children in the 1990s. Less costly projects, for example, replicating or adapting some of the interventions initiated in developing nations and the quasi-experimental methodology used to assess them, may be a very cost-effective way to learn more about the relative merits of formal and informal programs, the inter-actions between health, nutrition, and educational components, and the most effective ways to involve parents in early-childhood programs.

Of course, quality research is not a guarantee of governmental support. It has been noted that the United States dominates the world in the quantity and quality of its research on early-childhood programs, yet the weight of empirical evidence showing the benefits of such programs has not produced the political will to support a universal system of high-quality services. Researchers who compared child and family policies in the United States and several European nations concluded that research has played the largest role in guiding policy and practice in those nations where it "starts with a policy choice made and uses child effects as the vantage point for designing ever more satisfactory programs" (Kamerman and

Kahn, 1981, p. 122). The importance of playing close attention to the political processes by which public policy is created and carried out, a major theme of the final chapter in this book, is also one of the major lessons to be learned from an international review of early-childhood programs.

Notes

Assembling the materials for this review in the time allowed would have been impossible without the advice and assistance of a worldwide network of researchers and members of organizations that gather data on early childhood care and education and/or provide support for evaluations of policies and programs for young children and their families. The author is very grateful to the following persons who provided information about their own research and suggested other relevant sources: Chaim Adler, Hebrew University of Jerusalem; Kathy Bartlett, Aga Khan Foundation; Judith Evans, Consultative Group on Early Childhood Care and Development; Martha Friendly, University of Toronto; Bruce Fuller, Harvard University, Graduate School of Education; Kathleen Gorman, University of Vermont; Susan Holloway, Harvard University; Marlaine Lockheed, World Bank; Avima Lombard, Hebrew University of Jerusalem; Ki Sook Lee, Ewha Women's University (Seoul, Korea); Theresa Moran, World Bank; Peter Moss, University of London; Patricia Olmsted, High/Scope Educational Research Foundation; Alan R. Pence, University of Victoria; Hans-Gunther Rossbach, Universitat Munster; Seng Seok-Hoon, National Institute of Education, Singapore; Harold Stevenson, University of Michigan; Kate Torkington, Bernard Van Leer Foundation; Herbert J. Walberg, University of Illinois at Chicago.

1. At the same time, Olmsted notes important intercountry differences—for example, the proportion of single-parent households headed by women is considerably larger in the United States than in most other countries.

2. The most comprehensive are Cochran, 1993; and Woodill, Bernhard, and Prochner, 1992. Publications covering specific areas of the world include Bairrao and Tietze, 1993; Moss, 1990; Feeney, 1992; and Myers, 1992 (the latter on projects and research in Third-World countries). The best comparative statistics can be found in UNESCO, 1993, and OECD, 1993.

3. The most extensive is the IEA Preprimary Project, results of which are presented in Olmsted & Weikart, 1989, 1994.

4. The only such review in English, conducted by a Danish scholar (Sjolund, 1973), covered research through the 1960s.

5. For a fuller discussion of these issues, see, Olmsted, 1989; or Cochran, 1993, especially the introductory chapter.

6. A notable omission is research from the former Soviet Union and Soviet Block countries, whose preschool institutions and services were once viewed by many scholars and practitioners as model programs. Due to the economic and other crises these nations are now experiencing, all human services have been sharply curtailed, and little research on early-childhood care and education is being done. For discussion of public policy regarding children and families and research on early-childhood programs conducted in Eastern Europe during the 1960s and 1970s, see Kamerman and Kahn, 1981. More recent trends are discussed in Zimmerman et al., 1994; Ipsa, 1994; and Young, 1996, pp. 10–11, 63–64.

7. This finding is reported in Wylie, 1994, p. 12.

8. One shortcoming of the latter study is that there is no distinction made between care in the home by parents or by childminders; another shortcoming is that children in group care are studied only in the day-care center, children in home care only in the home.

9. It is noteworthy that comparable research carried out in the Netherlands, where maternal employment has been discouraged and the actual employment rate of mothers is one of the lowest in Europe, showed similar results—i.e., no consistent or statistically significant relationships between mothers' working patterns and children's welfare. See, for example, van Ilzendoorn and van Vliet-Visser, 1988. For a comparison of Swedish and Dutch ideology and public policy regarding mothers and children, see the chapter in this book by Stafford and Gustafsson.

10. Similar results were obtained in two British projects initiated in the late 1960s, reported in Woodward, 1977.

11. Other Latin American projects that show positive effects of combining nutrition supplementation and education with cognitive enrichment activities are PRONOEI, in Peru, PROMESA, in Columbia, and PROAPE, in Brazil, all discussed in Myers, 1992. A longitudinal study of Jamaican children hospitalized for severe malnutrition concluded that a "psychosocial stimulation" intervention produced the most, and most sustained, health, cognitive, and social benefits (Grantham-McGregor et al., 1994). Assessment of an educational intervention implemented by Israeli public health nurses found developmental advantages among the children who received the experimental treatment, compared to children who did not, five years afterwards (Palti, Adler, and Baras, 1987).

12. Two-generation interventions have been attempted in several developing nations. For example, the Early Childhood Enrichment Program (ECEP), a national program in the Philippines, provides training and materials (including children's books, games, and toys) to day-care workers, home-management technicians (employees of the Bureau of Agricultural Extension), and parents. A longitudinal study comparing children in home-based (informal) ECEP, center-based (formal) ECEP, and no preschool

program, found that children in home-based ECEP displayed more rapid motor-skill development, while children in center-based ECEP had stronger cognitive skills, but that children in either ECEP program tested better than children who had not participated (Child and Youth Research Center, 1988).

A secondary analysis of data gathered in connection with the Cali, Columbia, project, found that the long-term nutritional health of preschoolers could be significantly improved by equipping their mothers with basic reading skills, and, moreover, that the literacy training for mothers was more cost effective than the interventions focusing on children (Lomperis, 1991).

13. For example, a recent study of day-care centers in four states rated the quality of care in most (84 percent) of the centers as poor or mediocre, on a scale based on multiple developmental outcomes (Helburn, 1995).

14. The cross-national studies directed by Harold Stevenson and colleagues, comparing Taiwanese, Japanese, and American children's behavior and academic achievement, using larger samples and more quantitive modes of data gathering and analysis than Tobin, Wu, and Davidson, found similar differences, and concluded that these could be explained more by differences in beliefs, attitudes, and goals of teachers and parents in the three countries than by differences in the children's cognitive and other abilities (Stevenson and Stigler, 1994). For a fuller discussion of comparative perspectives on human development, family, and early child care and education, see Kagitcibasi, 1995.

3

E. C. Frede

Preschool Program Quality in Programs for Children in Poverty

Recently, experts have questioned whether the results from longitudinal studies of high-quality interventions for preschool children from low-income families can be generalized to widespread, poorly funded programs (see Chubrich and Kelley, 1994; Haskins, 1989; and Woodhead, 1988. For a review of the longitudinal studies see Barnett, this volume) The critics suggest that the quality and intensity of the preschool programs in the original efficacy studies are not being replicated by the public

Adapted from Frede, E. C. (1995). The role of program quality in producing early childhood program benefits. *The Future of Children* (Winter) 5(3):115–32, by permission of Center for the Future of Children, The David and Lucile Packard Foundation.

programs, and thus the same effects cannot be assumed. At the other extreme, some have assumed that one preschool intervention is much the same as the next and that positive benefits of the experimental programs studied in longitudinal research will automatically devolve on community-based programs. Thus, it is necessary to examine the specific services provided in the experimental programs and the mechanisms through which the programs influenced children's development. This chapter employs a sociocultural theoretical approach (Berk, 1996) to analyze descriptions of the curricula and program practices used across the longitudinal studies of programs that served three to five year olds to search for commonalties that may help guide program development and create testable hypotheses regarding effective intervention. This analysis is preceded by a review of the research and current thinking on program quality. The results are then combined and used as a basis for recommendations for policy and practice.

Effects of the Quality of the Preschool Experience on Child Outcome

Determining the effects of curricula or teaching methods on young children is a complex task. In assessing growth, pretest and outcome measures in early childhood are of questionable validity especially for children from minority cultures (Kamii, 1990). Measures of social development are problematic since they often fail to discriminate among children (Datta, 1976). Different curricular approaches have different goals; thus different outcomes should be expected, and comparing the curricula on the same outcome measures may be biased. This same bias can occur in trying to measure treatment implementation: The appropriate observation techniques for one approach may fail to discern important practices or failures in implementation of another approach.

Rarely are experimental or quasi-experimental methods used, which makes generalization questionable. Even when experimental methods are used, the researchers often fail to use the correct unit of analysis since the treatment is given to a whole classroom and not to individual children, which means they employ an incorrect test of significance. Differential attrition across programs can also cause analysis problems, particularly if one approach is having a positive effect on placement in special education or promotion, since school-administered tests often exclude those children from their cohorts (Barnett, 1995). Another major area of difficulty is that children's development is influenced by many factors, children shape their own environments, and development occurs in multiple domains that may be differentially impacted by particular methods.

Research concerning the effectiveness of various curricula or classroom practices can be grouped into three types with distinct but related purposes. One approach designs a theory-driven "horse race" to determine if a curriculum derived from Theory A is more effective than curricula derived from Theories B and C by comparing model programs in which each curriculum is implemented as completely as possible. The second research approach investigates programs in the community to determine which, if any, program characteristics are important predictors of positive child outcomes. The naturally occurring variation in program design, curriculum, and teacher practices is the focus of this research. A third type of research builds on the second approach but explicitly investigates the effects on children of programs that follow professional guidelines for developmentally appropriate practices (Bredekamp, 1987). Each of these research traditions is reviewed briefly below.

Curriculum Comparison Studies

The horse-race model was adopted in curriculum comparison studies in which children attended one of several classrooms using the various curricula (Karnes et al., 1983; Miller & Bizzell, 1983, 1984; Weikart, Epstein, Schweinhart, & Bond, 1978). Other possibly important variables were held constant such as teacher/child ratio, class size, teacher training, and child characteristics.

Reflecting the dominant interests of the era, the curriculum comparison studies reviewed here contrasted three basic types of curricula (Goffin, 1994). In a *didactic or direct instruction curriculum*, the teacher presents information to the children in structured, drill-and-practice group lessons that are fast paced, teach discrete skills in small steps, and involve frequent praise. *Open classroom or traditional approaches* flow from a belief that children must direct their own learning and will learn when they are ready, as long as the teachers provide stimulating materials and support for the children's choices. Socialization is often the main goal of this curriculum. *Interactive* or *cognitive developmental curriculum* adherents view learning as an active exchange between the child and her environment, one key element of which is the teacher. In this model, teachers initiate activities designed to foster children's reasoning and problem-solving abilities, and they interact with children during child-designed activities to add new ideas or enhance learning. The open classroom and interactive curricula are both considered nondidactic because teachers rarely instruct children directly on discrete skills.

No easily explainable differences were found among the various curricula's outcomes. Miller found that boys who attended the nondidactic programs had higher IQs and did better in high school achievement tests. However, this finding was not replicated by Karnes. Also, two of the longitudinal efficacy studies that had child-centered classrooms as their intervention method found positive results for girls and not boys on academic measures (Gray et al., 1982; Lally, et al, 1987). Even if this finding of differential effects by gender was replicated, it would be difficult to determine the practical applications of the finding. Should boys and girls be separated into classrooms with different approaches? How then do we meet the needs of boys or girls who do not develop in the same ways as their same-sex peers? This speaks to a need for more finely tuned research that looks at highly specific characteristics, not just gender or ethnicity but developmental ability, temperament, learning style, and personality as they interact with each other, familial characteristics, and other contextual issues.

Schweinhart, Weikart, and Larner (1986) found that a direct instruction model in preschool, as compared to child-centered approaches, may fail to reduce delinquency, may have little effect in other areas of social development, and may be less effective at developing problem-solving skills. These results have been questioned for methodological reasons by the developers of the direct instruction curriculum (Bereiter, 1986; Gersten, 1986). Their major complaint is that model developers should not be engaged in evaluating the effects of their own models. However, the Curriculum Demonstration Project staff were careful to protect against bias in the implementation of the curricula. Training in the direct instruction model was provided by the model developers, and the three approaches were observed by twelve national experts in the field of early-childhood education including Todd Risley, an expert in the application of behavioral psychology to intervention programs. All of the experts agreed that the classrooms, and the teachers' explanations of their teaching, were pure examples of the models (Weikart, Epstein, Schweinhart, and Bond, 1978). Data collectors throughout the process were never aware of the child's treatment.

Studies of Quality in Community-Based
Early-Childhood Care and Education

A second group of classroom practices studies investigated non-experimental, community programs to determine if observable program characteristics were related to child outcome. Some of the studies were motivated by the findings of the Westinghouse Learning Corporation (1969) study that Head Start had little effect on the children it served. One of the criticisms of the study was that evaluating a new program without attempting to consider the actual experiences provided was inappropriate. Government officials, researchers, and curriculum developers all became interested in investigating the elements of the experimental classrooms that made them successful. At first, this resulted in more informed opinion than new research findings (see, for example, Bronfenbrenner, 1974; Weikart et al., 1978).

More recently, studies have begun to measure classroom experiences through systematic observation and compare these findings to child-outcome data. As a result of concern for the number of children placed in care for long periods of time, much of this effort has focused on child-care centers. In both cases, researchers hypothesized that the effects of the program, whether a intervention or child care, depended on the actual teaching practices that took place in the classroom.

One large-scale study evaluated a statewide preschool program in the South Carolina public schools (Barnett, Frede, Mobasher, & Mohr, 1987; Frede & Barnett, 1992; and Frede, Austin, & Lindauer, 1993). Although children were not randomly assigned to attend the preschool program, the comparison group was taken from the waiting list of eligible children from disadvantaged families. Twelve classrooms with adequate waiting lists, in three locations across the state, were observed using an instrument that assessed fidelity of treatment implementation, and children were pretested on a screening test. Children were followed through first grade with analysis of school-related tests at both kindergarten and first grade. Some of the conclusions reached by the analyses were that: (1) teachers with master's degrees were better at implementing the developmentally appropriate curriculum (the High/Scope Curriculum was used throughout the state); (2) curriculum implementation increased over the course of the year, and increased more in classrooms where there was ongoing and individualized training for the classroom staff; and (3) classrooms in which the curriculum was moderately to well implemented had positive effects for children in kindergarten and first grade as measured by a test of school-related skills.

The study's authors wanted to go beyond this general look at treatment implementation and efficacy to tease out those aspects of teacher behavior that differentiated effective classrooms from ineffective or less effective ones. They identified twenty-two teacher behaviors that were significantly correlated with child outcomes. These included taking advantage of opportunities for incidental teaching during all parts of the day whether the activity was child initiated or teacher initiated, and including children's ideas, individual choices, and abilities in teacher-initiated activities. In addition, the more effective classroom staff observed children's activities, watching for appropriate times to enhance the learning by using some specific strategies such as incorporating emergent literacy, making specific comments or suggestions about children's work, asking both thought-provoking and divergent questions, referring children's questions and comments to other children, and modeling appropriate communication techniques. This attention to children's problem solving also extended to social development. Effective teachers were more likely to encourage children to think of positive ways to deal with their emotions and to encourage children to develop solutions to disagreements and arguments rather than imposing teacher-generated solutions.

Other researchers have examined classroom practices in community child-care centers. Noteworthy for its design and comprehensiveness is the Abt Corporation National Day Care Study (NDCS; Ruopp et al., 1979). In a unique mixture of experimental and quasi-experimental designs, the NDCS found that smaller groups of children and higher teacher/child ratios both resulted in better social and cognitive outcomes for children that seemed to be mediated by more positive interactions between care givers and children, among children, and between children and materials. These findings have been corroborated by other studies (Clarke-Stewart & Gruber, 1984; Cost and Quality Team, 1995).

Another variable that contributes to the quality of early-childhood settings is the training of staff. Many studies have found that formal schooling and specialized training result in more attentive and nurturing behavior by staff (Arnett, 1986; Berk, 1985; Feeney & Chun, 1985; Howes, 1983; Ruopp et al., 1979; Cost and Quality Team, 1995; Whitebook, Howes, & Phillips, 1989). The newest research has probed the working conditions confronting staff in early-childhood programs, finding that programs that offer higher salaries, better benefits, and supportive management also have better-qualified staff who remain longer in their jobs (Cost and Quality Team, 1995; Whitebook, Howes, & Phillips, 1989). Children in those programs seem to benefit from having stable relationships with teachers who are skilled and sensitive.

Researchers have developed global ratings of quality and related these to later development. These studies combined structural variables such as group size, physical environment, and staff qualifications with process variables such as teacher/child interaction, and developed an overall rating for the classroom or center. For the most part, these studies found that attendance at higher quality centers resulted in better social, language, and cognitive outcomes for young children (Bryant, Burchinal, Lau, & Sparling, 1994; Bryant, Peisner, & Clifford, 1993; McCartney, 1984; Phillips, Scarr, & McCartney, 1987; Cost and Quality Team, 1995; Vandell, Henderson, & Powers, 1989).

Research on Developmentally Appropriate Practice

Efforts in the research literature to describe and measure quality have been paralleled by attempts by the profession to acknowledge programs that are "developmentally appropriate." In 1985, the National Association for the Education of Young Children (NAEYC) first published the Guidelines for Developmentally Appropriate Practice, and subsequently published revisions and extensions (Bredekamp, 1987; Bredekamp & Rosegrant, 1992). These have formed the criteria for a nationwide accreditation system for programs that serve young children in a classroom setting. The criteria developed for the accreditation process have been used in a few studies to determine the effect of developmentally appropriate practice (DAP) on children.

Research conducted across many settings and with different groups of children indicates that developmentally appropriate programs in kindergarten, preschool, and child-care settings do promote better child-development outcomes. One set of these studies found an interaction between SES of the child and the developmental appropriateness of the kindergarten classroom. Children of low SES and African American background placed in developmentally inappropriate kindergartens experience more stress and did less well on achievement tests than did their counterparts in DAP programs (Charlesworth, Hart, Burts, & DeWolf, 1993). Holloway and Reichart-Erickson (1988) found more positive interactions among children in child-care classrooms rated as more appropriate. In a study of preschool programs, Hyson, Hirsh-Pasek, and Rescorla (1990) found that children who attended DAP programs did slightly better than those in highly academic ones on measures of academic skills and creativity, and were lower in anxiety. The children in this study were largely from middle-class families, and the researchers found a relationship between parental beliefs and practices and the type of center their child attended. Low-income parents have fewer choices regarding the type of program their child attends so this finding may not generalize to other populations. However, in a study of preschool programs for children from low-income families, those who attended developmentally appropriate programs were more likely to achieve academically and socially in elementary school (Marcon, 1994).

In most of the research cited above on the effects of early education and child care looking at classroom processes, quality was defined as DAP although different measures were employed to assess it, and they were not always explicitly based on NAEYC's guidelines. In fact, the most widely used measure, the Early Childhood Environment Rating Scale (ECERS) (Harms & Clifford, 1980), was one of the resources used for setting the guidelines, as were the results of some of the earlier studies. The practice of basing curriculum decisions on theories and knowledge of child development has recently come under criticism on a number of levels. Spodek (1991) points out that developmental theory may help us determine the processes of teaching most effective with young children but that it does not help us decide the content of the curriculum. Walsh (1991) states that DAP is based on the false assumption that early-childhood educators have a common understanding of DAP; that the theory of invariant, universal stages on which DAP is based is questionable; and that we may need to revise our concept of learning and development in light of the theories of Vygotsky and research from sociocultural perspectives. This belief in the importance of the social context of education is one of the primary bases of others' criticism of DAP (Swadener & Kessler, 1991) and gives rise to reconceptualizations of early-childhood education from feminist perspectives (Jipson, 1992) and from linguistic- and cultural-minority perspectives (Hale-Benson, 1990).

Overall, this review of the three strands of literature on classroom practices suggests that (1) early education and child care can be beneficial for children from low-income families; (2) the particular theoretical orientation of the curriculum used may have differential effects by gender but the evidence is contradictory, and didactic programs may be less effective in both cognitive and social domains; (3) teachers and caregivers who have specialized training, are attentive to individual children, have fewer children in their care, and use strategies associated with DAP generally are more competent at enhancing children's learning and growth; and (4) both equivocal results and new thinking about early-childhood curriculum point to intricate research questions that consider the interplay between the individual child's characteristics, the immediate contexts of the home and classroom, and the larger contexts of the formal school environment, the proximal microculture, and the distal macroculture. Building on that framework, a more detailed examination of the implementation of programs that proved to be effective over the long term offers insight into the mechanism by which early-childhood programs may contribute to development. This examination is based in the sociocultural theory of Lev Vygotsky (1978).

The Sociocultural Perspective

The issues of culture and context are important when considering how to conduct research, planning a curriculum, or interacting with a parent. The sociocultural perspective is an interactive, constructivist approach to child development. Theoreticians and researchers from this perspective believe that children construct knowledge through the interaction of biological maturation and environmental influences. However, they do not believe that features of the environment are universal across different cultures and contexts. In fact, experiences are filtered or interpreted through the varying cultures or contexts and may have differential effects on children's learning and development depending on the child's culture and the contexts he experiences. It is believed that much in the social context of the child has powerful influence on development (Cole, Gay, Glick, & Sharp, 1971). One aspect of the theory conceptualized by Vygotsky (1978) that is highly relevant to education is the zone of proximal development (ZPD). The ZPD is the range between the current level of functioning of a child without assistance and what she can accomplish with scaffolding provided by a sensitive adult, another child, or scripted routine (Bruner, 1962; Nelson, 1986). The idea here is not to match the child's current functional level (Hunt's [1961] idea of the "problem of the match") but to provide support for the child to work above his current ability and thus advance his development.

The best teachers seek to identify those challenges—the child's zone of proximal development—to individualize their efforts with each child. They then structure activities not to match the child's current functional level but to provide support for the child to work just above his current ability and thus advance his development. To help the child make that leap, the teacher needs individual knowledge of the child's current functioning and must understand the step that lies immediately ahead for that child.

For example, a five year old is pushing a small shopping cart through the house area in his preschool. His teacher notices that he is putting fruit in the small basket and all other groceries in the larger section of the cart. She has watched him sort objects over the past few weeks and thinks that he may now be able to classify along two dimensions at the same time, with some help from her. She goes to the cash register to pretend to be the cashier and says, "We need to be careful how we divide your groceries into bags. We want to use one bag for things that will go in the refrigerator, and other bags for the things that will go in the cabinet." Together they devise a system with one bag for each of the following categories: food in cartons that will go into the refrigerator; loose vegetables and fruit for the refrigerator; food cartons that go into the cabinet, and food cans for the cabinet. In this example, the child's unassisted level of classification was fairly gross—fruit versus nonfruit. With the teacher's help, he demonstrated an understanding of hierarchical classification.

Many of the curriculum practices used in the programs found to have lasting benefits for children can be seen as strategies that increased the ability of teachers to recognize and take advantage of each child's level of development. Teachers are more likely to gain the specialized knowledge they need to tailor their teaching when they work with relatively few children for a long period of time and when they have a chance to reflect on their teaching practices. Such teachers are more able to understand the children's individual learning and interests, and they can create activities and interactions within each child's zone of proximal development. The value of close relations between teachers and parents can also be seen as a means of improving the teacher's ability to understand the child and promote his or her learning. The teacher who has extensive contact with the child's family can better understand the child as an individual and have an appreciation for the contexts within which the child must function, the parents' aims and hopes for the child, and the values of the child's culture. When parents and teachers are teamed in such a collaboration, the adults do the work to build consistency in the world of the child, rather than leaving it up to the child to integrate disparate contexts.

Scripts to Cope with New Contexts

Routine activities can provide another kind of zone of proximal development and can help explain why consistency and continuity help children learn as they move from one context to another—from home to preschool or from preschool to kindergarten. Routine or repetitive activities, such as going to a restaurant or singing songs at circle time in preschool, provide scripts for children that help them make sense of other events and help them know how to behave. Having scripts makes it easier for children to learn because they are familiar with the structure and content of the event and can focus on mastering new information. When children lack scripted knowledge, their attention is drawn to the details of the new activity, and they may be unable to focus on learning tasks.

The lack of scripted knowledge challenges many children as they move from the home environment into school settings. The scripts of school are different from those in most homes and are likely to differ even more in some minority cultures, placing a double burden of learning on those children when they enter preschools and schools (Nelson, 1986). When children encounter similarities between settings in what happens and how it happens, it is easier for them to develop new scripts that help them make later transitions as well. Early-childhood programs can serve as a bridge for children between home and school, especially if the preschool curriculum emphasizes the traditional curriculum content and the varied interaction styles (large group, small group, one-on-one learning) that the child will encounter in school.

The following analysis draws on the sociocultural perspective to investigate the common elements of the curricula used by the preschool classrooms studied in the longitudinal research. The over-arching thesis is that the practices that were constructive helped teachers to work within children's zones of proximal development because of their increased knowledge of each child. This specialized knowledge was facilitated through (1) reflective teaching practices, (2) small class sizes combined with low child-to-teacher ratios, (3) intensity and continuity of the program, and (4) knowledge of the home and family. In addition, it is argued that the content of the curricula used in the studies did not differ significantly, or at least not in ways in which the measures of learning were sensitive.

Curricula and Classroom Practices in the Programs Studied Longitudinally

Expecting that program practices like those identified in the literature reviewed above may have contributed to the positive effects that experimental early-childhood interventions had on children, the author searched the longitudinal studies of the effectiveness of preschool programs for low-income children for common elements. This review focuses on seven programs with longitudinal study results at least through elementary school that provided center-based experiences for low-income children three to five years of age and included in their reports written descriptions of their curriculum and classroom practices (see Table 3-1). The three curriculum demonstration studies discussed earlier are included among the seven, as are several of the most influential early-childhood experiments analyzed in the articles by Barnett in this volume.

Reflective Teaching Practices

One major reason that many question whether the results of the longitudinal efficacy studies can be generalized is that the studies took place in "laboratory" settings (Farran, 1990). Although this criticism is not completely accurate (the Perry study, for example, was administered and conducted completely under the auspices of the Ypsilanti Public Schools in Michigan and, indeed, takes its name from the Perry Elementary School), it links with an important commonality across all of the programs: The teachers/caregivers were involved in conducting research and in model development. This is not simply the Hawthorne effect where involvement in any innovation results in enhanced outcomes. The teachers were engaged in regular reflection on their teaching practices with support from the research and curriculum specialists. As Neilson (1990) has suggested, teaching at its best is research: Teachers generate questions, gather data, test hypotheses, and draw conclusions. This process was systematized and augmented by the interactions with others on the research teams. As the following sample excerpts from program descriptions indicate, in the experimental programs teachers and other staff met often to discuss the program and individual children:

> The research staff offered consulting service on all aspects of the program. Weekly seminars were held for the entire preschool staff

Table 3-1.
Program Practices in Longitudinal Studies

Researcher		Ratio	Group size	Duration	Intensity	Activities for Parents
Garber[a]	infants	1:1	2	6 years	full day	Job training
	preschool	?	?			Different staff
Karnes (5 curricula)[b,c]		1:5	15	8 months	part day	1 curriculum
						Held parent conferences
Lally[d]	infants	1:4	8	5 years	full day	Weekly home visits
	preschool	?	?			Different staff
Miller (4 curricula)[e,f,g]		1:7	15	1 year	full-day	1 curriculum
						Made home visits
Ramey[h,i]	infants	1:3	?	5 years	full-day	Group meetings
	preschool	1:7	14			Different staff
Weikart (Perry)[j]		1:6	10–13	2 years	part-day	Weekly home visits
Weikart (3 curricula)[k]		1:8	15–16	2 years	part-day	Biweekly home visits

Sources: a. Garber (1988), b. Karnes (1983), c. Karnes (1977), d. Lally (1977), e. Miller (1983), f. Miller (1984), g. Miller (1975), h. Ramey (1991), i. Ramey (1982), j. Weikart (1967), k. Weikart (1978).

in order to discuss with authorities in various fields the topics pertinent to the operation of the program. . . . There was a constant effort to meet individual needs . . . to evaluate each child's understanding of an experience. (Weikart, Kamii, & Radin, 1967:24,76)

During the year, staff held weekly case conferences, in which the progress, problems and strengths of a particular youngster were discussed in depth. . . . Plans were drawn up for possible ways to enhance the child's participation in the program. . . . Input from every staff member was valued when such a problem arose and over time many became more skillful in helping individual children. (Lally, Mangione and Honig, 1987:8–9)

Teachers are given inservice training and consultative help in assessing children's needs, setting objectives, planning and implementing activities that will stimulate particular kinds of communication and in evaluating their own interactions with children. . . . Consultants helped them to select objectives to work on in the classroom each week, and guided them in devising activities that would help children reach the objectives set. (Ramey, McGinness, et al. 1982:163–65)

An ongoing training program that included group meetings, on the job training, and annual seminars was implemented by the curriculum supervisor. . . . The second portion of the group meetings centered around the personal needs of the caregivers and sensitizing the caregivers to the needs of the children. . . . Discussions emphasized personal attitudes toward specific children, education, . . . specific behavior. . . . This enabled placement of each child with a caregiver who felt positively about him/her. (Garber, 1988:42–43)

This same attention to teacher thinking, planning, and evaluating with outside support can be seen across very different curricular approaches. In discussing the traditional, child-centered curriculum employed in the High/Scope Curriculum Demonstration Project, Weikart quotes the classroom teachers, "The specific plans are formulated on a day-to-day basis, since the plans for one day depend on the successes or failures of the day before. Just as important as the planning is the evaluation immediately following each day" (Weikart, 1973:196). This was not limited to the nondidactic programs. Joseph Glick commented after observing all three of the classrooms in this study, "Common to all of the groups is the tremendous amount of preparation" (cited in Wiekart, Epstein, Schweinhart & Bond, 1978:50). There is evidence in both the Curriculum Demonstration Project and the Karnes comparison study that even the teachers in the "programmed" approach spent time reflecting on their practice, meeting with curriculum experts, and making adjustments to make the program fit the children they were teaching. By contrast, caregivers who work in community child-care programs and even many preschool teachers in public programs lack time for planning, reflection, and assessment, and few receive regular supervision by trained educational leaders (Fenichel, 1992; Jorde-Bloom, 1988).

The proponents of the teacher as a reflective practitioner believe that reflection leads to improved and more expert teaching (Richardson, 1994). From a sociocultural view, the improvement may come from the increased ability of the teacher to understand where the child's zone of proximal development is in a given area of learning. In the efficacy studies, teachers were given time to reflect and evaluate; the time was structured for this to occur through interactions with other teachers and with outside experts; the outside experts came into the classroom to observe, which enhanced their ability to facilitate the teacher's reflections; and the teachers discussed their reflections with the child's parents on a regular and intimate basis. In essence, the supervisor scaffolded learning within the teacher's zone of proximal development.

Teacher-Child Ratio and Class Size

As stated earlier, research has shown a relationship between the number of children assigned to a teacher, the amount of individual, positive interactions children receive, and child outcomes. This is confounded with the size of the class as a whole. The efficacy research literature supports the view that small class sizes and high teacher to child ratios result in positive, long-term benefits for children from low-income families. Ratios in the experimental literature rarely exceeded one teacher to every seven children, which is far below prevailing practices in Head Start and child care (U.S. General Accounting Office, 1995). Only one state requires child-care centers to maintain a ratio of one teacher to seven or eight children, and regulations in other states range from ten to twenty children per teacher. The reason that low ratios have a positive impact on learning, in this culture, seems obvious since it allows the teacher to know children better and interact with them more. Adults can create activities and interactions within the child's zone of proximal development. It may also create a more comfortable environment for children who do not thrive in groups and who prefer quiet, focused activities. Other cultures see a value in a larger group of children learning to function cohesively (Tobin, Wu, & Davidson 1989; also, see the chapter by Boocock in this volume) and larger class sizes in this context may facilitate learning because children create scaffolds within each other's zones of proximal development. However, it seems most of the children in our culture are not socialized this way, and neither are our teachers, who rely on whole-group instruction and giving directions when the class size increases (Ruopp et al., 1979; Seppanen et al.; 1993). For some microcultures within our country in which association is stressed, we may need to research the effects of larger class size with different teaching strategies in developing collaborative peer relationships that enhance learning.

Intensity and Continuity

Although one would expect the most effective programs to be those with the most intense and long-lasting interventions, comparisons

among the longitudinal research studies allow only general conclusions regarding the benefits of program intensity and duration.
(See the chapter by Barnett in this volume.) As Table 3-1 shows,
some effective programs offered only a half-day program during the
school year and others began intervention in infancy and continued
through to elementary school; one of these continued intervention in
the early grades for some of the children. Another study began in
preschool but provided intervention into the elementary school. Two
of the studies that began in infancy are the only longitudinal studies
to find lasting IQ gains for the experimental group with the
exception of the Harlem Study. The Harlem Study offered one-to-one
tutoring to boys in Harlem twice a week at age two or three. In
addition, the Perry Project that offered one or two years of preschool
intervention has shown remarkable effects of the program into
adulthood (Schweinhart et al., 1994). Intensity and continuity of
service must be viewed as more than a matter of hours of services.
Obviously, two one-hour one-for-one sessions per week with the
same teacher are intensive in a different way from the typical classroom program. Other ways that programs have provided intensity
are very small classes, home visiting, and low teacher turnover.

Relationships with Parents

Many believe that helping parents improve their skills as caregivers
is an effective method of improving children's life chances; however,
according to the chapter by St. Pierre, Layser, and Barnes in this
volume, experience has shown that programs for parents alone do
not influence children's development as strongly as do programs
that involve children directly. Most of the longitudinal studies
reviewed here combined center-based experiences for children with
extensive parent involvement components. Weekly or biweekly
home visits by the child's teacher, parent-group meetings, and
parent involvement in the classroom were methods used by many of
the successful programs. In most programs, the staff strived to
establish a collaborative relationship with the parents in which
knowledge about the child was shared from both the home and the
classroom perspective. It would seem likely that this intimate and
collegial relationship would not only help parents in their
interactions with the child, but would help the teacher understand
the child better and thus be more effective in interacting with the
child. Not only would this understanding of the child as an
individual be beneficial, but the teacher would have a better

understanding of the contexts within which the child must function, of the parent's aims and hopes for the child, and of the values of the child's culture. This collaboration then would result in the adults making the world of the child make sense, rather than leaving it up to the child to integrate disparate contexts.

A seeming contradiction to this view is the Harlem Study, which had no formal parent component. However, parents and other family members were encouraged to observe the tutoring sessions and were provided transportation to the center with their child. It is likely that parents learned a great deal about their child in these observations, and it is equally likely that they discussed the session with the teacher when it was over. Also, if a collaborative relationship between teacher and parent is effective in part because it increases the teacher's knowledge of the child, then working intensively with only one child at a time may provide the same knowledge, thereby negating the need for closer contact with the parent.

Few current early-childhood programs continue to offer the kind of parent-involvement program that existed in the experimental studies. In most Head Start programs, if home visits are offered, they are not weekly, and they are not conducted by the child's classroom staff (Brush, Gaidurgis, & Best, 1993; Zigler & Styfco, 1994). Child-care centers and other community programs are unlikely to involve parents beyond occasional meetings or parent conferences (U.S. Government Accounting Office, 1995).

Classroom Processes and Curriculum Content

Detailed descriptions of the curricula used across the longitudinal studies exist for some programs (Bereiter & Engelmann, 1966; Garber, 1988; Karnes, Zehrbach, & Teska, 1972; Lally & Honig, 1977; Miller & Dyer, 1975; Palmer, 1972; Ramey et al., 1982; Weikart, 1967; Weikart, 1972; Weikart et al., 1978). Actual classroom observation of the teacher practices are rare (see Weikart et al., 1978 for an exception). Based on the descriptions, some generalizations about the process and content of the curricula can be made. The focuses of the teachers and program developers were clearly different in many of the programs. For example, in an early description of the Perry program, Sonquist and Kamii (1967) state that "The basic function of the preschool . . . is facilitating the transition from sensory-motor intelligence to conceptual intelligence (89)." Garber (1988) describes the preschool curriculum in the

Milwaukee Study: "The stimulation program gradually shifted from social-emotional development to perceptual-motor development and then to cognitive-language development (58)," which became specifically a school-readiness program. The Bereiter and Engelmann (1966) curriculum used in three of the projects was based on behaviorist principles and used a direct instruction mode of teaching.

Even across these disparate approaches, some common processes and content are evident. Many of the programs consciously exposed children to classroom processes that differed from the children's interactions at home but were similar to those that they would experience in formal school: whole-class, small-group, and individual interactions with teachers. Preschool teachers used a discourse pattern, at least some of the time, which is typical of schooling: the initiation-reply-evaluation sequence (Mehan, 1979). This sequence is also very like the discourse of individually administered intelligence and achievement tests. For example, the teacher asks, "Which of these do you think will float in the water?" The child replies, "The cork." The teacher says, "Let's see if you're right." The preschool children also learned school-like strategies for remembering such as rehearsal and categorization since this is a by-product of schooling in our culture (Cole et al., 1971;Wagner, 1978). All of these experiences were apt to give the children advantages when they began school, which were the beginning of abiding differences in the way school was experienced.

Even though the programs applied new theories of development to help children develop thinking skills, the content relied on by most teachers was drawn from the traditional kindergarten and nursery school. Consistent across every program is a strong focus on language. The teachers provided a model of standard English, and the programs were strongly oriented toward getting children to talk and be understood, to understand others' speech, and to experiment with symbolic concepts through speech. The classroom materials and teacher-planned activities and discussions involved typical concepts such as shapes, colors, sizes, numbers, animals, transportation, prepositions, seasons, holidays, and the like. The fact that the process and content of the interactions was similar across differing approaches, all of which were successful in helping children, indicates that, as Spodek (1991) has said, content is also important.

From the sociocultural perspective, these similarities in both content and process may be effective because they provide scripts for children that help them make sense of other events and help them know how to behave in certain contexts (Nelson, 1981, 1986). The scripts of school are different from those in most homes, and seem to differ even more for minority cultures since "the acquisition of scripts is central to the acquisition of culture" (Nelson, 1981:110).

If exposure to traditional preschool content is the essential factor of effective programs, then why don't all preschool programs have outcomes like the longitudinal studies? It is not the essential factor, the other factors already mentioned are also important. In addition, there is some indication that community programs do not expose children to this content. Seppanen and colleagues (1993) found that public school preschool classrooms funded through federal government's Title I program for schools serving a high percentage of disadvantaged children did not provide regular activities dealing with math, language, and science and were lacking in small-group interaction and individual attention.

Conclusion and Recommendations

This analysis of the longitudinal studies of experimental preschools and newer studies of the effects of quality in early education and care suggests that the benefits of early-childhood programs are influenced by the interrelated factors of program structure (class size, the ratio of children to teachers, and service intensity); processes that help teachers respond to individual children (reflective teaching practice and close relationships with parents); and curricula that serve as a bridge between home and school.

The prevalence of these quality factors in the experimental preschools contrasts with their absence in many of today's typical community programs for low-income children. If preschool intervention is to live up to the promise of the longitudinal results, then Head Start, Chapter 1, child-care, and other programs should approximate the standard of quality suggested by the research reviewed here and endorsed by professional groups. The following recommendations spell out steps that can be taken by policy makers, practitioners, and researchers to ensure that early-childhood programs are good enough to benefit the children who attend them. The recommendations pertain particularly to center-based programs for children from low-income families, but they may be equally important for all children across early education and care settings.

Policy

State and federal policy makers affect early-childhood programs in two primary ways: by establishing regulatory standards that

GOVERNORS STATE UNIVERSITY
UNIVERSITY PARK
IL 60466

define the type of care that is legal or expected and by providing funding for programs and for quality-improvement activities. Both types of policy action have an immense impact on the nature of early-childhood programs because they define the legal and resource context in which programs must exist.

Review regulatory requirements and program guidelines

State regulatory requirements that child-care centers must meet to operate legally should be reviewed, focusing especially on group size and child-staff ratios and on teacher qualifications, because these factors create the program conditions that permit positive interactions to take place between teachers and children. Similar reviews should be conducted by the state and federal agencies that set guidelines for Head Start and for preschool programs operated by the public schools. Despite pressures to increase the availability of care, the temptation to increase permitted class sizes and ratios of children per staff member should be resisted.

Provide funds sufficient to pay for quality services

Many early-childhood programs that serve low-income children derive their funds from public sources, and their efforts to improve quality are directly linked to the level of that funding. Increasing the funding provided per child enables programs to improve quality; for example, by paying more to attract qualified teachers. Funding cuts are likely to decrease quality. Some state policy makers use funding formulas to encourage programs to become accredited by professional groups by paying higher rates per child for child care provided in accredited programs.

Support initiatives to improve program quality

In addition, public funds can be designated to pay for quality improvement costs by making free training available, for example, or by offering grants to help programs meet licensing or professional accreditation standards. The Child Care and Development Block grant passed by Congress in 1990 allowed 25 percent of the funds to be used to support efforts to increase the quality and availability of child care.

Professional Practice

Although policy changes in both regulations and funding levels are needed to achieve widespread improvements in early-childhood programs, the responsibility for creating change will remain with practitioners—program administrators, center directors, and teachers. Professionals have the task of translating research findings and professional knowledge into practical approaches in several key areas:

1. *Create new staffing patterns.* Design cost-efficient staffing patterns that yield favorable ratios of children to staff and allow stable relationships to develop between individual children and teachers.

2. *Find new ways to give teachers on-site supervision and support.* Develop training and models of supportive supervision and mentoring for new and experienced teachers to inform their work with individual children in actual classrooms (Child Care Employee Project, 1991; Morgan, Azer, & Costley et al., 1993).

3. *Implement comprehensive curricula.* Create and faithfully implement coherent curricula that attend to all facets of children's development and meet the needs of children with different backgrounds and different needs.

4. *Work toward coherence and continuity.* Design expansion and collaboration efforts to ensure that children experience both coherence and continuity in early-childhood programs, whether services can be provided by a single agency or must be coordinated across several programs.

5. *Help teachers work with parents.* Provide time and appropriate training to enable teaching staff to work collaboratively with parents.

Research

Research can serve policy and practice in the field of early-childhood programs in two major ways: by pointing out areas in which new approaches are needed and guiding the development of those approaches, and by assessing the impacts of innovations once they are put into practice. Several directions that research might take are described below:

1. *Identify ways curriculum and teaching should be individualized.* Mount finely tuned studies to document how children's developmental ability, temperament, learning style, personality, and familial characteristics affect their responses to different curricula and teaching practices.

2. *Examine continuities and discontinuities across contexts.* Conduct studies of the interplay between the individual child's

characteristics, the immediate contexts of the home and classroom, the larger contexts of the formal school environment, and the surrounding cultures of home and society.

3. *Assess the impact on teachers of classroom-based training.* Examine the changes in teaching practices that result when teachers receive support and guidance from supervisors or peers who have been trained in observation and consultation.

4. *Document the costs and impacts of changing regulatory requirements.* Pioneering studies have measured the effects that raising regulatory standards for child care has on the quality of care provided (Howes, Smith, & Galinsky, 1995; Love, Ryer, & Faddis, 1992) and have assessed the impact that raising requirements has on program costs (General Accounting Office, 1990). These studies should be replicated and extended to give policy makers reliable information about the fiscal and programmatic impacts of their actions.

As this chapter has shown, much is known about how to provide beneficial programs for children from low-income families, but this knowledge is only gradually influencing the decisions made by policy makers. Excitement over the promise of early-childhood programs persuaded many state leaders to create statewide preschool programs to prepare young children from low-income backgrounds to succeed in school. Federal funding for child-care services is at an all-time high. Concern over indications that Head Start programs vary widely in quality led federal authorities to protect one-fourth of the funding intended to expand the program for investments in quality improvement (U.S. General Accounting Office, 1994). Building on those positive trends, the combined efforts of policy makers, practitioners, and researchers are needed to support continued progress that will extend the benefits of high-quality early-childhood programs to all the children who need them.

Note

This chapter is based on a previously published article, used by permission: E. C. Frede (1995). The role of program quality in producing early-childhood program benefits. *The Future of Children: Long-Term Outcomes of Early Childhood Programs*, 5 (3):115–32. The author is grateful to Mary Larner and Deanna Gomby for extensive and useful editing on the prior draft and also to anonymous reviewers for helpful comments.

4

R. G. St. Pierre
J. I. Layzer
H. V. Barnes

Regenerating Two-Generation Programs

In spite of three decades of persistent antipoverty efforts, U.S. Census data have been used to make the case that the number of children living in poverty has increased greatly in recent years (Carnegie Task Force, 1994). Reasons include an increase in the number of single-parent families, a poor labor market, and declines in benefits to poor families (Duncan, 1991). For children and families, the correlates of living in poverty are many.

Adapted from St. Pierre, R. G., Layzer, J. I., & Barnes, H. V. (1995). Two-generation programs: Design, cost, and short-term effectiveness. *The Future of Children* (Winter) 5(3):76–93, by permission of Center for the Future of Children, The David and Lucile Packard Foundation.

Traditional Programs

One strategy, developed more than twenty-five years ago, is to intervene in the preschool life of children from disadvantaged families, at a time of great plasticity, in an attempt to improve the child's social competence and prepare him or her to enter school on equal terms with more fortunate children. Head Start has been the major federal early-childhood program for preschoolers.

An alternative approach that has been tried in many different settings over the past few decades is to attempt to affect childrens' development indirectly, through their parents. Programs adhering to this model believe that parents are their childrens' first and best teachers, and that while high-quality early-childhood programs are important, parents must be made into first-rate teachers in order for their children to succeed. This approach has resulted in the development of programs such as Head Start's Parent-Child Development Centers, Missouri's Parents as Teachers (PAT) program, and Arkansas's Home Instruction Program for Preschool Youngsters (HIPPY) program.

A third strategy, developed in response to increased concern about long-term welfare dependency, has focused on the adult single parent of a child or children. Welfare, welfare-to-work programs, and adult education programs have the dual aim of moving women off welfare into work and improving their economic well being. Enhancing a family's economic well being, it is argued, will by itself improve children's life prospects.

Two-Generation Programs

Individually, and even when taken in combinations of two, none of these approaches has proven to be a panacea for the nation's social and educational problems. Disadvantaged children and families need a more intensive and broader treatment than a year of preschool education, and it is unrealistic to expect that such a brief experience can counteract the pervasive effects of poverty, violence, and social dislocation that inner-city children experience. Further, there is little or no evidence that intervention with adults, either in terms of parenting education or adult education or literacy, will translate into effects on children that would, in the long run, lift them out of poverty.

In response, a new set of "two-generation" programs has adopted a strategy that recognizes the multigenerational, multidimensional aspects of family poverty and which sets out to attack it on several fronts simultaneously by using key features of each of the three approaches discussed above (Smith, 1991). In the absence of much research on the effectiveness of such a comprehensive and coordinated approach, two-generation programs have proliferated at the local, state, and federal levels. Under the umbrella of an integrated approach, two-generation programs seek to solve the problems of parents and children in two contiguous generations— to help young children get the best possible start in life and, at the same time, to help their parents become economically self-sufficient.

A model of how two-generation programs hope to produce effects for adults and children is shown in Figure 4-1. Two-generation programs share three features, to a greater or lesser degree: (1) a developmentally appropriate early-childhood program, (2) a parenting education component, and (3) an adult education, literacy, or job skills and training component. Two-generation programs typically feature case managers, whose job can be wide ranging; for example, they try to coordinate services, ensure that families are enrolled in appropriate services, cajole families to participate fully, provide on-the-spot counseling and crisis intervention, provide some direct service, and so forth. Two-generation programs often rely on educational and social services that exist in the community instead of creating duplicate service structures, and they typically provide "support" services such as transportation, meals, or child care so that families can participate in the main programmatic services. The hypotheses underlying two-generation programs are that:

- Early-childhood education has a direct effect on children's cognitive performance prior to school entry and may have long-term effects on child outcomes.

- Parenting education has a short-term direct effect on parenting skills, which, prior to school entry, will have an indirect effect on children's cognitive performance.

- Adult-focused programs has a direct effect on the literacy and skill levels of parents. However, this is not expected to translate into short-term child-level effects.

- Children's school performance will be enhanced both by their own experience in an early-childhood program and by their parent's enhanced parenting skills.

Figure 4-1.
Two-Generation Program Model

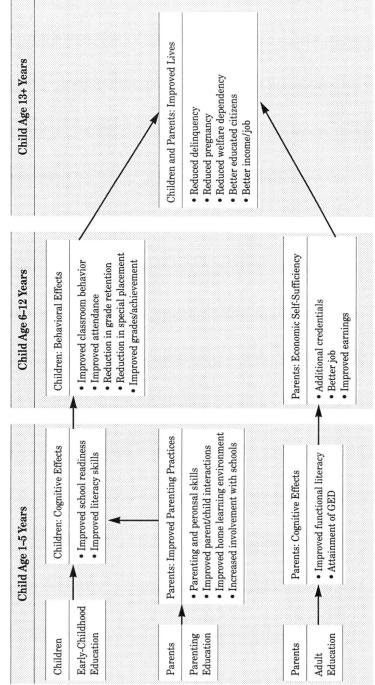

- In the long run, all three program components will enhance the life chances of parents and their children. In this view, there are no differences in anticipated outcomes for the two generations—the desired outcomes are reduced delinquency levels, reduced pregnancy rates, the ability to be an informed and responsible citizen, and improved economic self-sufficiency, including a job that provides adequate income.

Programmatic Variation

Here we describe a selection of two-generation programs representing federal, state, and local efforts (Table 4-1). Some are based on a clear model in which the duration, intensity, and nature of the program is specified ahead of time and guided by formal performance standards, while others provide the broad outline of a program and leave implementation to local discretion.

- AVANCE: The Avance Family Support and Education program began in the 1970s in San Antonio, Texas, and is designed to help school children by teaching parents to teach their children and by meeting the parents' needs for education and job training.

- CFRP: Funded from 1973 to 1983 by the U.S. Department of Health and Human Services, the premise of the Child and Family Resource Program was that the best way to promote childrens' growth and development is to support families and help parents become more effective caregivers and educators.

- CCDP: The Comprehensive Child Development Program was first funded in 1990 by the U.S. Department of Health and Human Services. Five-year grants are provided to thirty-four projects that provide comprehensive, continuous, coordinated social and educational services to low-income families with a newborn child.

- EVEN START: The Even Start Family Literacy Program began in 1990 as a demonstration program funded by the U.S. Department of Education. Even Start allows great local discretion to more than four hundred grantees, but mandates that participating families take part in each of three

Table 4-1.
Summary of Two-Generation Program Characteristics

Program/ Sponsor	Early-Childhood Education	Parenting Education	Adult Education, Literacy, Job Training	Other Notes
Avance Family Support and Education (San Antonio, Texas, 1973 to present)	Children age birth through two participate in educational day care for three hours a week while parenting services are delivered to mothers.	Mothers attend three-hour classes, once per week for year one of program. Avance staff make monthly home visits.	Year two adult literacy component added in 1981 provides basic literacy and advanced education for families who complete the parenting program.	Enhanced early-childhood component being added as part of involvement with CCDP.
Child and Family Resource Program (U.S. Dept. of Health and Human Services, 1973 to 1983)	Services provided from child's birth through age five. Children from birth to three years served through monthly home visits and twice a quarter center-based sessions. Fifteen minutes of home visit time devoted to this service. Sporadic attendance at center. Children age 3 to 4 participated in regular Head Start.	Parenting, child development, social services delivered through monthly home visits and twice a quarter center-based activities. Thirty minutes of home visit devoted to parenting. Sporadic attendance at center activities.	Offered by case managers on an as-needed basis. Not a strong component of CFRP.	No performance standards, much site-to-site variation in each component. Strong case-management component.
Comprehensive Child Development Program (U.S. Dept. of Health and Human Services, 1990 to present)	Services provided to families from child's birth through age five. Services based on DHHS performance standards. Children from birth to three years receive developmental screening and child development experience through center-based or home-based instruction. Aim for six or more home-based contacts per quarter, which focus on training parent as a teacher (about forty-five minutes per contact). Head Start is primary source of ECE at age four.	Parenting education includes child development, health care, nutrition, parenting skills, life skills, mostly delivered through case management visits, which occur on a bi-weekly basis.	Adult literacy education, vocational training, employment counseling, job training and place-ment are typically done through linkages and referrals to local com-munity colleges and other local educational institutions. Job linkages made with employers and agencies.	Strong case management. CCDP provides physical health, mental health, child care, substance abuse, other support services. 20% dropout in first year, 40% dropout by 2.5 years.

Table 4-1. (*continued*)
Summary of Two-Generation Program Characteristics

Program/ Sponsor	Early-Childhood Education	Parenting Education	Adult Education, Literacy Job Training	Other Notes
Even Start Family Literacy Program (U.S. Dept. of Education, 1990 to present)	No performance standards. Ages served, intensity, duration all determined locally. Obtain services from local Head Start, Chapter 1 preschool, other local preschool, public schools, Even Start preschool. National average of 232 total hours.	Intensity, duration determined locally. National average of fifty-eight total hours. Services typically provided by Even Start case managers.	Services typically provided by local programs in adult basic education, adult secondary education, GED preparation, English as a second language. National average of 107 hours.	Heavy use of existing services, provision of support services to enable participation. Average of seven months participation.
Head Start Family Service Centers (U.S. Dept. of Health and Human Services 1990 to present)	Normal Head Start services for four year olds, based on Head Start performance standards.	Case-management approach builds on Head Start parent involvement services. Great variation in the extent to which parenting education goes beyond Head Start requirements.	Case management includes needs assessment, service referral, support services. Adult literacy and employment training provided through partnerships with local agencies.	This demonstration adds adult-focused services to regular Head Start early-childhood services.
New Chance (MDRC, 1989 to 1992)	Free child care in high-quality centers. No special curriculum. including life skills, parenting	Phase one is full-day, full-week program for mothers including GED preparation, education, pediatric health education.	Phase one is full-day, full-week program for mothers visits. Program adult education. Phase two is vocational training, internships, job placement.	Case management through biweekly designed for eighteen months; average participation was six months.

core services: early-childhood education, parenting education, and adult education.

- HEAD START FSC: The Head Start Family Service Centers began operation in 1990 as a demonstration program funded by the U.S. Department of Health and Human Services. Sixty-six projects provide normal Head Start child-development and parenting services augmented by case managers who assess needs, deliver services, and make referrals for adult literacy, substance abuse, and employment training.

- NEW CHANCE: New Chance was a comprehensive program for disadvantaged young mothers and their children. It was funded by a consortium of public and private funders and operated between 1989 and 1992 at sixteen locations. Program components were case management, intensive educational services, and free child care.

Variation in the Early-Childhood Component

Two-generation programs vary substantially on almost every dimension of early-childhood education—for example, age of targeted children, duration of services, and intensity of services. Some programs target preschool three and four year olds and intend to provide services for about a year (Head Start FSCs), some intend to provide continuous services for multiple years to children from birth to entry to school (CFRP and CCDP), and others specify a wide age range (birth through age eight) but leave the exact age and duration of service to the discretion of local grantees (Even Start).

Some programs intend a set period of service duration, while others believe that this dimension should vary according to the needs of the family (Even Start), and still others simply try to involve families for as long as possible. The intensity of child-focused services also varies across programs and is related both to the program's service delivery model and to the age of the child. For example, both CCDP and CFRP are broad-based programs that provide relatively low-intensity services to children from birth through age three. Most of CCDP's early child-focused services for CCDP are delivered through weekly home visits that focus on teaching parenting skills and last about thirty minutes. The early-childhood component of CFRP was even less intensive, providing fifteen minutes of child development during monthly home visits. For four year olds, most CCDP and CFRP projects enroll their children in Head Start, which provides moderately intensive services—a half-day, center-based program for nine months of the year.

Other programs base their early-childhood component on a child-care model. Avance began as a parenting education program and has added a minimal early-childhood component that provides educational day care for infants and toddlers for three hours a week while their mothers are in parenting classes. Similarly, New Chance provides free child care in high-quality centers while mothers are taking part in program activities—no special curriculum is used in these centers.

Programs such as Even Start do not have implementation standards, preferring to let delivery model and program intensity vary according to local preferences. Consequently, Even Start projects exhibit huge variation in the intensity of early-childhood services, with children in the middle 50 percent of the projects receiving between 21 and 330 total hours of service.

Variation in the Parenting Education Component

Parenting education is at the core of many two-generation programs. Most of them include a set of services designed to affect areas such as parenting skills, involvement of parents in schools, parental self-esteem and coping skills, parental depression, and parents as teachers and role models in terms of their use of reading and writing in the household.

Programs with a high-intensity parenting component include Avance and New Chance. In Avance (initially a parenting-only program where mothers attended a center for three hours a week for a school year), one hour is spent on parenting skills in child development, one hour is spent on toy making, and one hour on learning about community resources. In New Chance, mothers receive parenting education as part of their full-day classes.

Other parenting components are lower in intensity. For example, the Head Start FSCs rely on the basic Head Start model of involving parents in governance and service delivery with occasional parenting workshops. CFRP and CCDP both deliver parenting education through home visits (monthly for CFRP and biweekly for CCDP). With its emphasis on local determination, Even Start allows local projects the flexibility to design their own parenting component— on average Even Start adults receive fifty-eight hours of parenting education over a seven-month period, sometimes delivered in the home, sometimes in group sessions.

Variation in the Adult Education/Employment Training Component

The adult-focused component exhibits the greatest amount of variation across two-generation programs. Some programs include fully functioning adult literacy and job training components. For example, New Chance has a two-phase approach including full-day, full-week, classroom-based adult education leading to GED attainment, followed by vocational training, internships, and job placement assistance. Even Start mandates that parents take part in an adult education program; however, local projects vary in the degree to which they include a job training, counseling, and search component. Adult-focused services are the unique part of the Head Start FSCs, where each grantee augments normal Head Start services by adding an adult literacy or employment training component, typically through case management and referrals.

A program such as CCDP relies heavily on case manager assistance to parents so that they can obtain necessary adult literacy education, vocational training, employment counseling, job training, and placement. This is typically done through brokered or referred services, and the level of intensity of this component varies substantially across projects.

Still other programs are relatively weak in this area, providing little more than a referral service (CFRP). Avance added a low-level adult literacy and job training component to its existing services in order to provide basic literacy instruction for mothers who complete the parenting program; if desired, these services are available for multiple years.

Program Costs

The preceding discussion describes how two-generation programs differ from one another for each of the three key program components. The cost of these quite different constellations of services also varies, both across programs, and across projects within a given program.

When measuring the costs of two-generation programs it is important to distinguish between direct program costs and the costs of all leveraged or brokered resources. CFRP, CCDP, Head Start FSCs, and Even Start are federally funded programs that prohibit grantees from using their funds to duplicate services that can be obtained locally. Rather, they are required to build on existing services, and to use program funds to "fill the gaps" in service provision. These programs often use Head Start to provide early-childhood services for four-year-old children, and Even Start and CCDP use local adult education programs to satisfy their adult literacy components, thus ensuring that families receive services with less expenditure of program funds.

Direct Program Costs

Costs for the programs cited here vary widely, both on a per-year basis and also in terms of the number of years that a family participates in the program (Table 4-2 contains cost estimates, converted to 1994 dollars). At the upper end of the cost spectrum, CCDP costs $8,632 per family per year, with the intent that a family participates for five years. New Chance costs $8,311 per family for an intervention in which the mothers can participate for up to eighteen months. Even Start, CFRP, and the Head Start FSCs each cost between $2,500 and $3,500 per family per year. Avance costs about $1,616 per family per year. Families in CFRP can participate for up to five years, families in Head Start FSCs can participate for up to three years, families in Avance can participate for up to two years (53 percent participate for nine or more months), and there is no set length of participation in Even Start (the average length of participation is less than a year).

Per-family costs vary substantially across program sites. In Even Start, 45 percent of the projects spent $2,000 to $4,000 per family, 22 percent spent less than $2,000 per family, and 33 percent spent over $4,000 per family. For New Chance, site-level costs ranged from a low of $4,758 per family to a high of $16,846. In CCDP, site-level costs ranged from $4,592 to $13,413 per family.

Full Program Costs

The cost figures discussed above are based only on the direct program funds provided by the program's funding agency and include none of the costs of referred or brokered services. Two studies have attempted to calculate the "full" costs of one of the above programs: the New Chance evaluation (Quint, Polit, Bos, & Cave, 1994) and the Even Start evaluation (St. Pierre, Swartz, Gamse, Murray, Deck, & Nickel, 1995).

A cost analysis conducted in a subset of Even Start projects showed that in 1991 leveraged or referred services added 54 percent to the federal cost of the program. Thus, federal Even Start costs

Table 4-2.
Summary of Two-Generation Program Costs

Program	Age of Child at Entry	Program Duration	Direct Program Outlays per Family
Avance (San Antonio)	Birth to two years	One or two years intended	$1,616 per year
CFRP (Federal HHS)	Birth	Five years intended	$3,222 per year
CCDP (Federal HHS)	Birth	Five years intended	$8,632 per year
Even Start (Federal ED)	Birth to eight years	Varies	$2,663 per year
Head Start FSCs (Federal HHS)	Four years	Three years intended	$3,507 per year
New Chance (Private/MDRC)	Varies	One and one-half years intended	$8,311 for average participation of six months

were $2,663 per family and total costs, including $1,438 worth of all referred and leveraged services, were $4,101. For New Chance, the cost of services supplied by other agencies added 18 percent ($1,496) to the cost of services supplied by the sponsoring agency ($8,311) so that the total cost per family was $9,807.

Allocation of Program Costs and Variation Among Sites

The Even Start study also examined the allocation of program costs among service components and found that about two-thirds of program funds were spent on the direct provision of services (31 percent for early-childhood education, 15 percent for adult education, 9 percent for parenting education, and 9 percent for support services), while the remaining third was spent on program administration and coordination (14 percent), evaluation (10 percent), case management and recruiting (4 percent), and a variety of other functions (8 percent).

Similar analyses conducted as part of the New Chance demonstration show that child care (29 percent) and case management (27 percent) accounted for over half of program costs. The remainder was spent on basic education (16 percent), skills training (8 percent), health and personal development (5 percent), recruitment and intake (4 percent), coordination (4 percent), parenting education (3 percent), employability development (3 percent), and college (3 percent).

The fact that the per-family costs vary widely across programs makes sense, given the great range in services provided. In addition, the studies that examined site-level variation in cost per family served found that variation in per-family costs among sites is as large or larger than cost variation among programs. Even Start provides data on some of the correlates of variation in costs between sites (size of program, extent to which services are provided internally versus through a collaborating agency), but unfortunately, we have only the beginnings of research evidence that can be used to help local program implementers decide which of these programs is most cost effective.

Comparative Cost of Single-Component Programs

For comparative purposes, the most intensive and effective child-focused program, the Infant Health and Development Program (IHDP, 1990), costs about $10,000 per family per year with the intent that families would participate for a three-year period. Head Start, the largest and oldest child-focused program in the nation costs about $4,000 per child per year. Since few families have more than one child in Head Start at the same time, we consider $4,000 as Head Start's annual cost on a per-family basis. At less than $1,000 per year, the Missouri PAT program is a much less intensive and inexpensive child-focused program. It involves hourly home visits once a month, primarily for parenting education, and occasional group meetings.

A range of estimates are available for the per-participant cost of an adult education/job training program. Basic adult education programs funded by the federal government cost quite little— between $100 and $500 per participant (Development Associates, 1994). Gueron and Pauly (1991) reviewed data from seven JOBS programs and found that costs ranged from $100 to $1,000 per participant. More comprehensive JOBS programs including the Teenage Parent Demonstration (Maynard, 1993) and the Minority Female Single Parent Demonstration (Burghardt & Gordon, 1990) had correspondingly higher costs—between $1,400 and $3,900 per participant. Finally, California's Greater Avenues for Independence (GAIN) program had costs of about $3,000 per experimental subject (Riccio, Friedlander, & Freedman, 1994).

A final comparative assessment can be made by examining data on the allocation of Head Start federal funds, available from the Head Start cost management system. In 1991, about 70 percent of Head Start federal costs were spent on direct service provision (41 percent on education, 8 percent on transportation, and about 3 or 4 percent each on health, nutrition, social services, parent involvement, and disabilities services). The remaining 30 percent was spent on administration (13 percent), occupancy (13 percent), and other (4 percent).

Program Effects

All of the programs reviewed here have been evaluated using high-quality, experimental studies (see the citations in Table 4-3). Most of these evaluations have reported only on the relatively short-term effects of two-generation programs. According to the model of two-generation program effects presented in Figure 4-1, this corresponds to effects on children from birth through age five. We hope that follow-up data will be collected on the mothers and children participating in at least some of these evaluations so that it will be possible to determine whether the hypothesized linkages between effects on parents and effects on children do, in fact, hold true.

Variation in Short-Term Effects on Children

Two-generation programs have positive effects on the participation of children in early-childhood programs; that is, by taking part in a two-generation program, young children are more likely to have an early-childhood educational experience than they would be in the absence of the program. However, scanning the summary of effects of two-generation programs on children leads us to conclude that there are small or no effects on a wide range of measures of child development (Table 4-3). Neither Avance nor CFRP had any effects on several measures of child development. CCDP had a small positive effect (about 0.10 standard deviations) on the Bayley Scales of Infant Development for children at age two. Even Start had a medium-sized effect of about 0.5 standard deviations on the Pre-School Inventory nine months after entry to the program; however, children in the control group caught up once they entered school and this early effect disappeared. Even Start children also demonstrated gains on the Peabody Picture Vocabulary Test; however, control-group children achieved similar gains.

Table 4-3.
Summary of Two-Generation Program Effects

Program	Effects on Children	Effects on Parenting	Effects on Adults	Who Benefits Most?
Avance Family Support and Education (Johnson & Walker, 1991)	No effect on the Bayley Scales of Infant Development, Kaufman-ABC, or Stanford-Binet. No effect on maternal report of child behaviors.	Positive effect on the home learning environment, maternal behavior and attitudes about child rearing, maternal role as a teacher, sense of parental efficacy, use of community resources.	Positive effect on enrollment in GED courses. No effect on maternal self-esteem, depression.	Mothers who were married with more education had more positive education and parenting outcomes.
Child and Family Resource Program (Travers, Nauta, & Irwin, 1982)	No effect on Bayley Scales of Infant Development, PreSchool Inventory, High/Scope Pupil Observation Checklist, Schaefer Behavior Inventory; no effect on child health. Positive effect on Head Start enrollment.	Positive effect on parent as a teacher, parent/child interaction.	Positive effect on employment and training; greater use of AFDC, food stamps, WIC, Medicaid. No effect on locus of control.	"Active" participants gained more from the program, as did mothers whose "coping" scores were high. No differences by demographic subgroups.
Comprehensive Child-Development Program (St. Pierre, Layzer, Goodson, & Bernstein, 1994)	At age two, positive effect on participation in work-related child care, Bayley Scales of Infant Development, child health behaviors, cooperative behaviors.	Positive effect on delayed pregnancy, heavier and healthier infants. Positive effect on use of case management, participation in parenting classes, parenting attitudes (AAPI), expectations for child's success, time spent with child, mother/child interaction (NCATS). No effect on home environment.	Positive effect on enrollment in academic, vocational training classes, literary activities, job satisfaction. Increased AFDC, food stamps. No effect on employment, income. No effect on use of health services, maternal physical health, depression, locus of control, coping, positive outlook, social supports, self-esteem, life skills, social connectedness.	No difference by demographic subgroups. No difference by length of participation.

Table 4-3. (continued)
Summary of Two-Generation Program Effects

Program	Effects on Children	Effects on Parenting	Effects on Adults	Who Benefits Most?
Even Start Family Literacy Program (St. Pierre, Swartz, Gamse, Murray, Deck, & Nickel; 1995)	Positive effect on participation in early-childhood programs. At nine months, positive effect on PreSchool Inventory, which disappears at eighteen months. Children moved from ninth to nineteenth percentile on PPVT, but no significant effect.	Positive effect on participation in parenting programs, presence of reading materials in the home. No effect on home environment, parental expectations for child, parent/child reading.	Positive effect on participation in adult education programs. Positive effect on GED attainment. No effect on CASAS reading literacy (same size gains as in other adult education studies). No effect on employment income, sense of mastery, depression, family resources.	Positive relationship between amount of participation in parenting and child's PPVT score. Positive relationship between amount of instruction and PSI, PPVT, CASAS gains as well as GED attainment.
Head Start Family Service Centers (Swartz, Smith, Berghauer, Bernstein, & Gardine, 1994)	No measurement in this area.	Findings not yet published: measures including reading at home, depression, drug/alcohol use, health rating.	Findings not yet published: measures include amount of participation in literacy and employment services, employment, income, literacy skills.	Findings not yet published.
New Chance (Quint, Polit, Bos, & Cave, 1994)	At eighteen months, positive effect on use of child care. No effect on health outcomes. No child-development outcomes measured.	At eighteen months, positive effect on participation in parenting, family planning, health education, emotional support for children, child-rearing attitudes. No effect on birth rate, maternal health, home environment.	At eighteen months, positive effect on participation in skill-building activities, educational programs, GED attainment, college credit. Negative effect on earnings. No effect on literacy, employment, use of AFDC, level of stress, depression.	No differences by demographic subgroups. No clear site-level effects. Amount of participation positively related to GED attainment, reduced pregnancies.

Variation in Short-Term Effects on Parenting

Two-generation programs have positive effects on participation in parenting programs. However, parenting is a broad concept and the hypothesized outcomes are many and varied. The only parenting outcome variable that seems to be consistently affected by multiple programs has to do with the attitudes of parents toward child rearing. In particular, Avance reported positive effects on the home learning environment, child-rearing behaviors and attitudes, maternal role as a teacher and sense of parental efficacy, and use of community resources; New Chance showed positive effects on child-rearing attitudes and on emotional support for children; Even Start had a positive effect on the presence of reading materials in the home; CFRP had positive effects on the Parent-as-a-Teacher scale and on parent/child interactions; and CCDP had positive effects on parenting attitudes, expectations for child's success, time spent with child, and mother/child interaction.

Variation in Short-Term Effects on Adult Education/Job Training

Two-generation programs increase the rate of participation of mothers in adult education and job training programs including academic classes and vocational training. Further, programs such as Even Start, New Chance, and Avance were able to achieve large effects on the percentage of mothers who attained a GED certificate. Unfortunately, in each of these studies, attainment of a GED was not accompanied by a corresponding effect on tests of adult literacy, such as the CASAS or the TABE. This fits with research suggesting that while the GED is an important credential, it bears little relationship to literacy skills (Cameron & Heckman, 1993).

Two-generation programs did lead to increased use of Federal benefits such as AFDC and Food Stamps. This occurred in CCDP, CFRP, and New Chance, each of which explained this finding as resulting either from new eligibility for benefits because of increased participation in educational classes, or simply as an increased awareness of the availability of these federal benefits. None of the programs that measured household income (Even Start, New Chance, CCDP, CFRP) had a measurable effect on this variable, and only CFRP had a positive effect on maternal employment. None of the programs had measurable effects on maternal depression, maternal self-esteem, or the use of social supports.

Who Benefits Most from Two-Generation Programs?

Some of the evaluations reviewed here attempted to address questions about what types of families benefit most from participation in a two-generation program and what types of services are most beneficial. These analyses were correlational in nature, and conclusions drawn from them are subject to a host of competing explanations. However, the findings are provocative and are suggestive of potentially important trends.

Evaluations of Even Start, New Chance, and CFRP all investigated the relationship of amount of participation to outcomes and all found a positive relationship. That is, higher levels of participation were associated with greater program benefits. The Even Start evaluation found that high levels of participation in early-childhood education were associated with larger gains on the PreSchool Inventory and on the Peabody Picture Vocabulary Test, and that high levels of participation in adult education were associated with larger gains on the CASAS and with GED attainment. The New Chance evaluation found that amount of participation in the intervention was positively related to GED attainment and to reduced pregnancies. The CFRP evaluation found that "active" participants gained more from the program than participants who were less active.

Additional analyses were conducted in several of the evaluations in order to determine whether program effects varied across demographic subgroups, such as teenage mothers versus older mothers, mothers with a high school diploma versus mothers without a diploma, male children versus females, relatively high income versus relatively low-income families, and so on. None of the evaluations in which these questions were addressed (CCDP, CFRP, New Chance) found important subgroup differences among program effects, except for Avance, which found better educational and parenting outcomes for better-educated, married mothers.

All of the evaluations that investigated effects for individual sites (Even Start, New Chance, CCDP, CFRP) found large site-to-site variation. One of the strengths and at the same time one of the weaknesses of large-scale research conducted on ongoing demonstration programs is that such studies are based on data from individual projects that vary widely in terms of the quality of implementation and even in terms of the activities implemented from project to project within the same general program. For example, Even Start mandates that each project deliver three core instructional services (adult education, early-childhood education, parenting education), but makes no demands about the amount of these services to be offered, the intensity of the services, how they are to be delivered, the types of staff involved, and so on. Naturally, an evaluation based on data from many Even Start projects will end up averaging together the results from sites that have taken some quite different approaches to implementation. This same issue holds with all of the evaluations described in this chapter—the amount of site-to-site variation within an individual program is large, and the relative effectiveness of individual sites varies considerably.

Conclusions

The randomized studies reviewed here show that two-generation programs increase the participation of mothers and children in early-childhood education, parenting education, and adult education/ job training. Case management services are delivered, services are brokered, and support services are made available and utilized. These comprehensive, multigenerational programs can and have been implemented, with varying degrees of success, in a very wide range of settings.

Evidence about Effects is Mixed

Evidence about the short-term effects of participating in two-generation programs is mixed. The evidence supports the following conclusions:

- Two-generation programs increase the rate of participation of children and their parents in relevant social and educational services.

- As currently designed, two-generation programs have small or no short-term effects on a wide set of measures of child development.

- Two-generation programs have scattered short-term effects on measures of parenting including time spent with child, parent teaching skills, expectations for child's success, attitudes about child rearing, and parent/child interactions.

- Two-generation programs have large short-term effects on attainment of a GED, but these are not accompanied by effects on tests of adult literacy. There are few effects on income or employment and no effects on the psychological status of participating mothers as measured by level of depression, self-esteem, or use of social supports.

• There is little evidence that two-generation programs are differentially effective for important subgroups of participants.

• Where there are positive effects, those effects are generally small (except for effects on GED attainment).

This is a mixed assessment of the short-term effects of two-generation programs. It says little about anticipated long-term effects, but many researchers believe that it is not reasonable to expect long-term effects in the absence of substantially large short-term effects.

Provide Services Directly to Children and Adults

There is substantial evidence cited in this volume to support the assertion that effects on children are best achieved by services aimed directly at children, and effects on parents are best achieved by services aimed directly at parents. There is only limited evidence to support the indirect method of achieving large effects—that is, achieving effects on children through earlier effects on parents.

This means that it is important for a two-generation program to provide early-childhood education services directly for the benefit of children, and not to assume that it is just as good to provide parenting services to mothers who will then act as enhanced intervenors in their childrens' lives. This may well be a reasonable theoretical approach, but the evidence is that large short-term effects on children are best achieved through direct, intensive intervention with children and not with mothers.

Intensity Is Important

Intensity of services matters for each component of a two-generation program. No program reviewed here (and no others to our knowledge) provide anything close to the intensity of child-focused services provided by high-end early-childhood programs such as the IHDP, which calls for a full-day, full-week, full-year, center-based early-childhood program for children from age one through age three, under the assumption that the home environments of many disadvantaged children are inimical to optimal development and that substantial amounts of time must be spent in an improved environment in order to make an importantly large difference to childrens' development.

The parenting component of some (not all) two-generation programs also is weak. Karweit (1994) compared the effectiveness of interventions that included both parent-focused and child-focused components of different degrees of intensity. "Low-intensity" parenting interventions consisted mainly of weekly or biweekly home visits along with occasional parent meetings. This level of intervention is similar to what is provided in many of the two-generation programs described in this chapter. Karweit concluded that the most effective interventions were ones that included intensive child and parent components, and that a low-intensity parent component did not add much, if anything, to the effectiveness of a high-intensity child component.

The same worry applies to the intensity of adult education/job training services—two-generation programs may not deliver enough of any particular service to match the service levels offered by the best of the single-component programs. Because all three components must be included in a two-generation program, along with a range of case management and support services, two-generation programs are in danger of taking a broad-based approach that does not provide enough of any single type of service to be effective.

High-Intensity, High-Quality Programs Are Expensive

There are practical limits on the amount of public funds that program administrators (and taxpayers) are willing to allocate to disadvantaged families. However, programs that provide high-quality infant stimulation as one component (IHDP) cost at least $10,000 per child per year. We estimate that high-quality parenting programs, such as Avance's, add at least an additional $1,000 per year, and a high-quality adult education and job training program, such as California's GAIN, costs another $3,000 per year. This means that a two-generation program that incorporates three high-intensity components could easily cost $12,000 to $15,000 per family per year. This is 50 to 100 percent greater than the most expensive two-generation programs (CCDP and New Chance).

Thinking about the annual costs of several other educational or social "programs" for which we commonly pay helps us to better judge the magnitude of two-generation program costs. For example, a year of public schooling costs about $6,000 to $10,000; a year of special education in the public schools costs about $20,000; a year of private schooling costs about $10,000 to $15,000; and a year of private higher education costs $20,000 to $30,000. Viewed from this perspective, the costs of a high-quality, two-generation program do not seem so intimidating. Why should we expect high-quality preschool, parenting, and adult education services, delivered to disadvantaged children and parents, to cost less than high-quality educational services delivered in other settings?

Regenerate Two-Generation Programs

The two-generation intervention strategy was initiated with limited evidence about the most effective way to implement the parenting and adult literacy components. A conservative strategy for enhancing two-generation programs would be to conduct planned variation research by building on known effective practices. A reasonable approach would be to conduct a series of small-scale research studies where we append different promising parenting and/or adult education strategies to a single high-quality early-childhood program in order to test experimentally their differential effectiveness in producing positive outcomes for parents and enhancing children's development.

One problem with this approach is that while considerable research evidence exists on what constitutes a high-quality early-childhood program, no consensus exists on what constitutes a high-quality parenting or adult education/job training program. The research on adult education programs cited earlier in this chapter, as well as our own observations, suggests that most adult education programs tend to replicate the poor high school settings in which participating adults initially failed. When this is the case, the common two-generation strategy of using existing community-based adult education services is doomed to failure. If we are serious about incorporating high-quality adult education into two-generation programs, then better approaches need to be developed.

Longitudinal Research Is Needed

The modest results described here are sobering but not surprising—two-generation programs may well be struggling to fix problems that are beyond their grasp. Many families recruited to participate in these programs are deep in poverty, facing the most adverse circumstances of substandard housing, substance abuse, inadequate incomes, and dangerous neighborhoods. Given the history of small effects commonly associated with programs aimed at alleviating poverty (as mentioned earlier), it is naive to think that there will be quick, easy, or inexpensive fixes. Further, our conclusions suggest that current welfare reform efforts face an uphill task. There is no evidence that the two-generation approach, as currently structured, can move substantial numbers of families from the welfare rolls in two years, or for that matter, in any amount of time.

The studies reviewed here follow children only up through their fifth birthday, although some of the programs are designed to continue until children are age eight or older. If future follow-up data are collected, we can determine whether hypothesized longer-term effects and linkages between effects on parents and effects on children do, in fact, occur.

5

J. L. Aber
J. Brooks-Gunn
R. Maynard

The Effects of Welfare Reform on Teenage Parents and Their Children

Welfare reform is on the public agenda, as policymakers at the state and federal levels design strategies that promise to reduce the cost of public assistance by discouraging out-of-wedlock births and by assisting welfare recipients to find work. Aid to Families of Dependent Children (AFDC), the cornerstone of the welfare system, was established to provide benefits for children in families with no breadwinners, and two-thirds of those who receive benefits are children (Congressional

Adapted from Aber, J., Brooks-Gunn, J., & Maynard, R. (1995). Effects of welfare reform on teenage parents and their children *The Future of Children* (Summer/Fall) 5(2):53–71, by permission of Center for the Future of Children, The David and Lucile Packard Foundation.

123

Research Service, 1995a). As a result, welfare reform initiatives designed to affect the behavior of adults—by reducing benefits or by increasing employment, earnings, and skills—will directly affect the lives of young children. Although there have been many experiments with welfare reform, few have systematically examined the effects of alternative policies on the parenting role of adults or on their children. One notable exception is the federally funded Teenage Parent Welfare Demonstration, which combined the threat of benefit reductions with supportive services designed to support the teenagers as workers and parents, and which is the focus of this chapter.

The Challenge of Welfare Reform

The nation's welfare system is characterized by leading policy makers, practitioners, and recipients alike as a system that fosters long-term dependency and offers limited direct assistance to those eager to become self-sufficient (Bane & Ellwood, 1989). In 1993, AFDC supported almost 15 million individuals each month, including 9.6 million children, at a cost of about $28.1 billion (Congressional Research Service, 1995b). A rapid rise in caseloads, continuing upward trends in child poverty rates, and concerns over state and federal budget deficits have led to widespread bipartisan demands for welfare reform. The Clinton Administration has proposed to achieve this goal by promoting parental responsibility for the support of children, changing the welfare and tax systems to "make work pay," demanding that all welfare recipients who can work do so and placing time limits on welfare eligibility. Other proposals, from the states and Congress, include provisions that would deny cash benefits to teenage parents under age eighteen, eliminate benefit increases for children born after a family first comes onto welfare, and institute a lifetime limit on the receipt of welfare benefits (Congressional Research Service, 1994).

Substantial evidence suggests that most welfare recipients would welcome an opportunity to provide for themselves and their families through work. However, they confront problems in finding jobs that pay well, arranging and paying for child care, finding transportation, and retaining their jobs. Many lack the skills demanded by employers for well-paid jobs, and the job training programs available to them have proven to be marginally effective (Bloom, Orr, Cave, Bell, Doolitle, & Lin, 1994; Friedlander, Freedman, & Riccio, 1993; Maynard, 1994). As many as half receive such low scores on tests of basic skills that they are precluded from even entering many training programs (Strain & Kisker, 1989; Hershey & Rangarajan, 1993; Martinson & Friedlander, 1994).

The welfare recipients most often singled out for attention are teenage parents. A large body of research conducted by sociologists, demographers, and economists has examined links between early child bearing and later income, education, marriage, fertility, and employment (Bachrach, Clogg, & Carver, 1993; Chase-Lansdale, Brooks-Gunn, & Paikoff, 1991; Hayes, 1987; Upchurch & McCarthy, 1989). Young women who become parents as teenagers often find themselves on trajectories that result in more reliance on public assistance and less engagement in the work force (Furstenberg, Brooks-Gunn, & Morgan, 1987; Furstenberg, Brooks-Gunn, & Chase-Lansdale, 1989). Teenage mothers who work are less likely than older women to have full-time jobs, to be stably employed, and to earn incomes adequate to support a family (Hayes, 1987; Brooks-Gunn & Furstenberg, 1987). A recent report by the General Accounting Office states that 42 percent of all families receiving AFDC at any given time were begun by a mother who was under the age of twenty when she gave birth (U.S. General Accounting Office, 1994). Other researchers report that teenage parents who receive welfare depend on it for an average of two years longer than do older first-time recipients (Ellwood, 1986), increasing policy makers' interest in welfare reform initiatives that target this group.

The importance of helping teenage parents embark on a path that will lead them toward self-sufficiency goes beyond the financial savings that should result from reduced welfare rolls. Child developmentalists who study how the timing of parenthood affects children suggest that the children of teenage parents fare less well than children born to older women in school readiness and high school performance (Baldwin & Cain, 1980; Brooks-Gunn & Furstenberg, 1986; Brooks-Gunn & Chase-Lansdale, 1995). One comparison showed that black youth with teenage mothers were one-and-a half to two-and-a-half times more likely than those with older mothers to experience delinquency, early sexual activity, teenage pregnancy, grade failure, running away from home, and other behavior problems (Furstenberg, Brooks-Gunn, & Morgan, 1987; Furstenberg, Brooks-Gunn, & Chase-Lansdale, 1989). Later changes in the family's circumstances also affect outcomes for children born to teenage mothers. For instance, one group of researchers have followed the lives of over 300 low-income African American mothers in Baltimore who gave birth as teenagers in the late 1960s (Furstenberg, Brooks-Gunn, & Morgan, 1987; Fursten-berg, 1976). Researchers found that the early arrival of siblings hampered the school readiness of the first-born children of teenage parents. However, children whose mothers left welfare before the child began high school performed better in school than those whose mothers remained welfare dependent (Brooks-Gunn, Guo, & Furstenberg, 1993; Baydar, Brooks-Gunn, & Furstenberg, 1993). Events such as subsequent births and employment appear to affect not only the life chances of the mother, but also those of her children.

Policy Responses at the State and Federal Levels

Propelled by concerns about rising AFDC costs and its apparent ineffectiveness at improving the prospects of recipients like teenage parents and their children, policy interest in welfare reform grew throughout the 1980s. The Teenage Parent Welfare Demonstration described in this article was the first and largest of a number of experiments implemented to learn what might be required to help welfare recipients to move into the world of work (Gueron & Pauly, 1991). Begun in 1986, the Teenage Parent Welfare Demonstration anticipated the provisions aimed at teenage AFDC recipients that would be included in later national welfare reform legislation, giving an early window into the impacts welfare reform might have on this vulnerable population.

The first attempt to reform the federal welfare system in over two decades took shape in the Family Support Act of 1988. This legislation broke new ground by conveying the expectation that mothers with young children should engage in out-of-home activities that would increase their capacity to provide for themselves and their children. It endorsed the idea that welfare should be a transitional program involving mutual obligations: the government should help welfare families work toward self-sufficiency; while parents have an obligation to help themselves even when their children are young.

In keeping with these principles, the legislation established the Job Opportunities and Basic Skills Training (JOBS) Program to provide education and training to adult welfare recipients and facilitate their transition to employment and self-sufficiency. Key features of the JOBS program are mandatory participation in employment-directed activities by adult recipients whose children are three years of age or older, mandated school enrollment for teenage parent recipients; access to education and job training programs, assistance finding employment, and subsidies for child-care services during participation in approved training or employment activities (Chase-Lansdale & Vinovskis, 1995).

The federal government required only modest participation rates in the Family Support Act, however, and the states were slow to build up their JOBS programs. Pressures on state welfare budgets limited state investments in the program, and so states tapped no more than 70 percent of the federal matching funds allocated for the JOBS program in 1993 (U.S. General Accounting Office, 1994). Despite the fact that teenage parents are to be a priority group for JOBS services, few states have worked aggressively to get out-of-school teenage parents back in school. A contributing factor may be ambivalence on the part of public officials regarding the economics, ethics, and implications of requiring that welfare recipients with young children engage in activities outside the home.

Early experience from studies of state- and foundation-initiated welfare demonstrations suggests that it may be possible to change the welfare system to emphasize self-sufficiency by offering, as President Clinton has said, "a hand up, not a handout." For instance, studies have found that welfare recipients view JOBS participation mandates as fair and reasonable if they are associated with real services to assist individuals in working toward self-sufficiency (Maynard, 1994). Clear participation expectations and strong case management services seem to be most successful in promoting employment and earnings gains (Cohen, Golonka, Maynard, Ooms, & Owen, 1994). Special JOBS programs that link teenagers to employment and training services, and provide child care and support services to them have been examined in a number of reports, as well (Hagen & Lurie, 1993; Cohen, Golonka, Maynard, Ooms, & Owen, 1994; Levin-Epstein & Greenberg, 1991; Hill, Greenberg, & Levin-Epstein, 1991; Bloom, Kopp, Long, & Polit, 1991). The methods for providing child-care assistance range from provision of free care in on-site centers, to referrals to child care in the community, to subsidy approaches that pay the cost of any type of child care, including that offered by relatives (Cherlin, 1995; Clewell, Brooks-Gunn, & Benasich, 1989; Schochet & Kisker, 1992; Kisker & Silverberg, 1991). Detailed evaluations of practical experience with program implementation can serve as an important guide to the development of new strategies.

The Teenage Parent Welfare Demonstration

In 1986, two years before the Family Support Act was passed, the U.S. Department of Health and Human services initiated the Teenage Parent Welfare Demonstration to test a new model of welfare that might stem the burgeoning of welfare caseloads by reducing teenage child bearing and improving the employment incentives and prospects of teenagers who do have babies (Hershey & Nagatoshi, 1989). Three principles undergirded this model: (1) parents have primary responsibility for their own health and welfare and for the health and welfare of their children; (2) the government has an obligation to help welfare-dependent mothers overcome barriers to self-sufficiency; and (3) intervention should begin early, before welfare dependency patterns develop.

Demonstration programs were established in Chicago and in two sites in New Jersey (Camden and Newark). In each site, teenage parents eligible for welfare who were assigned to the demonstration group received the maximum grant only if they actively pursued skills and experience that would boost their earnings potential and promote their self-sufficiency. Special program offices administered the new welfare requirements and provided comprehensive services to reduce the barriers that impeded the young mothers' participation in required activities. Thus the demonstration programs linked education, job training, and employment opportunities for the young mothers to services such as child care, parenting supports, and case management assistance that addressed the needs of children, following the model of two-generation programs (Smith,1995; Smith & Zaslow,1995).

The Teenage Parent Welfare Demonstration was designed as an alternative approach to routine welfare services that should apply to all the teenage parents entering the welfare system in each site, not only individuals who might volunteer to receive special assistance in redirecting their lives toward self-sufficiency. By contrast, most previous program initiatives targeted volunteers (Furstenberg, Brooks-Gunn, & Morgan, 1987; Polit, 1992; Polit & White, 1988; Quint & Riccio, 1985; Quint, Polit, Bos, & Cave, 1994). Each Teenage Parent Welfare Demonstration program identified all teenage mothers of a single child when they applied to receive AFDC, and enrolled all who completed applications into the experiment (approximately 6,000 mothers over the two-year demonstration period). About half of these young mothers were randomly assigned to participate in the enhanced services program in their city, and the remainder were assigned to a control group who received regular AFDC services. This chapter summarizes information gathered after two years on the effects that the demonstration programs had on the activities, educations, earnings, and child bearing of the young women (Polit, 1992; Maynard, Nicholson, & Rangarajan, 1993; Maynard & Rangarajan, 1994), and on parenting behavior and child outcomes (Aber, Berlin, Brooks-Gunn, & Carcagno, 1995).

Program Components

Participation in self-sufficiency activities was mandatory for those individuals assigned to the enhanced services group. To continue receiving their full welfare benefits, these young mothers had to develop and comply with approved plans for engaging in school, job training, or employment. Case managers worked with fifty to eighty young women at a time and helped them decide what education or training to pursue, found open slots in education and training programs, coaxed them to persist in their plans, and counseled them when problems arose (Hershey, 1991a). They also helped the young mothers find child care, deal with personal and family crises, and take advantage of program and community support services. If a young mother failed to persist in her planned activities despite the program's help addressing obstacles, the case manager applied financial sanctions by cutting her welfare benefits by the amount normally allocated to the mother's needs. For instance, the young mother's monthly AFDC grant (in 1991, a mother with one child received $322 in New Jersey, and $268 in Chicago) would be reduced by about $160 until she resumed participation.

Early on, participants were required to attend workshops focusing on personal skills, their new parental responsibilities, and the demands they would face in later education, training, and employment activities (Hershey, 1991b). Program staff linked participants to education, training, and employment services both in-house and in community agencies. All three programs offered classroom high school equivalency (GED) courses, on-site job readiness workshops, and referrals to counseling and job-skill training provided in other agencies. Each program also conducted problem-solving workshops to help selected participants cope with particular problems or pursue particular goals. After the initial workshop series, case managers helped the participants handle parenting issues on an individual basis, and they occasionally made home visits.

The programs provided child care and transportation subsidies to participants, and they paid for training and education expenses such as uniforms, registration fees, and tools. Parents who used licensed child-care centers and approved family child-care providers could receive child-care payments, and when they were at the program site they could use on-site child care. The Chicago and Newark programs provided specially equipped child-care rooms, and in Camden the program staff were available to care for children on an as-needed basis (Schochet & Kisker, 1992).

The costs of the demonstration program were relatively modest. About $6.8 million covered operating costs in all three sites, including $4.1 in federal demonstration funds (Hershey & Silverberg, 1993). Total expenditures for the four years of program operations averaged about $2,000 for each of the approximately 3,500 participants. Aggregate resource costs, including the costs of community-provided services such as alternative education and job-training services, were about $2,400 a year for each young mother. This sum included about $500 per person for child care and transportation services, including the on-site child-care facilities in Chicago and Newark.

The Participants

As mentioned above, the demonstration's target population consisted of all teenagers beginning to receive AFDC who had only one child or who were in the third trimester of a pregnancy. Although only 6 percent to 17 percent of new AFDC applicants in the three sites were teenage parents, because they typically depend on welfare for a long time, past experience suggests that they would eventually make up about half of the welfare caseload in each site. The Family Support Act, passed after this demonstration was well underway, made participation in JOBS activities mandatory for AFDC recipients between sixteen and nineteen years of age who had dropped out of school. Roughly one-third of the Teenage Parent Welfare Demonstration participants fit those criteria and would be considered mandatory participants in the JOBS program, and another third were likely to become mandatory when they reached sixteen or dropped out of school. The JOBS program would not require participation of the final third, because they had either completed high school or were older than nineteen. They were, however, required to participate in the Teenage Parent Welfare Demonstration activities.

As a group, the mothers in the demonstration were highly disadvantaged, and virtually all faced significant barriers to self-sufficiency (see Table 5.1). They were young—averaging eighteen years of age, and 5 percent were fifteen or younger. About 30 percent had dropped out before completing high school, and most who were still in school were behind grade level. Some 55 percent to 60 percent of the demonstration participants had reading scores below the eighth-grade level, which is the minimum level often required for participation in Job Training Partnership Act (JTPA) job training courses. Over half of the young mothers had had some work experience. One third reported child-care problems, and one-fourth cited transportation problems that had limited their employment options. Many of these teenage mothers had left their parents' homes—only about half were living with other adults who potentially could offer economic and social support. Only one-third received financial assistance from the child's father (30 percent received child support, 4 percent lived with the father). The profile of teenagers in this sample is one of young mothers who clearly need a great deal of help if they are to make progress toward economic self-sufficiency.

The Research Questions and Procedures

The demonstration was designed to address a number of important policy questions. At the most basic level, it sought to increase understanding of the size and characteristics of the population of teenage parents on welfare. Even today, most state welfare agencies cannot review their caseloads and distinguish the teenagers who are themselves parents from those who receive benefits as children in AFDC households. Little is known about the particular strengths and service needs that characterize the teenage parent population.

Another central goal of the demonstration concerned the feasibility of implementing a universal-coverage, mandatory employment and training program for young parents on welfare. Could states design and operate programs on a sufficient scale to meet the needs of all their clients? Could they develop enough education and training opportunities and address adequately the child-care needs of large numbers of infants? How important and effective would the financial sanctions be in promoting program participation among this special population?

The ultimate questions posed by the architects of the demonstration concerned whether this reformed welfare program would reduce significantly the incidence of long-term welfare dependency. In the short run, this meant looking at the effects of the

Table 5-1.
Characteristics of the Participants at Program Enrollment

Age (in years)	18 years
Race/ethnicity (percent)	
Hispanic	17%
Black, non-Hispanic	76%
White, non-Hispanic/other	8%
Marital status	
Never married, not cohabitating	92%
Living together, married or not	4%
Separated, widowed, divorced	4%
Age of youngest child (in months)	10 months
Living with parents	48%
Family received welfare during childhood	
Most/all of the time	29%
Occasionally to half the time	33%
Never	38%
Non-English speaking	3%
Completed high school/GED (percent)	33%
Ever held a job	52%

Note: Sample includes 5,297 teenage mothers who applied for AFDC in three sites: Camden, N.J.; Newark, N.J.; and Chicago, Ill.

Source: Adapted from R. Maynard (1993), *Building self-sufficiency among welfare dependent teenage parents: Lessons from the Teenage Parent Welfare Demonstration.* Princeton, N.J.: Mathematica Policy Research.

program on progress toward self-sufficiency. Did the reformed welfare program promote higher levels of participation in activities such as school or job training? Did the young mothers in the reformed system experience higher employment and earn more? Did they delay subsequent child bearing? Were they likely to receive greater financial assistance from the fathers of their children as a result of special efforts by the welfare program to establish paternity and secure child support awards? Over the longer run, the evaluation will also reveal beneficial or harmful impacts on children that might result from the mothers' activities outside the home, their parenting behaviors, or their decisions concerning child care.

The evaluators used a multipronged approach to answer these questions. They gathered baseline information from 5,297 young mothers prior to their assignment into the regular or the demonstration welfare programs, and made site visits to observe the programs. A follow-up telephone interview was conducted with 3,867 randomly selected mothers about thirty months after they enrolled in the demonstration, with a response rate of 88 percent. In addition, seventy mothers responded to indepth interviews, eighty-eight participated in focus-group discussions, and the experiences of forty-six were discussed in case conferences with program staff. The evaluators also reviewed state agency administrative records to gather longitudinal data on the young mothers' receipt of AFDC, food stamps, child support, unemployment compensation, and wages. Finally, a special study involving interviews and videotaped observations conducted in one of the sites assessed parenting abilities and styles, as well as aspects of the children's development. From these multiple sources of data, a picture emerges of how the Teenage Parent Welfare Demonstration was implemented, the experience of the teenage parents in the demonstration, and the short-term effects of the demonstration on the mothers and their children.

Mothers' Responses to the Program

No program takes place in a vacuum, and the interviews and focus-group discussions brought to light many differences in the ways the teenage mothers responded to the opportunities and demands of participating in a welfare-to-work program (Polit, 1992). All the young women lived in poverty, often in dangerous neighborhoods that provided relatively few role models to guide them toward social and economic independence. They differed considerably, however, in personal characteristics such as motivation, cognitive skills, self-esteem, and social support that can impede or facilitate their participation and progress. Examples of these differences are offered here to bring the experiences of the participants to life, and comments by the participants are included in Figure 5-1.

Experiences with education

As a group, the 30 percent who were high school dropouts faced the greatest barriers to self-sufficiency. Some had extremely poor basic skills and no family resources to support them; many confronted barriers compounded by deep personal problems, dysfunctional

Figure 5-1.
In Their Own Words:
Participants in welfare-reform programs
describe their perspectives

On pregnancy

I didn't plan it, and then again I knew that it was going to happen because I wasn't like really taking the pills like I was supposed to. I couldn't remember every day to take a pill. And I still don't.

On motherhood

I like being a mom. I love my son, nothing could change that. He's, how can I say it? I don't know, he's everything to me anyway. I don't care about nothing else but him, how he is.

On child care

I have to know the person real good to let them take care of the baby, because these days you can't trust a lot of people taking care of babies. I would be scared because these days babysitters abuse little kids and you don't know it until you find out for yourself.

On mandated participation

At first I didn't go. They used to send me letters and call me. I still wouldn't go. And then they sent this man [a case manager] out to my house. And, I was like, I'll go and see what it was about. Then the first time I went I didn't like it because they would ask me little personal questions. Then, after I did that, I never came back, and they came out to my house again and called: "Could you please come to the program." And, I finally went, and then after I went I liked it. I really liked it then.

On achieving self-sufficiency

I'm happy I got a job because I was on welfare and I was tired of staying home waiting for the first of the month check, and there wasn't enough for me and my child. Then when I got a job I was happy because it keeps me out of being bored and quite responsible for my kid. I'm making money and supporting my kid. It shows me to be more responsible.

On the future

I might have a child years from now. My daughter will probably be in high school by then. I want to get my life together. I want to be married, have a good husband, a good home, and know I could afford another one.

home situations, and welfare system entrenchment. Others had dropped out of school because of transitory circumstances—for instance, when the pregnancy coincided with another major family crisis—and they were more responsive to the programs' pressure to return to school.

Similar contrasts were found among groups of mothers who had more success and stronger attachments to school. Some of the mothers had enough ambition or family support to remain in school after giving birth; others needed the assistance provided by the demonstration program to maintain attendance. In still other cases, even the program's support failed to keep the teenagers enrolled in school. The high school graduates varied, as well. Some already had the skills they needed to pursue employment or higher education but they lacked motivation, or faced family problems and other impediments. Others, on the path to self-sufficiency, took advantage of program resources to expedite their achievement of this goal.

Resiliency and determination

In spite of the difficult circumstances in which they were living, many of the mothers were highly motivated to improve their own lives and to provide their children with a better childhood than they had experienced. Almost none of the young mothers envisioned permanent dependence on welfare. On the contrary, there was a strong and almost universal hatred of it. Many of the teenagers who participated in the focus groups commented that women on welfare often become "addicted" to receiving public assistance and, over time, they lose the motivation and ability to care for themselves.

Child care

As new parents, the teenagers were inexperienced with child care. Although the demonstration programs helped participants find and pay for licensed child care, many young mothers reported they were afraid to trust a stranger to care for their children and would not even consider care provided by nonrelatives. Ultimately, most of the young mothers were able to rely on relatives to care for their babies (Schochet & Kisker, 1992). While they were generally satisfied with the child-care arrangements they made with relatives, recent research raises concerns that the quality of the care provided by relatives compares poorly with the quality of licensed forms of child care (Galinsky, Howes, Kontos, & Shinn, 1994).

Child support by fathers

Only a handful of mothers in the sample cooperated with the efforts of child-support enforcement agencies to secure support payments from the children's fathers. Half of the mothers who were interviewed in person indicated that they were in touch with the fathers of their babies, who provided groceries, diapers, and baby clothes, or small amounts of cash. Yet, the young women felt it was in their best interest not to cooperate with child-support enforcement agencies. Many who received no child support stated that they preferred to have nothing further to do with the babies' fathers.

Repeat pregnancies

Although most of the young mothers wanted to postpone further child bearing until they were more financially secure, many acknowledged having problems managing their fertility. Two years after program enrollment, one third of the seventy mothers interviewed in depth had experienced a repeat pregnancy (Maynard & Rangarajan, 1994). Typically, the young mothers had not planned these pregnancies; rather, many commented that it had "just happened."

Rewards of parenthood

The young mothers emphasized the positive aspects of having a child. Their children provided a source of love and affection, enhanced their self-esteem, and made them feel more mature and responsible. Given the limited rewards many teenaged parents derive from their lives, these benefits of motherhood can seem quite powerful to them. Some saw working or attending training programs as interfering with their parenting responsibilities. Most teenagers, however, felt it was not only acceptable but desirable to work before their children started school—primarily because they wanted to provide for their children's needs.

Program Design and Implementation Lessons

The experience of implementing a large-scale, supportive welfare-to-work program for this population of young parents afforded many lessons relevant to future initiatives in welfare reform (Hershey & Maynard, 1992).

Staff commitment

To implement a mandatory program successfully, welfare staff had to accept an approach that required teenage mothers to go to school, job training, or work, and that imposed consequences on mothers who failed to accept this responsibility—even though it meant the mothers had to leave their babies in the care of another person for substantial blocks of time. This represented a major shift in thinking for those staff accustomed to approving AFDC benefits for mothers who stayed at home.

The program staff also had to recognize and deal creatively with the problems that prevent some young mothers from maintaining a full-time schedule of work or school, spending project resources to resolve those difficulties. For instance, when one case manager visited the home of a young mother with poor attendance, she found the mother and her partner were sleeping in shifts at night to guard the baby's crib from rats. The case manager helped the couple find better housing, and the young woman began attending program classes. Specialized training was needed to prepare staff who were experienced with adults to work supportively with a teenage population.

Flexibility

Services for teenage parents—those offered by community agencies as well as by the program itself—had to be tailored to respond to individual circumstances that often changed rapidly. For instance, many teenage parents would not return to their former high schools for a variety of reasons, including boredom, embarrassment, and conflicts with school staff; yet, many also found it difficult to enter educational programs focused on adults. Imaginative programs that combined academics, work experience, and intensive personal attention seemed to work best at sparking their interest and commitment. Schedule flexibility was also imperative to enable the teen mothers to deal with sick children, child-care breakdowns, transportation problems, and other crises.

Child-care support

This demonstration underscored that any program intent on engaging teenage mothers in out-of-home activities must deal sensitively with their child-care needs. Money to pay for care is needed by those who cannot use free care by relatives: 60 percent of those who used paid care relied on the subsidies provided by the program. However, most of these young mothers were acutely aware of the widely publicized (if rare) incidents of child abuse in child-care settings, and they were reluctant to leave their infants with anyone whom they did not know well and trust. Moreover, the part-time nature of the mother's activities often prevented her from using center-based child care, and the difficulty of using public transportation when carrying a baby and a day's worth of baby supplies limited the choice of child care to the immediate neighborhood, where quality was questionable (Kisker, Maynard, Gordon, &

Strain, 1989; Larner, 1994). Subsidies were only part of the child-care assistance needs of this population.

Program Impacts on the Behavior of Mothers

The Teenage Parent Welfare Demonstration program showed that it is possible to achieve high rates of participation in activities oriented toward self-sufficiency—such as education or job training—so long as program staff are committed to work with the young mothers to remove the barriers they face and are willing to use financial sanctions constructively to underscore the responsibilities of parenthood (Maynard, Nicholson, & Rangarajan, 1993). Table 5-2 presents results showing the program's effects on the mothers—their involvement in education and employment, their incomes, their ties to the fathers of their children, and their subsequent child bearing.

The three programs succeeded in enrolling nearly 90 percent of the teenage mothers they targeted. However, this high enrollment rate rested on the emphasis given to mandatory participation requirements, and on the efforts of case managers to coax, pressure, and cajole troubled and uncooperative teenage parents into joining the program (Hershey, 1991a). Only one-third of these young mothers responded to routine notices about the program parti-cipation requirements, but follow-up communications and threats of grant reduction increased the percentage joining the program by an additional 50 points. The 10 percent who did not complete the enrollment process did not receive any welfare benefits; they were not considered AFDC recipients.

Over 80 percent of the mothers in the enhanced services group developed a self-sufficiency plan that established long-term goals and specified the steps required to move toward these goals—such as attending school, enrolling in job training, or finding work. Through persistent monitoring and provision of assistance by case managers, the programs were able to keep between 40 and 60 percent of the teenage mothers involved in approved activities each month. Over the course of the two-year program, two-thirds of the young mothers in the enhanced services group received formal warnings that they were in jeopardy of having their grant reduced, and one-third suffered a grant reduction. The majority of those warned or sanctioned subsequently came into compliance with the participation requirements. Participation in program activities was highest among those who entered the program with relatively strong basic skills, were still enrolled in school, did not have any health problems, were black, or lived at home with nonworking mothers.

Table 5-2.
Outcomes after Two Years of Program Participation

	Regular Services	Enhanced Services	
Involvement in Self-Sufficiency Activities			
Any activity	66%	79%	p<.05*
In school	29%	42%	p<.05
In job training	23%	27%	p<.05
Employed	43%	48%	p<.05
Income, by source			
Monthly earnings	$114	$137	p<.05
Monthly AFDC benefits	$261	$242	p<.05
Monthly food-stamp benefits	$127	$125	p<.05
Monthly child support	$ 23	$ 20	n.s.**
Social and Demographic Status			
Has income below poverty	86%	85%	n.s.
Living with spouse or male partner	9%	10%	n.s.
Paternity established for child	46%	50%	p<.05
Receiving regular financial support from child's father	10%	9%	n.s.
In regular contact with child's father	26%	28%	n.s.
Number of repeat pregnancies	1.00	1.01	n.s.

* A difference of this magnitude would occur by chance only five times out of 100.

** n.s. = Not statistically significant, indicating that any apparent difference between the two groups is so small that it likely reflects the effects of chance.

Note: Information on earnings, AFDC, food-stamp benefits, and child-support payments are based on a sample size of over 4,559 (2,275 in the regular-services group, 2, 284 in the enhanced-services group). Other entries are based on a sample size of 3,867 (1,924 in the regular-services group and 1. 943 in the enhanced-services group).

Source: Adapted from R. Maynard (1993), *Building self-sufficiency among welfare dependent teenage parents: Lessons from the Teenage Parent Welfare Demonstration.* Princeton, N.J.: Mathematica Policy Research.

The two-year demonstration programs improved the life chances of many of the teenage parents they enrolled. Among the program participants, rates of school attendance, job training, and employment increased compared to the mothers in the regular-services group, while the mothers in the control group faced their challenges with little assistance. The differences between the groups were all statistically significant, though several are only modest in size. The teenage mothers who were assigned to the enhanced services program were considerably more likely to be enrolled in school (42 percent vs. 29 percent of the regular services group attended school). They were also somewhat more likely to be receiving job training (27 percent vs. 23 percent), and more of them held a job at the end of the two years (48 percent vs. 43 percent in the regular services group).

Understandably, the programs increased school attendance most among younger mothers, those with low basic skills, and those who had not graduated from high school. Their impacts on job training and employment were especiallly large among participants who began with higher basic skills and among older youth. Program impacts on all three self-sufficiency activities (school enrollment, job training, and employment) were the largest among Hispanic participants, the group who were least likely to succeed without the assistance the program provided (Maynard, Nicholson, & Rangarajan, 1993). Of the Hispanics in the enhanced services group, 42 percent attended school, 23 percent took job training, and 42 percent had a job. The comparable percentages for the Hispanics in the regular services group were 21 percent in school, 17 percent in job training, and 25 percent employed.

Gains in earnings that averaged $23 per month followed from the increased employment among the mothers in the enhanced services group. Also, the combination of those increased earnings and the financial sanctions imposed on the mothers who failed to participate as expected reduced the amount of public assistance received by the program group. They averaged $21 less in AFDC benefits, and $2 less in food stamps. As a result, program involvement yielded little or no overall change in the economic welfare of the teenage mothers.

The programs did not succeed in convincing the teenage mothers to limit or delay repeat pregnancies and births—perhaps because they did not offer specific services, such as family planning, that would directly affect childbearing. Nor did the participants in the enhanced services group secure more financial support from their children's fathers. Both child bearing decisions and negotiations concerning child support are more personal than choices about education and employment, yet they also influence a teenage mother's prospects for self-sufficiency. Endeavors with this population could considerably strengthen those aspects of the intervention that deal with family planning and parenting to minimize the challenges to success in school and employment posed by continued child bearing.

Effects of Participation on
Parenting Behavior and on Children

The evaluation of the Teenage Parent Welfare Demonstration went beyond assessing the mothers' abilities to move toward self-sufficiency, to determine whether participation in welfare-to-work activities had positive or negative effects on the parents' behavior with their children, and on the development of the children themselves (Aber, Berlin, Brooks-Gunn, & Carcagno, 1995). Unintended negative consequences for children could result if the stress of juggling work and child rearing leads mothers to spend less time with their children, or to be harsh or unresponsive. On the other hand, self-sufficiency activities might enhance parenting skills if they include parenting classes, or if they increase the mother's confidence and feelings of efficacy. To explore the effects of program participation on parenting and child outcomes, the researchers conducted an observational study of 182 mothers and their three- to five-year-old children, all of whom were African American, from the Newark site. The sample included mothers from the enhanced services program and the group that received regular services for AFDC recipients. The mothers were very disadvantaged—only 20 percent had finished high school after their two years in the Teenage Parent Welfare Demonstration, and 40 percent had worked.

Researchers visited the mothers and children at home to conduct interviews and videotape play sessions in which the child tried to complete a puzzle that required help from an adult. During the play session, observers noted the mother's use of harsh control (authoritarianism) and her negativism toward the child. They also recorded the child's enthusiasm, persistence, and anxiety. In addition, the mothers rated their children on checklists of sociability and mental-health problems, and the evaluators administered a standard brief test of verbal ability, the Peabody Picture Vocabulary Test (PPVT-R).

The results of comparisons on these outcomes showed that being assigned to the mandatory enhanced services program did not influence the behavior of the mothers or children during the play session, nor did it affect the children's development. The mothers in the enhanced services program were not more positive with their children, nor more negative and harsh. Their children did not behave differently in the play sessions, nor differ on the other developmental measures. Policy makers may be encouraged by the suggestion that mandating participation in self-sufficiency programs like the Teenage Parent Welfare Demonstration does not, in itself, impose hardships that express themselves in negative parenting or problems for children. On the other hand, these results also suggest that in the short term, welfare-to-work programs do little to enhance the development of the children of poor teenage parents.

Of course, mothers in both groups participated to differing degrees in self-sufficiency activities. To determine whether involvement in education, job training, or employment affected parenting overall, the program and control groups were combined. The videotapes of the mothers who did not participate in any self-sufficiency activities were compared with those who were moderate or very active participants. Here a number of differences emerged. The mothers who were more active in activities outside the home were less controlling, less negative, and more engaged when they played with their children than were the mothers who were not involved in school, job training, or work. The children of the more active mothers, in turn, showed more enthusiasm and persistence as they played and completed the puzzle task.

While these results are likely to reflect preexisting differences between the mothers who are motivated to take advantage of self-sufficiency opportunities and those who remain indifferent, they also fit with the idea that both employment and preparation for work can be a positive influence in the daily lives of poor adults and their families (Klebanov, Brooks-Gunn, & Duncan, 1994; Wilson, 1991).

Conclusion

The Teenage Parent Welfare Demonstration experience yields lessons that can be useful to policy makers eager to reform the welfare system. This effort showed that large-scale, supportive welfare-to-work programs for teenage parents can be implemented at relatively modest cost through typical human service agencies. The program's participants were not volunteers but representative samples of the teenage parents coming onto welfare in three cities. Consequently, the demonstration staff experienced the full spectrum of opportunities and challenges facing young parents as they attempt to move to a more stable and independent lifestyle, and the comprehensive evaluation provided further insights into the social, psychological, and economic forces that shape these young mothers' lives.

The demonstration program's combination of mandatory requirements and supports increased participation by teenage parents in activities thought to promote human capital development and self-sufficiency, such as school, job training, and employment. Moreover, the demonstration showed that, if it is coupled with supportive case management and other social services, a mandatory participation requirement for teenage parents need not add to the stress on young, poor mothers. Nor does that requirement appear to harm their parenting or their preschool children's development. Nonetheless, causing no harm is not the same as providing benefits.

These findings suggest that welfare reformers who hope to replicate or improve on the outcomes of the Teenage Parent Welfare Demonstration should focus their efforts in several areas: (1) communicate clear expectations about the need for education, training, and employment; (2) recognize and flexibly respond to the diverse needs and abilities represented in the teenage parent population; (3) be prepared to solve practical problems that keep teenage mothers from fully participating in activities that promote self-sufficiency; and (4) build in direct supports for both parent and child development, if the aim is to improve the life chances of the children of poor, teenage parents.

Note

The research reported in this paper is based on a demonstration program and evaluation funded by the Administration for Children and Families and the Assistant Secretary for Planning and Evaluation, U.S. Department of Health and Human Services. The primary evaluation was conducted by Mathematica Policy Research, Inc., under contract HHS-100-86-0045. Supplementary data collection and analyses were funded by the Rockefeller Foundation and the Foundation for Child Development, and conducted in collaboration with Dr. Aber and Dr. Brooks-Gunn at Columbia University under contract to Mathematica Policy Research, Inc. The authors are listed in alphabetical order.

The authors express their appreciation to many who participated in the demonstration and evaluations underlying this paper: Reuben Snipper and Nancye Campbell, DHHS project officers for the evaluation; Phoebe Cottingham, project officer from the Rockefeller Foundation, and Sheila Smith, project officer from the Foundation for Child Development; Janet DeGraaf, Kathy Abbott, Yvonne Johnson, Melba McCarty, and Denise Simon, who were responsible for the demonstration program operations; Alan Hershey, Ellen Kisker, Denise Polit, and Anu Rangarajan who were the senior researchers on the Mathematica Policy Research, Inc., evaluation; John Homrighausen who directed the survey data collection for Mathematica Policy Research, Inc.; and the field researchers at Mathematica Policy Research, Inc., and Columbia University who worked on the embedded study, especially Susan Sprachman, Geoff Goodman, Pam Morris, and Alice Michael.

6

F. A. Campbell
R. Helms
J. J. Sparling
C. T. Ramey

Early-Childhood Programs and Success in School

The Abecedarian Study

This chapter describes correlates of long-term academic outcomes for participants in the Carolina Abecedarian Project, a randomized experimental trial of intensive early childhood education for children from low-income families. This longitudinal study provided an opportunity to examine adolescent scholastic performance as a joint function of early intervention, personal characteristics, and family factors.

The Abecedarian study began in the early 1970s, at a time when disappointment at the quick erosion of Head Start benefits (Cicirelli, 1966; McKey, Condelli, Ganson, Barrett, McConkey, & Plantz, 1985) led policy makers to question the value of early-childhood programs for poor children. Some theorists suggested that, to be effective, early intervention should be offered during the period of most rapid cognitive growth—that is, birth to age four (Hunt, 1961; Bloom, 1964). Partly based on this assumption, the Abecedarian study was designed to learn the degree to which intellectual/academic development could be enhanced if intervention began in infancy.

Abecedarian Project

Program

The study was multidisciplinary, involving a prospective, longitudinal experiment with a 2 x 2 crossover design. The original investigators included developmental and educational psychologists and pediatricians. Treated children were provided educational intervention delivered in a full-time child-care setting (Ramey, Collier, Sparling, Loda, Campbell, Ingram, & Finkelstein, 1976). Child-care arrangements for control children, if any, were at families' discretion. Study participants were from families who met a predetermined level of sociodemographic risk for having a child with cognitive delays or academic problems. The High Risk Index included such factors as low levels of parental education, low income, single-parent families, evidence of social disorganization, and the like (Ramey & Smith, 1977).

A very important feature of the Abecedarian program was the random assignment of participants to the treatment or control conditions. The preschool program was primarily child centered, although it could be argued that the provision of full-time, free child care was itself a parental treatment. Parents were invited to visit the classroom as often as they could and were also offered an optional series of programs focused on parenting skills, nutrition, and health. Some parents served on the Center's Advisory Board. Supportive social work services were available to families in both the treatment and control groups on an emergency basis (Ramey et al., 1976; Ramey, 1992).

The components of the preschool program have been described in numerous earlier publications (see, for example, Ramey, Yeates, & MacPhee, 1984; Ramey & Campbell, 1984; 1987; Sparling & Lewis, 1978, 1979, 1984). Infants could begin attending the child-care program as young as six weeks of age; mean age at entry was 4.4 months, with a range from six weeks to six months. The program was housed in a university-owned Child Development Center; it operated five days per week, fifty weeks of the year (approximately two additional program weeks were lost across the year because of holiday closings). Free transportation to and from the center was provided. Primary medical care was available on site. A systematic curriculum, covering development in the cognitive and fine-motor, language, social-emotional, and gross-motor domains was used (Sparling & Lewis, 1978, 1984; Sparling, undated).

Before children entered public school kindergarten, the preschool treatment and control groups were randomly divided into primary school-age treatment and control groups. The school-age phase lasted for three years during which treated families had a Home School Resource Teacher (HST) who provided customized learning activities for mothers to use at home with the child. The goals were to increase parent involvement in the educational process and to reinforce basic skills being taught at school. The HST also served as a liaison between the school and family (Ramey & Haskins, 1981; Ramey & Campbell, 1991).

Subjects

Four cohorts of infants from low-income families entered the Abecedarian study between 1972 and 1977. The condition of random assignment to treatment and comparison groups was explained during the enrollment process. In addition to qualifying on the High Risk Index, a further condition for enrollment was that infants had to appear at birth to be biologically healthy and free from conditions associated with mental retardation. One hundred twenty families (to whom 122 children were born) agreed to consider enrollment. Of these, however, eight refused their random assignment once known, two children were reassigned from the control to the day-care group at the request of local authorities and consequently dropped from the research, and one child was identified very early as having biologically based mental retardation and was therefore ineligible. Thus, the original base sample for the Abecedarian study was 111 children born to 109 families, 57 randomly assigned to the treatment group and 54 controls. Ninety-eight percent were African American.

Later attrition included four children who died (2 E, 2 C); one who proved to have a seizure disorder associated with mental retardation (E); thirteen who moved out of the area (5 E, 8 C), and three who withdrew (1 E, 2 C). Of the fifty-seven subjects originally assigned to the E group, forty-eight remained in the study through the eight-year treatment period (84 percent retention); of the fifty-four controls, forty-two remained (78 percent retention). Analysis of the key demographic factors for the nineteen families lost to attrition showed no significant differences from those retained, with the exception that 71 percent of the lost subjects were female (Chi Square = 4.63, df = 1, p = 0.03).

Descriptive statistics for selected demographic and predictor variables in the preschool treatment and control groups are shown in Table 6-1. At birth, 76 percent of the children lived in single-parent or multigenerational households. Maternal IQs averaged in the mid-80s in both groups. Control children averaged approximately twenty-four months in preschool or day care in contrast to the fifty-nine months experienced by youngsters in the educational treatment program.

Data collection

From infancy, children and their families were assessed following an established protocol that included cognitive/developmental evaluations of the children, psychological studies of the parents, and measurements of the home. Academic achievement was assessed with standardized instruments and teachers rated classroom adjustment in each of the first three years in school. In the spring of the third year, at the treatment endpoint, teachers and parents made ratings of the children's socioemotional adjustment. Follow-up intellectual, academic, and socioemotional data were collected four and seven years later, when children were twelve and fifteen years old. Examiners who collected the cognitive and academic follow-up data were unaware of the subjects' previous treatment histories.

Early Outcomes

Treated preschoolers scored significantly higher on standardized tests of intellectual development during infancy and early childhood (Ramey & Campbell, 1984). After three years in school, scores on standardized tests of reading and mathematics were significantly higher for children who had preschool treatment. In contrast, there were not significant academic or intellectual benefits associated with the school-age phase alone, although age eight academic test scores displayed a linear increase as the number of years of early intervention increased (Ramey & Campbell, 1991). Follow-up studies four and seven years later, when children were twelve and fifteen years old, confirmed that the earlier significant academic advantage associated with preschool persisted through ten years in school (Campbell & Ramey, 1994, 1995).

Table 6-1.
Entry-Level Demographic Data for
Preschool Experimental and Control Families

	Group		
Variable	Experimental ($N = 55$)	Control ($N = 54$)	Total ($N = 109$)
Maternal age (years)			
M	19.56	20.28	19.91
SD	5.77	4.90	4.90
Maternal education (years)			
M	10.45	9.98	10.22
SD	1.75	1.91	1.84
Maternal full-scale IQ			
M	85.49	84.18	84.84
SD	12.43	10.78	11.61
Percent intact family	23%	26%	24%
Percent African American	96%	100%	98%

Model for Present Study

The theoretical framework for the present analysis is loosely based on Bronfenbrenner's (1979) ecological system in which development is assumed to vary as a function of nested levels of influence that include the characteristics of the individual, interpersonal processes, and the environmental context, including social and cultural features. Table 6-2 summarizes how factors that might represent each level have been assessed across the longitudinal period covered by this study. At six periods, starting in infancy, predictors are grouped to approximate Bronfenbrenner's hierarchy of Person (attributes of the target subject), Process (mediating processes such as involvement of the parent in learning activities at home), or Context (structural aspects such as treatment group assignment).

Five years of Abecedarian educational intervention significantly affected the early environmental context of treated children. To determine if such a major contextual alteration was associated with long-term academic gains, it was necessary to control for background variables that might account for differences seen between treated and untreated groups. At the earliest chronological stage, these factors would include such individual "baseline" characteristics as gender, genetic potential for cognitive development (indexed by the biological mother's IQ), and temperament, defined

Table 6-2.
Predictors of Mid-Adolescent Academic Scores

Level of Influence	Development Stage					
	Infancy	Preschool	Kindergarten	Grades One, Two	Grade Six	Grade Nine
Person	Maternal IQ Child temperament	Child IQ	Child IQ Academic motivation Social adjustment	Child IQ Academic success Academic motivation Social adjustment	Child IQ Academic success Social adjustment	Child IQ Social adjustment
Process	Maternal attitudes Absence of punishment Home support for learning	Absence of punishment Home support for learning	Teacher's perceptions	Teacher's perceptions Absence of punishment Home support for learning	Home support for learning	Home support for learning
Context	Preschool treatment Learning materials Home organization	Preschool treatment Learning materials Home orgnaization	School-age treatment Learning materials Home organization	School-age treatment Learning materials Special education Grade retention	Special education Grade retention	Special education Grade retention

here as inborn patterns of adaptability, activity levels, and sociability (Bates, 1987).

Moderating processes from infancy through adolescence include parental attitudes and behaviors that might be more or less supportive of learning (Bradley, et al, 1989; Kelly, Marisset, Barnard, & Patterson, 1996) and the extent to which learning materials were provided at home (Bradley et al., 1989; Duncan, Brooks-Gunn, & Klebanov, 1994).

School-age personal characteristics include child IQ at school entry, academic motivation (indexed by teacher ratings of on-task behavior, distractibility, curiosity, and creativity); behavior problems in school; and early academic success. Teachers' perceptions of children's ability levels were construed as representing interpersonal processes within the classroom. Interpersonal processes at home should also remain important. Context variables at this time would include the school-age educational intervention, special class placements, and retentions in grade.

Table 6-3 describes the instruments and procedures used in the present study. Where possible, subsidiary scores from individual instruments were consolidated into single scores to reduce the number of variables. This procedure is briefly illustrated below by describing how data from the longitudinal assessments of the home environment were treated in the present analysis.

The quality of the preschool home environment was assessed when children were six, eighteen, and thirty months of age using the *Home Observation for Measurement of the Environment*, birth to thirty months (HOME) (Caldwell & Bradley, 1979) and at forty-two and fifty-four months using an early eighty-item version of the *Inventory of Home Stimulation (Ages 3–6)* (Caldwell, undated). A third version of the HOME, the *Inventory of Home Stimulation (Ages over 6)* (Caldwell & Bradley, 1979) was administered when children had completed the third year in elementary school. After an initial analyses in which every scale at every age was correlated with all concurrent and later outcomes, scales showing little or no significant relationships with outcome criteria were dropped from further consideration and some of the others were combined to create a reduced set of variables.

The constructs thus defined included the absence of restrictiveness and punishment, home support for learning, provision of appropriate toys and learning materials, and an organized and stable environment within the infant home (six, eighteen, thirty month and combined), the preschool home (forty-eight and fifty-four month combined), and the school-age home.

Table 6-3.
Measures Used in Present Analysis of Abecedarian Study Results

Domain	Instrument	Age Administered
Cognitive	Stanford-Binet Intelligence Scale (Terman & Merrill, 1972)	Thirty-six months
	Wechsler Preschool and Primary Scale of Intelligence (Wechsler, 1967)	Five years
	Wechsler Intelligence Scale for Children—Revised (Wechsler, 1974)	Eight, twelve, and fifteen years
Academic	Peabody Individual Achievement Test (PIAT; Dunn & Markwardt, Jr., 1970)	Spring of Kindergarten, spring of first grade
	Woodcock-Johnson Psychoeducational Battery (WJ; Woodcock & Johnson, 1977). Age-referenced Skills score	Spring of second grade (age eight); after seven (age twelve) and ten years in school (age fifteen)*
Temperament	Infant Behavior Record (IBR) of the Bayley Scales of Infant Development (Bayley, 1969). Cooperativeness, Activity Level, and Goal Directedness combined into a measure of adaptive engagement	Six, twelve, and eighteen months
Maternal attitudes	Emmerich's (1969) adaptation of the Parental Attitudes Research Inventory (PARI; Schaefer and Bell, 1958). Democratic Attitudes factor score	Mother completed when child was six, eighteen, and thirty months
Infant home environment	Home Observation for Measurement of the Environment, birth to three (HOME; Caldwell & Bradley, 1979). Scores included Absence of Punishment, Support for Learning,* Provision of Appropriate Play Materials, and Provision of Stable Environment	Six, eighteen, and thirty months
Preschool home environment	Inventory of Home Stimulation (Ages three to six) (Caldwell, undated). Scores included Absence of Punishment, Encouragement of Learning,* and Learning Materials	Forty-two and fifty-four months
Middle childhood home environment	Inventory of Home Stimulation (Ages over six) (Caldwell & Bradley, 1979). Scores included Elementary Home Learning Support, Avoidance of Punishment, Environmental Stability, and Learning Materials	End of third year in school (age eight)

Table 6-3. (*continued*)
Measures Used in Present Analysis of
Abecedarian Study Results

Domain	Instrument	Age Administered
Adolescent home environment	Family Environment Scale (Moos & Moos, 1981). Encouragement of Learning*	Ages twelve and fifteen
Classroom adaptation	Classroom Behavior Inventory (Schaefer, Edgerton, & Aaronson, 1977). Teacher ratings used to create indices of Academic Motivation,* Task Orientation, Introversion, and Verbal Intelligence	Spring of K, grade one, and grade two
Problem behaviors	Walker Problem Behavior Identification Checklist (Walker, 1983)	Spring of grade two
Social competence	Child Behavior Checklist and Profile (Achenbach and Edelbrock, 1983). Parent ratings. Constructive Activities T-score and Social Competence T-Score	Ages eight, twelve, and fifteen

* Starred items represent combined scores based on multiple subscales.

At age twelve and fifteen, each adolescent and his or her parent completed the *Family Environment Scale* (Moos & Moos, 1981). Scales from the Personal Growth dimension (Achievement Orientation and Intellectual-Cultural Orientation) were combined into an index of home encouragement of learning.

Major Outcomes

The dependent variables for the current analysis were preschool IQ scores (Stanford-Binet at thirty-six months and Wechsler Preschool and Primary Scale of Intelligence at sixty months) and school-age academic achievement-test scores. For kindergarteners the academic test score was the total score on the Peabody Individual Achievement Test (PIAT) (Dunn & Markwardt, 1970). At the third, seventh, and tenth school year, the outcome scores were age-referenced Standard Scores on the Skills subscale of the Woodcock-Johnson Psychoeducational Battery, Part 2, Tests of Achievement (Woodcock & Johnson, 1977). This score combines individual subscales measuring reading, math, and written language.

Analysis Plan

It would be desirable to obtain separate estimates of the impact of each of the study's independent variables and mediators on early IQ and later academic scores. However, the variables used as predictors are so highly multicollinear that the data do not support separable estimations of effects. This situation is not a statistical artifact; the characteristics of the underlying study population are highly correlated (i.e., maternal IQ, maternal attitudes, characteristics of the home environment). Therefore, a more general approach of separately examining the marginal joint distribution of each outcome variable and each predictor (or related set of predictors) was taken. Statistics were computed from the joint distribution of outcome and independent variables, conditional upon (i.e., "adjusted for") important baseline characteristics. Parental characteristics including maternal IQ, parental educational levels at the child's birth and the initial HRI score and child characteristics, such as gender, Apgar scores, and birth order were evaluated. Of these, only maternal IQ was persistently and significantly correlated with outcome variables. Consequently, subsequent correlations were computed from the conditional joint distribution of outcome variable and predictor (or set of predictors), given maternal IQ measured near the time of birth. Partial correlations were computed by SAS PROC CORR. Because this procedure is based on casewise deletion, analyses were executed for a few independent variables at a time to minimize the reductions in numbers of subjects available for estimating the correlations.

In the interest of compactness, groups of closely related variables were considered as a set, examining the multiple partial correlation of the criterion variable with the set of predictors, conditional on (adjusted for) maternal IQ. Operationally, in each of these cases, residuals were computed from regressing the outcome variable and each of the set's other variables on maternal IQ, as described above. The outcome variable residual was used as a dependent variable in a multiple equation regression using the predictor variable residuals as regressors. The multiple partial correlation was computed as the square root of the R^2 from the regression. This procedure produces the highest possible partial correlation between the outcome variable and a linear combination of the set of predictors. In such cases, these values, rather than partial rs, are entered in the table summarizing the outcomes.

Results

Mean scores on the major outcome variables, arrayed by preschool treatment group and by child gender are given in Table 6-4. The scores show that children treated in preschool consistently outperformed preschool comparison children on IQ and academic scores at every point. None of the gender differences in mean achievement scores were statistically significant.

Simple correlations of the baseline variables with the major outcomes are given in Table 6-5. This Table shows that neither gender, the Apgar score, birth weight, birth order, nor the presence of the father in the home was significantly correlated with long-term academic outcomes. Interestingly, parental educational levels and the High Risk Score (which are confounded) increase in association with child academic performance the longer students stay in school.

Table 6-6 summarizes the results of the major correlational analysis. The figures in this table, with the exception of the figures relating maternal IQ to the outcomes, are partial correlations in which the effects of maternal IQ have been removed. Only correlations significant at the 0.05 level or higher are shown. For this sample, preschool intervention remained a significant predictor of academic outcomes across the full developmental span for which measures are now available. In contrast, the school-age phase of treatment was not associated with academic outcomes in these models. The most powerful predictor of academic performance at age fifteen was previous academic performance. The best predictors of early academic success were child IQ scores at age three and five.

The best predictors of IQ in early childhood were the infant temperament score and early intervention, followed by the degree to which the characteristics of the infant home environment supported early learning, and maternal IQ. Infant temperament significantly predicted early cognitive scores and academic performance through ten years in school, implying that personal characteristics play a strong role in later outcomes. Early interpersonal processes were also important. Having a mother who endorsed a democratic stance toward children was significantly related to long-term academic performance. HOME scores measuring encouragement of Infant and Preschool Learning remained significant predictors of academic outcomes through ten years in school. Absence of punishment in the home during the preschool period predicted long-term academic scores, but this factor in the infancy period did not. As to the contextual features of the home, having an organized and stable

Table 6-4.
Mean Scores on Child Cognitive and Academic Measures by Preschool Treatment Group and by Gender

| | Control | | | | | | Experimental | | | | | |
| | Male | | | Female | | | Male | | | Female | | |
	n	M	SD	n	M	SD	n	M	SD	n	M	SD
Stanford-Binet												
IQ Score, thirty-six months	20	83.90	11.80	23	85.87	15.25	26	101.35	13.15	23	101.04	14.48
WPPSI												
IQ Score, sixty months	20	90.80	13.47	23	95.91	13.93	26	101.00	10.46	23	191.91	11.71
PIAT, Spring-K												
Total Test Raw Score	20	70.20	11.45	22	71.82	11.19	24	76.50	12.95	23	79.65	13.78
WJ Skills Standard Score												
Year three	19	86.11	11.27	21	86.29	10.31	26	92.65	13.03	22	96.32	13.42
WJ Skills Standard Score												
Year seven	21	87.43	14.75	22	86.05	14.01	24	91.33	14.33	23	96.00	16.04
WJ Skills Standard Score												
Year ten	21	88.67	11.06	23	86.65	10.44	26	90.46	9.65	22	94.68	13.74

Table 6-5.
**First-Order Correlations of Background Variables with
Longitudinal Cognitive and Academic Outcome Measures**

Background Variable	Outcome Measure					
	SB 36	WPPSI 60	PIAT	WJ Y3	WJ Y7	WJ Y10
Maternal IQ	.30**	.42***	.29**	.42***	.42***	.44***
High Risk Index	−.15	−.20	−.11	−.33**	−.26**	−.23**
Number of Siblings	−.08	−.16	−.14	−.07	−.07	−.09
Gender	−.00	.01	.13	.06	.05	.04
Birthweight	.08	.11	.13	.18	.11.	.02
Apgar (1 min.)	−.07	−.01	−.11	−.14	−.08	−.03
Father Absent	−.03	−.00	.02	.11	.04	.12
Mother's Education	.06	.09	.09	.32**	.20	.25*
Father's Education	.10	.15	−.03	.06	.26*	.28*

* $p < .05$ ** $p < .01$ *** $p < .001$

environment in infancy predicted early cognitive and academic outcomes, but not later ones. Learning materials in the home during the preschool years predicted child IQ at age five and learning in kindergarten, but did not show significant correlations with later learning. Thus, with the exception of preschool treatment itself, the factors we defined as contextual in this analysis were not as strongly related to later outcomes as were individual characteristics and interpersonal processes.

In general, there was less association between the elementary-age home environment scores and measures of academic skills at age eight and thereafter than there was with the characteristics of the infant and preschool home and later academic scores. Home Learning Support as measured by the elementary school version of the HOME predicted age eight academic skills, but not those at age twelve or fifteen; organization of the environment at age eight predicted skills scores at age twelve but not at age eight or age fifteen. However, there was a significant relationship between the twelve year old's description of the emphasis on academic, intellectual, and cultural matters in the home and academic achievement at age twelve.

Once children were in school, earlier and concurrent IQ test scores consistently showed moderately strong associations with academic scores. Not surprisingly, variables measuring aspects of

Table 6-6.
Statistically Significant Partial Correlations or Multiple Partial Correlations between Predictor Variables and Academic Outcomes

			Outcome Variable at End of Time Period					
Time Period	Class of Variable	Variable or Related Group of Variables*	INFANCY SBIQ 36	PRESCHOOL WPPSI 60	EARLY ELEM. SCHOOL PIAT Total	ELEM. SCHOOL WJ Yr.3 Skills	LATE ELEM. SCHOOL WJ Yr.7 Skills	HIGH SCHOOL WJ Yr.10 Skills
BIRTH	Person	Mother's IQ (bivariate)	.30	.42	.29	.42	.42	.44
INFANCY	Process	Infant Temperament	.54	.38	.46	.33	.31	.27
		Maternal Democratic Attitude	.27	.31		.22	.30	.32
		HOME: Absence of Punishment	.28	.39				
		HOME: Encouragement of Infant Learning	.40	.48	.47	.33	.31	.35
	Context	HOME: Appropriate Toys		.24	.28			
		HOME: Organized and Stable Environment	.32	.26		.22		
		Preschool Treatment	.52	.38	.38	.39	.26	.27
PRESCHOOL	Person	Stanford-Binet IQ at thirty-six mos.		.71	.67	.34	.30	.24
	Process	HOME: Absence of Punishment		.33	.26	.25	.23	.24
		HOME: Encouragement of Preschool Learning		.49	.51	.38	.28	.26
	Context	HOME: Provision of Toys		.30	.28	.33		

Table 6-6. (continued)
Statistically Significant Partial Correlations or Multiple Partial Correlations between Predictor Variables and Academic Outcomes

			Outcome Variable at End of Time Period					
Time Period	Class of Variable	Variable or Related Group of Variables*	INFANCY SBIQ 36	PRESCHOOL WPPSI 60	EARLY ELEM. SCHOOL PIAT Total	ELEM. SCHOOL WJ Yr.3 Skills	LATE ELEM. SCHOOL WJ Yr.7 Skills	HIGH SCHOOL WJ Yr.10 Skills
KINDERGARTEN (Year One)	Person	WPPSI IQ at sixty mos.			.63	.46	.41	.36
		CBI: Achievement Motivation			.41	.27	.27	.25
		Task Orientation			.27	.40	.37	.32
		Distractibility				-.23	-.29	
		Introversion			-.23			
	Process	Teacher's Perception of Learning Ability (K)			.65	.50	.44	.38
	Context	School-Age Treatment						
ELEMENTARY SCHOOL (Years Two and Three)	Person	PIAT Total Raw Score, End of Kindergarten				.56	.49	.47
		WISC-R IQ at eight years				.42	.47	.44
		CBI: Academic Motivation				.47	.33	.39
		CBI: Task Orientation				.42	.28	.36
		CBI: Dependency				-.29		-.23
		CBI: Introversion				-.39	-.24	-.28
		CBI: Extroversion				.25		
		Walker: Acting Out				-.24	-.24	

Table 6-6. (*continued*)
Statistically Significant Partial Correlations or Multiple Partial Correlations between Predictor Variables and Academic Outcomes

Time Period	Class of Variable	Variable or Related Group of Variables*	INFANCY SBIQ 36	PRESCHOOL WPPSI 60	EARLY ELEM. SCHOOL PIAT Total	ELEM. SCHOOL WJ Yr.3 Skills	LATE ELEM. SCHOOL WJ Yr.7 Skills	HIGH SCHOOL WJ Yr.10 Skills
		Walker: Distractibility				-.38	-.26	-.29
		Walker: Disturbed Peer Relations			-.32	-.32	-.26	
	Process	CBI: Teachers Perception of Ability (Year Three)				.58	.49	.51
		HOME: Elementary Home Learning Support				.23		
	Context	HOME: Organized, Stable Environment					.23	
		Early Special Education (Gr. K–2)				-.38	-.42	-.43
		Early Grade Retention (Gr. K–2)				-.54	-.37	-.31
LATE ELEMENTARY SCHOOL (Year Seven)	Person	WJ Skills (Year Three)					.78	.74
		WISC-R IQ at ninety-six months					.47	.44

Table 6-6. (*continued*)

Statistically Significant Partial Correlations or Multiple Partial Correlations between Predictor Variables and Academic Outcomes

Time Period	Class of Variable	Variable or Related Group of Variables*	INFANCY SBIQ 36	PRESCHOOL WPPSI 60	EARLY ELEM. SCHOOL PIAT Total	ELEM. SCHOOL WJ Yr.3 Skills	LATE ELEM. SCHOOL WJ Yr.7 Skills	HIGH SCHOOL WJ Yr.10 Skills
	Process	*FES: Academic-cultural emphasis* (Year Seven)					.33	
		WJ Skills (Year Seven)						.88
HIGH SCHOOL (Year Ten)	Person	WISC-R IQ (Year Ten)						.49

Outcome Variable at End of Time Period

* Italicized variables represent sets.

the elementary school environment were more predictive of academic outcomes than were concurrent or earlier measures of the home environments. Academic motivation in the primary grades (based on CBI ratings of curiosity/creativity and independence) was strongly related to academic performance. Task orientation was positively related to academic scores and distractibility and introversion, negatively so. The most powerful academic predictor among the CBI variables proved to be the teacher's view of the child's verbal intelligence.

Teachers' ratings of problem behaviors in the third school year significantly and negatively predicted concurrent and later academic scores. On the other hand, parent ratings of social competence were not related to scholastic scores nor were parent descriptions of the degree to which the student was engaged in constructive activities or the adolescent's ratings of the degree to which the family was engaged in active, recreational endeavors.

In sum, for this sample of children from low-income families, cognitive level at school entry and the child's own early characteristics best predicted early school performance. Early school performance was, in turn, highly related to later academic scores. The relationship between one academic outcome and the next steadily increased in strength over the ten-year period covered by the academic data.

Discussion

The results of the Abecedarian study support a developmental model in which early experience provided a cognitive basis on which later academic success was built. Seven to ten years after intervention was terminated, the group treated in the Abecedarian preschool program earned significantly higher scores on academic skills. In contrast, there is little evidence that having a follow-through program in the first three years of elementary school, or having a school-age program alone, conferred long-lasting benefits (Campbell & Ramey, 1994, 1995). Farran (1990) concluded on the basis of a review of thirty-two early-intervention programs that a follow through into public school was necessary if early-childhood gains were to be sustained. Data from the Chicago Child Parent Center and Expansion program support her view (Reynolds, 1994), as do some data from Project Follow Through (Seitz, Apfel, Rosenbaum, & Zigler, 1983). The Abecedarian data do not support this conclusion, nor do results from the Houston Parent-Child

Development Center study (Johnson & Walker, 1991) or the Harlem Study (Palmer, 1983), in which relatively long-term gains were sustained in the absence of a follow-up intervention.

That the school-age phase of treatment added so little to the benefits of preschool intervention was unexpected and deserves further exploration. Intensive efforts were made to encourage treated families to become actively involved in their child's learning by providing them the materials and methods to work specifically on areas where the child needed extra support. Parents were referred to relevant agencies for help with problems that might have interfered with their ability to assist the child's scholastic efforts. Parents rated the program highly; teachers expressed regret that it could not continue past the first three years. But its benefits in terms of lasting academic change are dwarfed by the relative strength of the preschool program.

There could be a number of explanations for this outcome. Families were randomly assigned to treatment; it may be that such family-centered programs would be more effective if parents self-selected them. The emphasis may have been misplaced in this program. Implicit in the approach taken was that the family needed to change in relationship to the child's schooling and that the home environment was the place to intervene. It is possible that the school-age emphasis should have been in the classroom, on instructional methods. Some programs targeting students from low-income families have demonstrated significant gains through a classroom-centered approach (Becker & Gersten, 1982). The outcomes from a current study of the transition of Head Start graduates into public school may provide insights on this matter (Ramey & Ramey, 1990).

Although the Abecedarian sample is too small to justify the use of sophisticated hierarchical regressions or structural equation modeling, the descriptive analyses used here revealed a number of important links between the characteristics of the individual, the family, early school adaptation, and later academic outcomes. Even covarying the IQ of the biological mother, early-childhood education was significantly related to academic performance many years later, as were the mother's early attitudes toward children and the degree to which the family fostered learning within the home. These findings all affirm the importance of the quality of the early environment as a determinant of later outcomes (Baumrind, 1993). On the other hand, of all the variables examined, maternal IQ emerges as one of the best predictors of child attainment. Similarly, the child's own temperament played a surprisingly strong role in predicting later cognitive and academic outcomes. Infants who were rated as active, cooperative, and goal directed during the first and second years of life had higher IQs and higher scores on academic tests fifteen years later. To the extent that maternal IQ represents the inherited capacities of the individual and infant temperament reflects a biological tendency to react to the environment in a certain way, the data also support Scarr's (1992) contention that the individual's "more enduring characteristics of intelligence, interests and personality" (p. 9) will themselves contribute to the construction of the environment.

One conclusion to be drawn from this study is that intensive educational intervention, even if it began in infancy, does not eliminate the early home environment as an important contributor to academic success. These data do imply, however, that it is processes within the home environment during the early, as opposed to the later, years that are most strongly linked to long-term academic outcomes. Although scores on the scale operationalized as Elementary Home Learning Support were significantly related to academic skills at age eight, the relationship was not as strong as that seen between eight-year-old academic skills and Encouragement of Infant or Preschool Learning. Moreover, only infant and preschool HOME measures were significantly related to academic scores at age twelve and fifteen. This finding is inconsistent with a report by Bradley, Caldwell, and Rock (1988) that simple bivariate correlations between infant HOME scores and school achievement at age ten or eleven were not significant, whereas scores on the Elementary HOME at age ten were. One difference between the two studies is that the Abecedarian data are based on an earlier version of the Elementary HOME, containing additional items and having the items grouped into somewhat different scales. Another important difference between the two studies is that in the Abecedarian data, maternal IQ was covaried when considering the influence of the early home, thus removing a crucial component of the mother's contribution to the HOME scores themselves. It is possible, too, that the Abecedarian sample is somewhat less ethnically and economically heterogeneous than the Bradley, Caldwell, and Rock sample.

Infants whose mothers saw children as autonomous persons with rights of their own and espoused sharing of responsibility for decisions among all family members tended, years afterward, to display higher levels of academic attainment. Such mothers would tend to be "constructivists" as opposed to "structuralists" (Miller, 1988). Other research has shown that being more democratic in belief is associated with being more comfortable in the role of parent

(Emmerich, 1969), that brighter and better-educated women tend to adopt a more democratic stance toward children (Ramey & Campbell, 1976), and that higher SES mothers tend to hold attitudes that are linked to more positive outcomes for children (Miller, 1988). The present finding of a long-lasting link between maternal attitudes as described in infancy and child school performance fifteen years later is even more important considering that the link was found with maternal IQ covaried. The data do not show the ways in which having democratic attitudes toward children might translate into actual behavior toward them. Much previous research has been devoted to establishing links between attitudes and behaviors (Goodnow, 1988); the general consensus is that links can be shown, but not strong ones (Miller, 1988). Given the enduring nature of the association between this early self-description by the mothers and long-term child outcomes, it is a link deserving more research.

Elementary grade teachers' perceptions of students' learning ability provide one of the strongest predictors of long-term academic outcomes. As early as the fall of the kindergarten year, teachers made judgments that are significantly correlated with actual intelligence test scores (Schaefer & Campbell, 1996) and that remained predictive of academic scores ten years later. The implications of this finding should be further explored. This sample of young children was 98 percent African American, and most were from relatively poor families, in a school setting where the majority of the students were from affluent, university-connected families. In such a school context, an "average" child might appear slow. Teachers are believed by many to view minority children from low-income families in negative, even pejorative, ways (e.g., Rist, 1970; Hale-Benson, 1989), to have difficulty in communicating with such students (Heath, 1983), or to use culturally incongruent assessment criteria that are biased against them (Hale-Benson, 1989). Nevertheless, teachers predicted the academic performance of the Abecedarian participants with moderate accuracy, which implies that they were responding to more than simple ethnic and SES characteristics in judging ability. This finding raises many questions. On what basis did the teachers judge the children's ability? Do teachers provide differential treatment within the classroom for children perceived to be more capable? A better understanding of classroom processes is of enormous importance for today's multicultural schools because classroom adaptation was strongly linked to academic success. The child's academic motivation, as expressed in greater curiosity and independence was strongly linked to the acquisition of skills. Task orientation in the early years was linked to later success. Children who were rated by their primary grade teachers as introverted, dependent, and distractible did poorly. It is interesting to note, in this connection, that kindergarten teachers' ratings of considerateness and hostility did not show any relationship to academic performance. However, Walker Problem Behavior Identification Checklist scores obtained during the third year in school were negative predictors of academic attainment years later. In contrast, parents' ratings of social competence at age eight, twelve, or fifteen were related neither to concurrent nor later academic performance, nor were the students' involvement in constructive childhood sports, clubs, or hobbies.

Predictably, early placement into special classes or early retention were negative predictors of later academic scores. Both, however, are as likely to be consequences as causes of academic difficulties. In the schools attended by these children, special-class placements during the first three years were for speech/language delays or academic problems typically described as "unreadiness," or for behavior problems. Clearly, early retention and early special-education placement (not always within a self-contained classroom) bode ill for future progress. However, those who do not achieve are retained or placed because school officials or parents believe they have not mastered the necessary skills to permit them to move forward; retained children perform worse on academic tests. Yet, the question remains, would the child have fared better without the placement or the retention? Unfortunately, a truly scientific examination of this question is almost impossible to envision.

The implications of the Abecedarian study for public policy affirm the importance of environmental learning support in the earliest years. The provision of five years of high-quality, systematic, educational child care enhanced early cognitive development in treated children above the levels attained by comparison children, a factor strongly associated with success in school. It is crucial to note, however, that early educational intervention built upon but did not obviate the importance of individual characteristics, interpersonal processes within the family, and the home environment, as determinants of mid-adolescent academic performance.

The importance of the early environment was affirmed. We cannot trust that children will have sufficient developmental plasticity to overcome lacks in early childhood. In a society in which out-of-home care is increasingly needed for the very young, it is essential that such care be highly supportive of cognitive and socioemotional growth. Waiting until a child enters school to begin preparation for formal learning is too late.

7

W. S. Barnett
J. W. Young
L. J. Schweinhart

How Preschool Education Influences Long-Term Cognitive Development and School Success

A Causal Model

Information about the causal connections through which preschool education improves the cognitive abilities and school success of children in poverty is important for public policy. A clearer understanding of how preschool programs produce their effects would facilitate the design and implementation of highly effective programs and public policies to support effective programs. Of course, many people believe that they understand how preschool programs produce—or fail to produce—long-term effects on child development and school success. However, there are considerable differences of opinion among them.

Four major theoretical alternatives seek to explain the empirical evidence regarding the effects of preschool education on the cognitive development and socialization of children from low-income families. These four models can be characterized as follows:

1. Preschool education's long-term effects originate in effects on children's cognitive abilities, which contribute to later cognitive abilities directly through effects on learning and indirectly through the resulting early academic success, which generates increased motivation, improved socialization, and increased parental expectations for long-term school success (e.g., Schweinhart & Weikart, 1980; Lazar, Darlington, Murray, Royce, & Snipper, 1982; Zigler & Freedman, 1987).

2. Preschool education's long-term effects stem from initial effects on motivation and behavior that lead to improved test performance and more favorable assessments by teachers. Increases in early test scores do not represent increases in cognitive ability but result from increased self-confidence or greater willingness to persist in trying to answer difficult questions (e.g., Woodhead, 1988; Zigler & Freedman, 1987).

3. Preschool education's long-term effects are due to the effects of preschool education programs on parents (e.g., Reynolds, Mavrogenes, Bezruczko, & Hagemann, 1996). These may include changes in parents' beliefs, expectations, and values regarding education for their children, improved parenting practices, and increased ability to work with the schools to obtain the best education for their children. Clearly, the strongest effects would be expected from early-childhood programs that emphasized parent involvement and parent education. Family support programs that comprehensively address parents' needs together with the child's might be expected to be the most effective (e.g., Lally, Mangione, & Honig, 1988; Seitz, Rosenbaum, & Apfel, 1985).

4. Preschool education programs have no substantive effects on children or parents at all (e.g., Locurto, 1991). For a short time children may perform better on IQ tests because ECE programs directly or indirectly teach them the answers to test items. Long-term effects on school success are due to teachers' expectations about the effects of preschool program attendance or the use of misleading early IQ scores to make decisions about grade retention and special-education placement.

All four alternatives seek to explain the pattern of effects over time resulting from preschool education programs for children in poverty. The conventional wisdom about this pattern of effects is that initial effects on children's cognitive abilities and socialization fade out after a few years and are followed by effects on grade retention, special education, and, perhaps, high school graduation (e.g., Haskins, 1989; Herrnstein & Murray, 1994; McKey et al., 1985; Natriello, McDill, & Pallas, 1990). This pattern disappointed the hope that preschool education would produce large, permanent increases in IQ that would lead to increased school success and has been considered by some to be something of a mystery (e.g., Gramlich, 1986; Haskins, 1989). As Barnett's chapter in this volume reveals, the actual pattern of effects over time is more complex. Although initial effects on IQ often fade out, effects on other measures of cognitive abilities generally do not fade out. It is this more complex pattern of findings that must be explained.

All three alternative explanations hypothesizing real long-term effects can draw support from theories of learning and human development that emphasize interactions among cognitive, social, and emotional domains and the importance of social and cultural contexts for development (Bronfenbrenner, 1989; Brown, Collins, & Duguid, 1989; Resnick, 1987; Vygotsky, 1978). However, these theories do not provide much guidance for discriminating among the alternative explanations because all of the key variables (cognition, motivation, socialization and classroom behavior, parent involvement, and school responses to the child) are potentially important and might be directly or indirectly affected by preschool education programs. Indeed, even the portrayal of the alternatives above is to some degree an abstraction because advocates of these views tend to emphasize the relative importance of one explanation in a process in which all of the alternatives are operative to some degree.

This chapter employs data from the High/Scope Perry Preschool study (Schweinhart, Barnes, Weikart, Barnett, & Epstein, 1993) to examine the empirical support for each of the four alternatives. To do this we estimated and compared three models of the preschool program's initial effects and the links from initial effects to four long-term outcomes: IQ, achievement, special-education placements, and educational attainment. These three models correspond to the first three rival explanations described above. As the fourth alternative is the antithesis of the other three; it is rejected if any of the others are accepted.

Methods

Sample

From 1962 to 1965 the Perry Preschool study enrolled 128 African American children and their families in five waves from a single elementary school attendance area in southeastern Michigan. All families were low income and all of the children had IQs below 90 (an indicator of risk for educational difficulties). Five children were lost to the study because they moved away shortly after the study began or died during the preschool years. Thus, the sample available for follow-up had 123 members.

Assignment to the preschool program and control groups was performed by pair matching within each wave and randomly assigning one member of each pair to the program group. To permit mixed-age classes, the first wave consisted of thirteen children who entered the preschool program at age four and attended for one year. The forty-five program children in the remaining four waves entered the program at age three and attended for two years. The small number of children attending for one year greatly limits the study's power to detect differences in effects between one and two years, and this issue is not examined here. All of the children in the study entered kindergarten at age five.

Two minor deviations from randomization occurred. First, younger siblings of children who had entered the study in an earlier wave were assigned to the same group as the older sibling in order to prevent treatment diffusion. One hundred families were represented in the sample. Second, two children were shifted from the program to the control group because their mothers' employment interfered with attending the preschool classes or participating in the home visits. This resulted in a temporary difference between the two groups on mothers' employment. There was no difference in maternal employment between program and control groups when this was measured again at age fifteen (Schweinhart et al., 1993). If anything, the initial difference on employment tends to produce underestimation of program effects because it is negatively related to program participation, but positively associated with favorable outcomes.

Table 7-1 reports participants' characteristics at study entry. The only significant difference between groups is in maternal employment. Attrition throughout the study was low. Table 7-2 reports descriptive statistics for each variable used in this study. To facilitate their interpretation, IQ scores are reported in the tables

Table 7-1.
Background Characteristics of Subjects by Group at Study Entry (standard deviations in parenthesis, N = 123)

Characteristic	Preschool	No Preschool	p
Child's Stanford-Binet IQ	79.6	78.5	.38
	(5.9)	(6.9)	
Child's Age in Months	42.7	41.9	.44
	(6.2)	(5.9)	
Child's Sex: Percentage Male	57%	60%	.87
One-Parent Families	45%	49%	.76
Receiving Welfare	58%	45%	.23
Parental Employment			.02
Both employed	9%	11%	
Father alone employed	39%	34%	
Mother alone employed	4%	22%	
Neither employed	48%	34%	
Mother's Highest Grade	9.5	9.4	.84
	(2.4)	(2.0)	
Father's Highest Grade	8.4	8.8	.58
	(2.3)	(2.5)	
Persons per Room in Home	5.2	5.2	.93
	(1.2)	(1.6)	

rather than standardized scores (mean 0, s.d. 1). Attrition was not significantly different between groups and did not vary significantly with child and family characteristics (Schweinhart et al., 1993).

Treatment

The Perry Preschool program provided two-and-one-half hour classes each weekday morning and weekly ninety-minute, teacher-conducted home visits with mother and child in the afternoons during the school year. Classroom staff were certified public school teachers, and the staff-child ratio was one teacher to roughly six children. Across all years, the curriculum was child centered and explicitly focused on supporting children's cognitive development through individualized teaching and learning. However, the curriculum was not static but was continuously developed by the staff as their knowledge and experience grew. Over the years, the program became more clearly articulated and more systematically based on Piagetian theory. The variations in curriculum do not

Table 7-2.
Variables Employed in Causal Models: Means, Standard Deviations & Correlations with Maternal Employment
(N = 108)

Variable	Mean	s.d.	Corr.
Preschool (yes/no)	49.5%	—	−.260
IQ at Pre-K Entry	79.2	6.3	.114
IQ at End of Pre-K	88.7	12.2	−.019
IQ, Ages 6–8	89.0	10.7	.143
IQ, Ages 9–10	86.7	10.4	.170
IQ, Age 14	81.2	10.8	.098
Achievement, Age 7–8	0.0	0.9	.146
Achievement, Age 9–11	0.0	0.9	.148
Achievement, Age 14	108.1	39.0	.072
Personal Behavior	4.0	0.6	.177
Parent Participation	4.0	1.8	.019
EMI Placement	25%	—	−.182
Motivation	3.1	0.8	.188
Highest Grade, Age 19	11.4	1.3	.192

These variables correspond to those in the analyses as follows. Early IQ is the average of IQ at the end of preschool and ages 6–8. Later IQ is the average of IQ at ages 9–10 and 14. Early achievement is the average of achievement at ages 7 and 8. Later achievement is the average of achievement at ages 9–11 and 14.

appear to have produced differences in outcomes across the waves (Weikart, Bond, & McNeil, 1978).

Measures

The High/Scope Perry Preschool study provides an unusually comprehensive data set. Data on participants were collected at entrance to the study, annually through age eleven, and at ages fourteen, fifteen, nineteen, and twenty-seven. A complete description of the data set is beyond the limits of this chapter, but is provided by Schweinhart and colleagues (1993). Special features of the data set include: annual IQ test data from study entry through age ten and at age fourteen; annual achievement-test data from kindergarten through age eleven and at age fourteen; teacher assessment of academic motivation, personal and classroom behavior, and other affective characteristics in kindergarten and later grades; teacher assessment of parent participation in kindergarten and later grades; school progress and placement data for each year from school entry through school exit; and a wide range of other measures of family background, parent behavior, and parent attitudes before and after the preschool program. These data are critical for sorting out the differences among the alternative theories regarding how early intervention produces long-term effects.

The small sample size is an important constraint for the estimation of causal models. In order to maximize the number of cases with complete data and hold down the number of variables included in the models, averages over several years were calculated for some measures. Each of the variables that entered into the models is described below.

- *Preschool*: Coded 0 for members of the control group, 1 for members of the preschool program group.
- *Gender by preschool interaction*: The product of Gender (coded 1 for females, 0 for males) and Preschool.
- *Pretest IQ*: IQ score on the Stanford-Binet (3d revision, Terman & Merrill, 1960) at entry to the study (age three or four). All IQ scores were converted to standardized z-scores with a mean of zero and standard deviation equal to 1.
- *Early IQ*: The average of Stanford-Binet IQ z-scores obtained in the spring prior to kindergarten, and in kindergarten through second grades. Children were tested with their age mates regardless of whether they were actually at grade level. Average IQ score was calculated over all available scores as in a few cases children did not have scores for all three years.
- *Later IQ*: Average of Stanford-Binet IQ z-scores from the spring of the third- and fourth-grade years and the WISC-R (Wechsler, 1974) z-score obtained at age fourteen.
- *Early achievement*: Average of nonmissing California Achievement Test (CAT) (Tiegs & Clark, 1963) total scores (Lower Primary Level, sum of scores for reading, arithmetic, and language subscales) at ages seven and eight (from spring of the first- and second-grade years for most children). Prior to computing averages, raw CAT scores for each year were converted to z-scores with a mean of zero and standard deviation equal to 1.
- *Later achievement*: Average of nonmissing CAT total scores (Upper Primary Level, sum of scores for reading, arithmetic, and language subscales converted to z-scores) at ages nine through eleven (spring of the third-, fourth-, and fifth-grade years and at age fourteen (Level 4, sum of scores for reading, arithmetic, and language subscales converted to z-scores).

- *Mothers' participation*: A measure of parent involvement computed as the average of nonmissing teacher ratings from kindergarten through grade three. Maternal cooperation and predicted maternal participation in school were rated on scales of 1 to 7.
- *Motivation*: Average of nonmissing teacher ratings on a Likert scale (very frequently to very infrequently) of child's academic motivation in kindergarten through third-grade years. The scale included items on leadership and initiative, completing assignments, interest in school work, concern for learning, retaining learning, motivation for academic performance, and persistence and willingness to try difficult tasks.
- *Behavior*: Average of nonmissing teacher ratings on a Likert scale (very frequently to very infrequently) of child's personal behavior in kindergarten through third-grade years. Behaviors rated included absences and truancy, inappropriate personal appearance, lying or cheating, stealing, use of obscenity, and poor personal hygiene.
- *Ever EMI*: Whether a child was ever classified as educably mentally impaired (EMI) by the schools. EMI was the only special education placement found to be related to participation in the preschool program and was the placement type for twenty-five of the thirty-seven children who received special education services.
- *Attainment*: Highest grade completed in school by age nineteen. This was determined from school records.

Model Specification

Figure 7-1 depicts the basic theoretical specifications of the three models hypothesizing long-term effects. The key relationship specified in each model is the initial effect of preschool education. The models are labelled as the cognitive, socialization, and parent involvement models based on the hypothesized initial effect. Not all possible relationships in each of the alternatives are shown. Each model could incorporate relationships with all of the variables in the other models in some form.

The LISREL 7 program (in SPSS Version 4.1) was used to estimate simultaneous equations models by maximum likelihood for each alternative. The analyzed correlation matrix was estimated by the LISREL preprocessor, PRELIS 1.12. Model construction proceeded by adding paths as suggested by the results (LISREL recommends paths that would significantly improve the model) and

Figure 7-1.
Key Theoretical Paths Specified by Each Theoretical Model

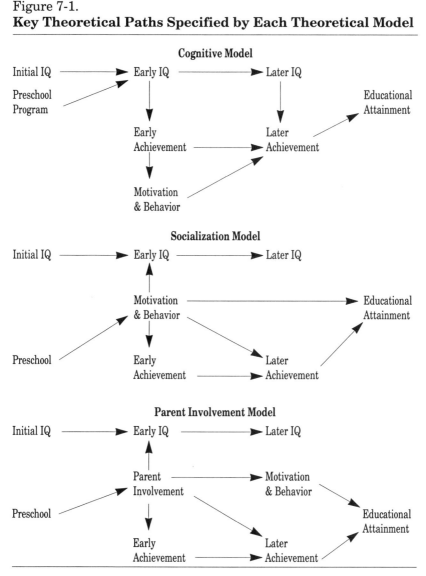

eliminating paths when they were strongly rejected. However, each alternative was constrained to include the initial path from preschool as specified in Figure 7-1. In general, paths that were inconsistent with temporal ordering were not added even if the results indicated that they would improve the fit of the model. At later stages of model building we tried to reintroduce paths that had been rejected, particularly paths hypothesized to be critical links in the various alternative theories. Goodness of fit was judged based on multiple criteria: significance of Chi-Square (p), the Adjusted Goodness-of-Fit Index (AGFI), and the Root Mean Square Residual (RMSR). When comparing models, larger values of p and AGFI and lower values of RMSR indicate a better fit between a model and the data.

Results

Figure 7-2 displays the path diagram for the cognitive model that emerged from our analyses. It was the only model for which the initially specified path from preschool education was found to be statistically significant. The socialization and parent involvement models were strongly rejected. None of the paths linking preschool program participation to the key theoretical variables in those models were found to be statistically significant (p>0.05), and these two models fit the data poorly as judged by all three measures of goodness of fit (Chi-Square, p<0.01; AGFI <0.70, and RMSR >0.10). By contrast, the cognitive model fit the data quite well. The key theoretical paths are statistically significant (p<0.05), and the model's overall fit was good (Chi-Square, p=0.358; AGFI=0.895; RMSR =0.046).

In the structural equations model estimated for the cognitive effects hypothesis, program participation, pretest IQ, mother's participation in elementary school, and a gender by treatment interaction were specified as exogenous variables. This may seem somewhat odd in the case of mother's participation in that this measure was not obtained until elementary school. However, when we specified mother's participation as an endogenous variable it was found to be unrelated to any of the exogenous variables and was indicated to affect early IQ. To examine this relationship further we separated the IQ measure into IQ at school entry (age 5) and IQ in early elementary school. Mother's participation was indicated to affect IQ at school entry, a variable that was measured earlier than mother's participation. This supports our view that the mother's participation variable should be viewed as a stable measure of mother's active involvement in the child's early learning and development, rather than a measure of involvement in elementary school per se.

As can be seen in Figure 7-2, the preschool program was found to have a significant direct effect on early IQ. The size of the program's effect on IQ declined over time as indicated by the nega-

Figure 7-2.
Estimated Cognitive Model of Long-Term Effects

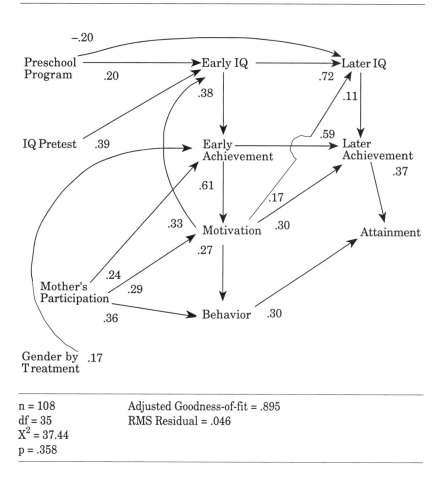

n = 108   Adjusted Goodness-of-fit = .895
df = 35   RMS Residual = .046
X^2 = 37.44
p = .358

tive "direct effect" of program participation on later IQ. Program participation was indirectly linked to achievement, motivation, personal behavior, and highest grade attained. Estimates of the total effects (direct and indirect effects combined) of preschool participation were statistically significant for three outcomes: early IQ, motivation, and later achievement. In addition, there was a direct path from the treatment by gender interaction to early achievement. We interpret this path as an indication that the effect of the program on early achievement through IQ was larger for girls than for boys (see also Barnes, 1989). Total effects estimates for the treatment by gender interaction were statistically significant for early and later achievement, motivation, and highest grade attained, and effects approached significance for later IQ and behavior. In sum, there were larger and more pervasive long-term effects for girls than for boys.

EMI classification does not appear in the model because the variable EVER EMI did not seem to fit into the same model as the other outcomes (nor did it fit into any of the models estimated for the other alternative explanations). No relationship was found between EVER EMI and achievement or educational attainment. Thus, effects on special-education placement are not a plausible explanation for the achievement and educational attainment effects. When separate models were estimated for EVER EMI, the best predictor of EMI placement appeared to be early IQ. The High/Scope Perry Preschool program has never been found to have a significant effect on whether children were placed in EMI. Rather, the program was found to have a significant effect on the number of years in EMI classes using statistical tests appropriate for count data (Schweinhart et al., 1993). In future studies, it might be useful to develop structural models that include measures of the number of years in special education at several points in the school career.

As indicated earlier, significant treatment by gender interactions were found in the cognitive effects model. These results suggest that completely different causal models might be warranted for girls and boys. Unfortunately, the sample size is too small to reliably estimate separate structural equations models for each gender to investigate this issue. To further investigate treatment by gender interaction, we estimated gender-specific single-equation regression models of each outcome on program participation and maternal employment at study entry (recall that this was not randomly distributed between preschool and control groups). Achievement and IQs for each year rather than multiple year averages were examined to obtain a view of year-to-year changes. These regressions provided estimates of the program's total (direct and indirect) effect on each outcome that were unbiased by the omission of other relevant variables because, due to randomization, program participation was uncorrelated with all background characteristics except maternal employment. Given our interests, the small sample sizes once the full sample is divided by gender, and the limited power of these analyses compared to the structural equations model, we concentrate on the size of the estimated effects of the preschool program rather than statistical significance. Table 7-3 reports estimated effects (Bs) and standardized effects (Betas), which are the effects measured in standard deviation units.

Table 7-3.
Estimated Total Effects of Preschool Education by Gender

Variable	Males		Females	
	B	**Beta**	**B**	**Beta**
IQ, End of Pre-K	10.29	.45	14.14	.49
IQ, Age 6	6.50	.28	5.12	.24
IQ, Age 7	4.14	.20	7.87	.33
IQ, Age 8	−0.27	−.01	5.82	.25
IQ, Age 9	−0.55	−.02	4.87	.22
IQ, Age 10	−2.16	−.10	7.00	.30
IQ, Age 14	−1.43	−.06	3.91	.22
Achievement, Age 7	7.14	.09	25.99	.33
Achievement, Age 8	11.51	.12	32.90	.37
Achievement, Age 9	25.37	.17	48.09	.32
Achievement, Age 10	29.01	.18	44.84	.29
Achievement, Age 11	14.31	.10	16.88	.14
Achievement, Age 14	22.45	.27	37.19	.47
Personal Behavior	0.15	.15	0.28	.28
Motivation	0.22	.13	0.51	.35
Parent Participation	0.05	.01	0.17	.06
Classified EMI	−0.20	−.22	−0.33	−.40
Highest Grade, Age 19	0.27	.10	1.26	.30

Sample size for each analysis is all cases available for that variable, unlike causal model, which is limited to 108 cases for all variables.

Beginning at age seven, the lasting effects of the program on cognitive development and academic success appear to be stronger for girls than for boys. However, the pattern of effects over time appears to be somewhat more complicated than revealed by the structural equations analysis. The preschool program had substantial initial effects on IQ for boys and girls (with roughly equal *Beta*s). After an initial dropoff in the IQ effect, an IQ effect of about 0.25 of a standard deviation (the *Beta*s) seems to have persisted for girls while the IQ effect for boys quickly faded out. Although it is not evident from Table 7-3, the dropoff in the IQ effect appears to result from both a decline in IQ for the program group and an increase in IQ for the control group during the kindergarten year (Schweinhart et al., 1993).

Turning to academic achievement, the size of the effects on raw scores grew over the early grades, but the standardized effect sizes were more stable. At age eleven (spring of grade five for most students), there was a sharp dropoff in the size of estimated effects. Possibly the Upper-primary level of the California Achievement Test (CAT) did not discriminate among students as well at age eleven because it had become relatively easy for the students or because of a ceiling effect for the higher achieving students. The effect on achievement rebounded at age fourteen when a more difficult level of the CAT was employed, at which time the program effect appeared to be larger than ever. Estimated effect sizes tended to be roughly twice as large for girls as for boys except at age eleven.

The results for EVER EMI, motivation, and behavior all followed the same general pattern as achievement—the estimated effects were two to three times larger for girls than for boys. One variable for which this was not the case was mother's participation in school. No significant program effect was found on this variable for either boys or girls and the estimated effect size was negligible in both cases.

Discussion

Overall, the results favored the view that the long-term effects of the Perry Preschool program on achievement and school success derived from its immediate effects on cognitive abilities rather than from program effects on parents or on children's socialization. Mothers' participation in the child's education, academic motivation, and personal behavior were all found to be powerful influences on achievement and educational attainment. However, mothers' participation in the child's education was not affected by preschool program participation. Motivation and personal behavior were affected only indirectly by the preschool program through program effects on IQ and achievement. Early achievement gains appeared to set in motion a cycle of lasting improvements in achievement, motivation, and behavior. These results are consistent with constructivist, ecological, and sociocultural theories of learning and development (Piaget, 1952; Vygotsky, 1978; Bronfenbrenner, 1989).

However, there are a number of complexities that must be dealt with in interpreting the results. Perhaps the most important is how the preschool program's cognitive effects could produce long-term increases in achievement and educational attainment at the same time that IQ gains gradually faded away. We believe that the explanation is that (a) learning is a cumulative process to which both general intellectual abilities and subject matter knowledge and skills contribute (De Corte, 1995; Weinert & Helmke, 1995), and (b) IQ tests measure general intellectual abilities while achievement tests assess subject matter knowledge and skills.

The extent to which the preschool program initially influenced general intellectual abilities rather than subject-matter-specific knowledge and skills is unclear because it is difficult for IQ tests to distinguish between general intellectual abilities and subject-matter knowledge during the preschool years. Arguably, the fade out in IQ test scores after school entry indicates that the chief effect of pre-school education was on subject-matter knowledge and skills. These abilities had a substantial effect on early achievement and set in motion the achievement-motivation-behavior cycle that produced long-term gains but had little or no effect on long-term general intellectual abilities (at least for boys).

This study's results also provided some support for the hypothesis that preschool education's effects on early cognitive abilities contribute to the reduction in special-education placements. However, effects on EMI placement were unrelated to program effects on other educational outcomes. Possibly a more complex representation of the process might yield different results. Whether the effect on EMI placement should be viewed as artificial or inappropriate because there was no persistent effect on IQ test scores cannot be entirely resolved on the basis of this study. However, there was no negative effect on achievement from the reduction in EMI placements. The implication is either that the reductions in special education were appropriate because the children really had higher abilities or that special-education placements were ineffective for these children.

As preschool education effects on grade retention are a common finding of other studies (see Barnett's review, this volume), the lack of such effects in this study deserves comment. The most obvious explanation is that the elementary school attended by virtually all of the children in the study made little use of grade retention. As few children were retained in grade, there was no room for preschool education to have much of an effect on grade retention. Studies of preschool programs in areas where children have higher rates of grade retention would be expected to yield different results.

Differences in program effects by gender also require an explanation. In the LISREL model, differences appeared to begin with a stronger effect on achievement for girls than boys that was then transmitted to effects on motivation, later achievement, and educational attainment. The more detailed year-by-year single-equation regression analyses revealed a more complicated picture in which gender differences in effects on IQ as well as achievement are evident by second grade. It appears that there may be small to moderate long-term effects on general intellectual abilities for girls. These could result from direct preschool program effects or from the (larger) effects on subject-matter knowledge and skills that, in turn, increase general intellectual abilities. The combination of effects on general intellectual abilities and larger effects on subject-matter knowledge and abilities could explain why there was a large effect on educational attainment for girls but not boys.

The treatment-by-gender interactions found in this study would be of less interest (perhaps even dismissed as the results of chance in a small sample) if similar interactions had not been found in other studies (e.g., Gray, Ramsey, & Klaus, 1982; Lally, Mangione, & Honig, 1988). Moreover, examination of the results of another true experiment—the Abecedarian study—through age fifteen reveals a strikingly similar pattern. Specifically, achievement effects for boys appear to decline in size over time while they remain steady for girls (Campbell, 1994).

A number of quasi-experimental studies of public preschool programs have employed much larger sample sizes than the Perry Preschool study and other studies of researcher-initiated programs. These studies generally do not find treatment-by-gender interactions (e.g., Reynolds et al., 1996). Similarly, the pooled analyses conducted by the Consortium for Longitudinal Studies failed to find differences in effects by gender (Lazar et al., 1982). One plausible explanation for these variations in findings is that differences in effects by gender depend on preschool program characteristics, school practices, and children's and families' attitudes that vary over time and across communities. For example, the program studied by Reynolds and his colleagues (1996) includes an enhanced early elementary school program with a continuing emphasis on parent involvement that may shape parent and child attitudes in ways that help produce and sustain effects for boys.

The limited evidence of treatment-by-gender interactions is enough to recommend that future research investigate the extent to which preschool education programs may produce smaller and less pervasive long-term gains for boys than girls in educational attainment and cognitive abilities. Such studies should consider the possibility that differences may result from later interactions with the school and larger social environments as well as from differential direct effects of preschool education and that differential effects need not always be in the same direction. Although the Perry Preschool program was found to produce larger effects on educational outcomes for girls, analyses published elsewhere found that the program produced larger effects for boys on such nonschool outcomes as arrests, earnings, and home ownership (Schweinhart, et al., 1993). This suggests a need to study the ways in which preschool program effects on learning and development are shaped by children's social and cultural environments including schools, families, and peer groups (Bronfenbrenner, 1989; Vygotsky, 1978). For example, social and cultural factors may lead girls to respond more positively to school and teachers to respond more positively to girls. Also, differences between girls and boys in anticipated future opportunities and responsibilities may lead them to respond differently to schooling even if they enter kindergarten with similar early cognitive gains from preschool education.

Returning to our major theme, this study found that a preschool education program for children in poverty had large initial effects on cognitive abilities and that these effects subsequently generated persistent effects on achievement and school success. The chain of effects found in this study is consistent with the view that children are active learners who continue to build on their own abilities using the resources available in school and elsewhere (Piaget, 1952; Vygotsky, 1978). The notion that effects would necessarily die out after special interventions ceased and experimental and control children experienced the same schooling environment would appear to be based on a model of learning and development in which children are passive and the school is active. It is interesting to note that the children who did not attend the preschool program appear to receive a boost in early IQ scores after they enter kindergarten, indicating that their schools were an effective intervention to some extent. When the child is recognized as an active agent in the process of development, it is no longer necessary to look for some other agent (the school or the family) as the source of persistent effects. Perhaps the popularity of the view that preschool-program-induced changes in parents are the primary source of persistent effects is due to an implicit assumption that children are purely passive learners while adults are the active agents at home as well as in school. In any case, preschool education for children in poverty does not appear to require continued special interventions in the schools or effects on parents to generate long-term effects on cognition and school success (see also Barnett this volume).

Of course, similar effects on long-term achievement and educational attainment might be produced by preschool programs that focus on parent involvement in the child's education or improving the child's motivation and behavior in school. This study does not directly address those issues, but it does provide evidence that noncognitive factors significantly influence achievement and educational attainment. Moreover, larger long-term effects might be produced by supplementing preschool programs that seek to influence school success through all these paths with programs to improve the quality of education in the elementary school (De Corte, 1995; Allington & Walmsley, 1995). Some support for this comes from a recent study of a preschool and early elementary program found to directly affect parent involvement as well as cognitive abilities (Reynolds et al., 1996) as well as from research on the effects of efforts to improve elementary education for children in poverty (Allington & Walmsley, 1995; Ross, Smith, Casey, & Slavin, 1995; Barnett, 1996).

Despite what has been learned from this and other studies, much remains to be learned about how preschool programs produce long-term effects, and our lack of knowledge is an impediment to effective public policy. There is a need for new randomized trials with sample sizes that are sufficiently large to address questions about alternative approaches, age at start, gender differences, and the effects of variations in later school environments. Without such studies it will be difficult to advance our knowledge about how much improvement in cognitive development and school success preschool programs can produce for children in poverty or about the ways in which early elementary school policies can be designed to build on the gains produced by preschool programs.

8

D. J. Hernandez

Economic and Social Disadvantages of Young Children

Alternative Policy Responses

Young children experienced a revolutionary transformation in child-care and educational circumstances during the past half century. Massive movement by mothers into the paid labor force since World War II and large increases in mother-only families since 1960 led to drastic reductions in young children with a parent available in the home to provide full-time care. Enormous increases in alternative care and educational arrangements have raised pressing questions about the cost, quality, and

Adapted from Hernandez, D. J. (1995). Changing demographics: Past and future demands for early childhood programs. *The Future of Children* (Winter) 5(3):145–60, by permission of Center for the Future of Children, The David and Lucile Packard Foundation.

availability of nonparental care for young children. Rising poverty since the early 1970s has magnified concern about the well being and developmental prospects of many young children. Parents simultaneously confront difficulties in providing their children with both good care and adequate economic resources, while government seeks public policies to maximize the opportunities for these children to become productive workers, successful parents, and responsible citizens when they reach adulthood.

This chapter briefly reviews the historical underpinnings of these revolutionary changes in the lives of young children and major sources of increasing inequality and diversity in the needs of young children. It then offers a conceptual framework for classifying the range of public policies that might reduce sources of economic and social disadvantage or ameliorate deleterious consequences. Finally, the chapter draws on existing scientific evidence to explore the likely efficacy of alternative policy responses to needs of young children for economic resources and educational experiences that effectively promote their long-term social, psychological, cognitive, and physical development.

Historical Roots of Increasing Nonparental Child Care

During the past 150 years, the family economy was revolutionized twice, as fathers and then mothers left the home to spend much of the day away at jobs as family breadwinners (Figure 8-1).[1] Corresponding revolutions in child care occurred, as children aged six and over and then younger children began to spend increasing amounts of time in school or in the care of someone other than their parents. The growing reliance of American families on nonparental care for young children after 1940 is rooted in these historical changes in parents' work (Hernandez, 1993a).

For one hundred years prior to 1940, in order to improve their relative social and economic status, parents had been moving off the farm so that fathers could work at comparatively well-paid jobs in urban areas, parents had been limiting themselves to smaller and smaller families so that available economic resources could be spread less thinly, and parents had been increasing their educational attainments to improve their employment prospects within urban areas.

By 1940, however, most families had already taken these steps. Because only 23 percent of Americans lived on farms and 70 percent of parents had only one or two dependent children in the home,

Figure 8-1.
Children Ages 0–17 in Farm Families, Father-as-Breadwinner Families, and Dual-Earner Families: 1790–1989

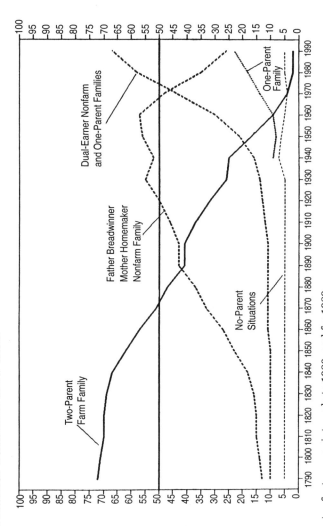

Note: Estimates for ten-year intervals to 1980, and for 1989.

Source: Hernandez, 1993, p. 103, © Russell Sage Foundation. Reprinted by permission.

these two historical avenues to improving their relative economic standing had run their course (Elder, 1974). In addition, beyond age twenty-five it is often difficult or impractical to pursue additional schooling. As of 1940, then, mothers' work had become the only major avenue available to most couples over age twenty-five who sought to improve their relative social and economic status.

With these enormous historical changes, many mothers were potentially available for and increasingly attracted to paid work. Increasing rates of school attendance by children aged six and over had freed many mothers from the need to stay home and, over time, public schooling increased the educational attainments of young women, making them better qualified as employees. After 1940, the economic demand for married women to enter the labor force increased substantially (Oppenheimer, 1979). Many also had strong incentive to work, because in a competitive, consumption-oriented society, families with two earners could jump economically ahead of families with only a single earner (Oppenheimer, 1982).

In addition, since more than one-fifth of children during the past fifty years have lived with fathers who, during any given year, experienced part-time work or joblessness, many mothers experienced a powerful incentive to provide economic support to the family through work for pay. Additional incentives for mothers' paid employment included, in the context of historic increases in divorce, the fact that paid work served as a hedge against losing most or all of the husband's income through divorce, as well as the personal nonfinancial rewards of productive involvement with other adults and the satisfactions of having a career.

After 1960, the proportion of young children living in one-parent, working-parent families also increased substantially. Underlying this increase are sharply rising rates of divorce and out-of-wedlock child bearing. During the prior century, remarkably steady increases occurred in divorce, in part because with an urban job a father could leave his family but keep his income, considerably weakening the economic interdependence experienced by husbands and wives living on farms that required parents to work together to sustain themselves. More recently, the incomes of working women helped to weaken further the economic interdependence of husbands and wives, setting the stage for an unprecedented rise in separation and divorce during the 1960s and 1970s (Figure 8-2). Economic insecurity associated with fathers' part-time work, joblessness, or difficulties finding employment also made marriage less attractive and less sustainable for many families, contributing both to divorce and out-of-wedlock childbearing (Hernandez, 1993a;

Figure 8-2.
Divorce Rate, 1860 to 1988 (Divorces per 1,000 married women age 15 years and over)

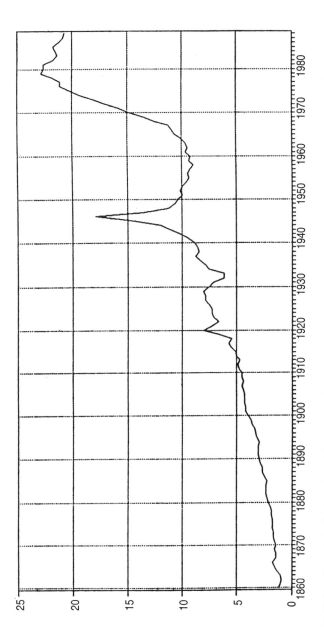

Sources: P. H. Jacobson (1950). *American Marriage and Divorce.* New York: Rinehart; U.S. National Center for Health Statistics. (1991). Advance report of final divorce statistics, vol. 39, no. 12, supplement 2. Washington, D.C.: USNCHS.

Conger et al., 1990; Conger & Elder, 1994, Elder, Conger, Foster, & Ardelt, 1992; Wilson, 1987; Liker & Elder, 1983).

The Need for Alternative Child-Care Arrangements

As a consequence of these trends, most children today live either in dual-earner families in which both parents work at jobs away from home, or in one-parent families (Figure 8-1). As a result, a growing proportion of children under age six need care by persons other than their parents for a significant portion of the day.

In 1940, only 8 percent of children aged birth to five lived in a dual-earner family or one-parent family with an employed parent. By 1989, this had increased to 51 percent (Figure 8-3). About three-fourths of this rise is accounted for by dual-earner families, which increased sevenfold from 5 to 38 percent, while the remainder is due to the fivefold increase from 2 to 13 percent in young children living with a lone working parent. The decline in young children living in a "traditional" two-parent family with a breadwinner father and homemaker mother has been even more precipitous, since the proportion living in such families declined from 83 percent in 1940 to only 32 percent in 1989.

The decline in breadwinner-homemaker families for infants under age one has been just as great as for children age five (Table 8-1). In 1940, the proportions under age one and age five living in breadwinner-homemaker families were 85 percent and 79 percent, respectively, for a 6 percentage point difference, but by 1989 the proportions had fallen to 34 and 30 percent, respectively, for a difference of only 4 percentage points. Corresponding increases have occurred in the proportions living in dual-earner families and in one-parent, working-parent families, although the increases were somewhat larger for parental part-time employment among infants, and for parental full-time employment among children age five.

Not all children without a specific parent home full time are cared for by someone other than parents; by 1989, about 12 percent of children lived in dual-earner families in which the parents worked different hours or days and could personally care for their children. Still, about 40 percent of preschoolers spent considerable time in the care of someone other than their parents while the parents worked (Hernandez, 1993a; O'Connell and Bachu, 1990; Presser, 1989).

If the labor-force-participation rate for mothers rises further, if out-of-wedlock child bearing continues to rise, or if recent welfare

Figure 8-3.
**Children Ages 0–5 in Dual-Earner Families and
One-Parent Families with an Employed Parent: 1940–1989**

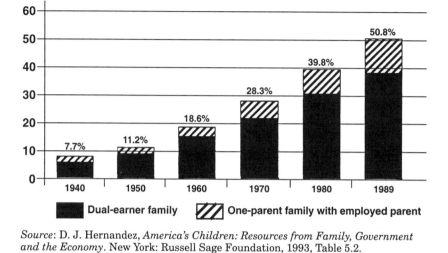

Source: D. J. Hernandez, *America's Children: Resources from Family, Government and the Economy*. New York: Russell Sage Foundation, 1993, Table 5.2.

reforms succeed in lifting employment rates of mothers with young children, then the need for nonparental care for young children may expand beyond the current, historically unprecedented level.

Increasing Inequality and Diversity in Children's Needs

After the Great Depression, economic inequality declined, but between 1969 and 1993 the official poverty rate for young children jumped from 17 to 25 percent and the "relative" poverty rate jumped from 24 to 31 percent. Meanwhile, the proportion living in families with luxury-level incomes expanded from 12 to 23 percent, and the proportion living in middle-class comfort or near-poor frugality shrank from 65 to 47 percent (Table 8-2) (Hernandez, 1993a, 1997). Since parents with higher family incomes can usually afford to provide resources and educational experiences that foster the development of their children, while children from poor homes may have less access to such resources and experiences, the quantitative increases in the need for nonparental care during the past quarter-century have been accompanied by increased qualitative differences in the educational needs of children who enter child care.[2]

Table 8-1a.
Children Ages 0–5 by Parental Presence and Employment Status: 1940–1989

	1940	1950	1960	1970	1980	1989
Total number (in thousands)	12,384	18,801	24,808	20,895	19,719	20,168
Percent	100.0	100.0	100.0	100.0	100.0	100.0
Breadwinner-homemaker total	82.9	78.3	72.9	60.7	45.5	31.6
Breadwinner-homemaker intact	70.7	65.6	61.0	50.4	35.2	NA
Breadwinner-homemaker blended	12.2	12.7	11.9	10.3	10.3	NA
Two-parents, father not breadwinner	2.1	3.0	1.8	2.5	2.6	4.9
One-parent family, not a breadwinner	2.3	2.9	3.9	5.6	7.2	11.0
Dual-earner family, employed full time	2.5	4.5	6.6	10.1	13.8	17.5
One-parent family, employed full time	1.4	1.7	2.4	4.4	5.6	7.0
Dual-earner family, employed part time	2.9	4.3	8.4	11.7	17.0	20.8
One-parent family, employed part time	0.9	0.7	1.2	2.1	3.4	5.5
No parent in home	5.0	4.7	2.9	3.0	4.9	1.7

Sources: D. J. Hernandez, *America's Children: Resources from Family, Government and the Economy.* New York: Russell Sage Foundation, 1993, Table 5.2.

Notes: Estimates derived from 1940–1980 Census PUMS and 1989 CPS. Estimates for 1940 and 1950 based on mother's marital history only.

Breadwinner-homemaker: Two-parent family with father in labor force and mother not in labor force.

    Intact: Two-parent family with all children born after parents' only marriage.

    Blended: Two-parent family other than intact.

Two-parents, father not breadwinner: Father not in labor force, mother may or may not be in labor force.

One-parent family, not a breadwinner: Mother-only or father-only family with parent not in labor force.

Dual-earner family, employed full time: Two-parent family, both parents employed thirty-five or more hours in last week.

One-parent family, employed full time: Mother-only or father-only family with parent employed thirty-five or more hours in last week.

Dual-earner family, employed part time: Two-parent family, both parents in labor force, at least one employed less than thirty-five hours in last week.

One-parent, employed part time: Mother-only or father-only family with parent in labor force employed less than thirty-five hours in last week

No parent in home: Child does not reside with biological, step, or adoptive parent.

Another trend affecting child-care and educational needs is the increasing racial and ethnic diversity of American children. Figure 8-4 shows that while in 1990, 69 percent of children under age eighteen were white (and not of Hispanic origin), 15 percent were black, 12 percent were Hispanic, and 4 percent were of another racial or ethnic group, the U.S. Bureau of the Census projects that by 2030, only 50 percent of children will be white, non-Hispanic, and one-half will be Hispanic, black, or of another nonwhite race.

Table 8-1b.
Children, Single Years of Age, by Parental Presence and Employment Status: 1940–1989

Age	1940	1950	1960	1970	1980	1989
Breadwinner-Homemaker, Total						
0	85.6	82.6	76.8	65.2	49.9	33.8
1	85.1	79.9	74.5	63.8	47.2	33.0
2	84.5	78.2	74.5	60.1	45.4	31.5
3	81.4	78.2	70.8	59.4	44.5	30.6
4	81.7	74.8	71.8	59.4	43.2	30.1
5	79.4	74.5	68.9	56.9	42.0	30.2
Breadwinner-Homemaker, Intact						
0	75.8	70.6	64.8	54.8	39.2	NA
1	74.4	67.6	63.3	52.8	35.9	NA
2	72.0	65.6	61.9	50.1	35.5	NA
3	68.6	65.3	58.5	49.6	34.3	NA
4	68.2	61.9	60.1	48.8	33.7	NA
5	66.1	61.1	57.0	46.7	32.0	NA
Breadwinner-Homemaker, Blended						
0	9.8	12.0	12.0	10.4	10.7	NA
1	10.7	12.3	11.2	11.0	11.3	NA
2	12.5	12.6	12.6	10.0	9.9	NA
3	12.8	12.9	12.3	9.8	10.2	NA
4	13.5	12.9	11.7	10.6	9.5	NA
5	13.3	13.4	11.9	10.2	10.0	NA
Two-Parents, Father Not Breadwinner						
0	2.3	3.5	1.7	2.9	2.9	4.2
1	1.6	2.9	1.9	2.2	2.7	5.0
2	1.9	3.3	1.8	2.6	2.6	5.4
3	2.4	2.9	1.7	2.2	2.4	5.7
4	2.3	2.9	1.7	2.0	2.6	4.1
5	2.3	2.6	1.9	2.8	2.5	4.9
One Parent Family, Not a Breadwinner						
0	1.8	2.8	4.2	6.6	7.6	13.1
1	2.2	2.8	4.1	5.2	7.4	11.6
2	1.6	2.6	3.9	5.9	7.6	11.0
3	2.7	2.7	3.9	5.5	6.7	9.8
4	2.6	3.2	3.5	5.4	7.1	10.2
5	2.7	3.2	4.0	5.3	7.0	10.3
Dual-Earner Family, Employed Full Time						
0	1.7	2.3	4.9	7.4	10.9	13.9
1	2.3	4.3	6.4	9.3	13.1	18.0
2	2.3	4.3	6.1	10.4	14.6	18.0
3	2.6	5.0	7.4	10.3	14.7	18.9
4	3.0	5.7	7.1	10.7	14.6	17.8
5	3.0	6.0	8.1	12.1	15.1	18.5

Table 8-1b. (*continued*)
Children, Single Years of Age, by Parental Presence and Employment Status: 1940–1989

Age	1940	1950	1960	1970	1980	1989
One-Parent Family, Employed Full Time						
0	0.9	0.6	1.8	3.4	2.9	4.8
1	1.2	1.4	1.9	3.8	4.8	6.5
2	1.3	2.1	2.3	4.5	5.9	7.2
3	1.6	1.7	2.8	4.8	6.3	7.5
4	1.7	2.3	2.4	5.1	6.6	7.7
5	1.6	2.5	3.0	4.6	7.2	8.7
Dual-Earner Family, Employed Part Time						
0	1.9	3.0	6.4	9.8	17.0	23.1
1	2.7	3.9	7.6	10.4	16.1	20.0
2	2.9	4.1	7.7	11.7	16.3	19.3
3	3.3	4.5	9.3	12.5	16.5	20.4
4	2.5	4.9	9.4	12.4	18.0	22.2
5	3.6	5.4	9.9	13.3	18.2	19.4
One-Parent Family, Employed Part Time						
0	0.6	0.5	1.0	1.7	3.4	5.5
1	0.9	0.6	0.9	2.2	3.2	4.7
2	1.0	0.6	1.0	2.0	3.2	5.5
3	1.0	0.6	1.3	2.2	3.9	5.0
4	1.0	1.0	1.4	2.2	3.5	6.3
5	1.1	0.6	1.2	2.2	3.4	6.1
No Parent in Home						
0	5.3	4.7	3.2	3.1	5.3	1.7
1	4.0	4.3	2.7	3.0	5.6	1.3
2	4.5	4.7	2.6	2.9	4.5	1.9
3	5.0	4.4	2.9	3.0	5.0	2.0
4	5.2	4.9	2.7	2.8	4.3	1.7
5	6.2	5.2	3.1	2.9	4.7	1.9
Total (in thousands)						
0	1,757	3,092	4.270	3.440	3,636	3,892
1	2,045	3,303	4,233	3,321	3,333	3,751
2	2,181	3,520	4,197	3,292	3,269	3,666
3	2,092	3,553	4,061	3,884	3,188	3,681
4	2,160	2,641	4,016	3,530	3,114	3,633
5	2,148	2,690	4,031	3,928	3,179	3,680

Source: D. J. Hernandez, *America's Children: Resources from Family, Government, and the Economy*. New York: Russell Sage Foundation, 1993, Table 5.3.

Notes: See Table 8.1 notes.

Table 8-2.
**Children Ages 0–5, by Relative Income Levels and
Official Poverty Rates: 1939–1988**

	1939	1949	1959	1969	Census 1979	CPS 1979	CPS 1988
Relative poverty	37.9	24.3	24.8	23.6	26.4	24.5	30.1
Near-poor frugality	10.9	14.8	20.2	20.7	17.0	16.8	15.4
Middle-class comfort	28.3	42.8	43.4	44.1	42.5	42.1	31.8
Luxury income	22.8	18.0	11.7	11.7	14.2	15.8	19.7
Official poverty	7.8	44.7	26.3	16.5	18.2	18.1	22.7

Variations in family living arrangements and in parental work arrangements also influence children's lives, including their risks of dropping out of high school, bearing children as teenagers, and not being employed by their early twenties (McLanahan & Sandefur, 1994). Children in one-parent families may have educational needs that differ from children in two-parent families, and within two-parent families there may be important differences between children with a parent home full time, children in dual-earner families where parents work the same hours of the day, and children in dual-earner families where parents work different hours or days and who, consequently, spend comparatively little time together (Presser, 1989; Hernandez, 1993a). All of these trends underscore the importance of creating policies and programs that correspond to the child-care and educational needs of an increasingly diverse population of children.

Alternative Approaches to Public Policy

Public policies to insure that the increasingly diverse developmental needs of young children are met might be directed either toward minimizing future growth in or reducing the number of children disadvantaged by poverty, racial or ethnic minority status, or family circumstances; or public policies might be directed toward providing services specifically designed to meet the particular needs of children in disadvantaged circumstances.

Figure 8-4.
**Percent of Children Who Are
Non-Hispanic White, Black, and Hispanic**

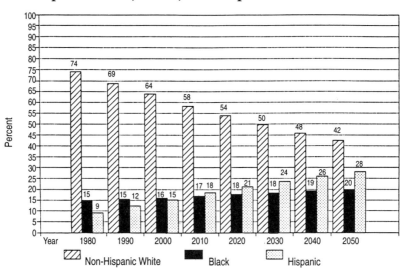

Source: U.S. Bureau of the Census, Current Population Reports, Series P-25, Nos. 1095 and 1104.

What is the nature and likely efficacy of policies taking each of these approaches? Due to limitations of space and of research evidence, definitive answers cannot be provided here, but a broad assessment based on existing knowledge is possible.

Policies to Reduce Economic Disadvantage

Current policy discussions involve three distinguishable approaches to reducing childhood economic disadvantage: (1) fostering two-parent families by discouraging divorce and out-of-wedlock child bearing, (2) bringing additional parental earnings into the home through increased child-support payments by absent fathers (or mothers) or through increased employment and earnings of parents, or (3) providing economic support through direct government income transfers to impoverished children and their families.

*Policies Discouraging Divorce and
Out-of-Wedlock Childbearing*

Policies to discourage divorce and out-of-wedlock childbearing can be distinguished further as seeking to (1) increase knowledge or change values of parents or potential parents, (2) reduce or eliminate benefits that welfare programs provide to one-parent families, especially compared to two-parent families, or (3) increase child-support payment by noncustodial parents (for example, see McLanahan & Sandefur, 1994; Blankenhorn, 1995).

Knowledge, Values, Divorce, and Out-of-Wedlock Child Bearing. Programs to influence knowledge or values include public education campaigns aimed at increasing parental knowledge about potential risks to children associated with divorce or out-of-wedlock child bearing, and they include government efforts to encourage or fund prominent national, religious, and community leaders to exhort their constituencies to refrain from these behaviors. Since such proposals have not been tried systematically on a large scale, their possible level of success is uncertain. Public health education campaigns designed to reduce cigarette smoking and drunken driving by increasing public knowledge about harmful consequences of these activities do, however, provide models for such programs.

Whatever success these education programs have had, it is important to note that many people continue to smoke and to drive drunk. More importantly, smoking and drinking are behaviors that do not have the same powerful socioeconomic underpinnings identified earlier in this chapter as fostering long-term increases in divorce and out-of-wedlock child bearing. Since these socioeconomic underpinnings would not be changed by educational or informational campaigns, such campaigns might have only small to negligible effects.

Welfare Benefits, Divorce, and Out-of-Wedlock Child Bearing. One purpose of efforts to reduce or eliminate welfare benefits to one-parent families is to discourage divorce and out-of-wedlock child bearing by reducing economic incentives seen as encouraging such behaviors. Proposals to cut programs are nearly as numerous as the total count of programs providing benefits to one-parent families, including Aid to Families with Dependent Children (AFDC), Food Stamps, Public Housing, and the Supplemental Food Program for Women, Infants, and Children (WIC) program.

Despite the plausibility of this approach, the weight of scientific evidence to date indicates that welfare programs have had little, if any, effect in fostering single parenthood. This conclusion has emerged both from research in the United States and from international comparisons which show that despite the more generous welfare programs in Western Europe, these countries generally have lower rates of divorce and out-of-wedlock child bearing than does the United States (Sorrentino, 1990; Hobbs and Lippman, 1990; Hernandez, 1993a, McLanahan and Sandefur, 1994).

   Child Support, Divorce, and Out-of-Wedlock Child Bearing. The third approach to discouraging the formation of one-parent families is to require noncustodial fathers (or noncustodial mothers) to make larger child-support payments. The underlying idea is plausible; namely, that some fathers will be discouraged from divorce or out-of-wedlock child bearing if economic costs to noncustodial parents are increased. Of course, from the perspective of mothers, increased child-support payments reduce the economic disincentive to divorce or bear children out of wedlock. It is too soon to tell whether recent laws (the Child Support Enforcement Act of 1984 and the Family Support Act of 1988), which are designed to increase these payments, have had such effects on divorce and fertility behavior.

Policies Increasing Parental Earnings Available to Children

Two potential policy approaches to increasing parental earnings available to children focus on increasing child support payments or on increasing parental earnings.

   Child Support and Income Available to Children. Increased child-support payments might also directly reduce childhood economic disadvantage by bringing additional parental earnings into the homes of children in one-parent families. How much more child-support can noncustodial fathers afford to pay, and which children would benefit? Until recently, answers to such questions were based on mothers' reports of child support income and on indirect inferences about the income of noncustodial fathers, but a major new study now provides answers based on the first national estimates of noncustodial fathers' income and child-support payments as reported by fathers themselves in a large nationally representative study (Sorensen, 1995).

   The estimates are derived using the Wisconsin child-support guidelines, that is, setting the value of child-support awards at a percentage of the noncustodial parents' income, specifically 17 percent for one child, and 25, 29, 31, and 35 percent, respectively, for parents with two, three, four, or five or more children. The results indicate that noncustodial fathers could pay much more as of 1990, $34 billion more than the actual payments of $14 billion, or a total of $48 billion.

   Many noncustodial fathers have little or no earnings available for child-support payments, however, because they do not work for part or all of the year. Classifying a noncustodial father as poor in 1990, if his income was less than the official poverty threshold for the family he lived in, or if his personal income was less than the poverty threshold for a single person, Sorensen (1995, p. 45) estimates that between 13 percent and 26 percent of noncustodial fathers were poor, with a range of 11 percent to 15 percent for nonblacks, and a range of 23 percent to 56 percent for blacks.

Sorensen develops a range of estimates to reflect the fact that the survey she uses, like all national surveys, undercount men, particularly black men in the prime fathering ages. Sorensen's lower-bound poverty estimates are derived assuming uncounted men have incomes and living situations identical to men who are counted, while the upper-bound estimates assume that the uncounted men all have incomes below the poverty threshold. If, as seems likely, uncounted men tend to have much lower incomes than men who are included in this and other major national surveys, then the actual poverty rates of noncustodial fathers are closer to the upper- than to the lower-bound estimates.

Furthermore, the value of child-support payments from fathers with low incomes will, of necessity, be quite small, because a child-support payment of 17 to 35 percent of a very low income is a comparatively small amount. Since men with limited education, restricted work opportunities, and low incomes tend to be divorced from or to bear children out of wedlock with women who are similarly disadvantaged, children in mother-only families who are most economically disadvantaged will also often have fathers who have little or no income to pay in child support.

For this reason, and because about one-half of officially poor children live in two-parent families where the child already has access to the father's entire income, Sorensen's estimates imply that a perfect child-support system would reduce the number of children officially classified as poor in 1990 by 1 million or less, that is, by less than 10 percent.[3] In other words, the official poverty rate for all children in 1990 would have been reduced by 1 or 2 percentage points or from 20.6 percent to about 19 percent. This suggests that with a perfect child-support system in 1993, the official poverty rate for children might have been reduced from about 23 percent to about 21 percent.

Instead of improving the economic situation of poor children, much of the potential increase in child-support payments would improve the economic situation of nonpoor children with comparatively high incomes. Sorensen (1995) estimates that $27 billion of the additional $34 billion that noncustodial fathers can afford to pay, that is, 78 percent of the total, would be paid by fathers in the top one-half of the income distribution of noncustodial fathers.

Hence, increased child-support payments would bring many additional billions of dollars into the homes of children in mother-only families, but since children in the most economically disadvantaged families would receive only a small portion of these payments, a policy of increased child-support payments will have comparatively little effect in reducing poverty among the most economically disadvantaged children. In fact, if a policy of increased child-support payments were combined with a policy that reduced or eliminated welfare payments to low-income, mother-only families, then the combined policies would have a still smaller effect, or no effect at all, in reducing economic disadvantage among the most needy children, or the combined effect might decrease economic resources available to these children.

Parental Earnings and Income Available to Children. A second set of policy approaches to increasing the earnings of parents involves increasing either the amount of time that parents work or their earnings per hour of work.

Public policies might encourage increases in the amount of parents' work by providing resources that facilitate work, such as child care, access to transportation,and so on. For example, it appears that a substantial minority of mothers with young children would seek employment, or work more hours, if child care were available at a reasonable cost (Presser and Baldwin, 1980). Since the lack of availability of child care constrains mothers' employment most among mothers who are young, black, single, and have low education and little income, additional public support for child care for young children might help raise the amount of income available to many children who are especially disadvantaged.

Public policies focusing less on the amount of work and more on increased earnings per hour of work include those to increase the minimum hourly wage or the work skills of parents through education and training programs. Raising the legal minimum hourly wage would immediately increase the income available to children in families with parents earning the very lowest wages, while education and training programs could enhance the marketability and value of parents' work skills. Policies to expand the number of available jobs, either directly or through subsidy programs, might also improve work opportunities for parents of economically disadvantaged children.

Since officially poor children are split about equally between one-parent and two-parent families, policies to increase parental employment and earnings could reduce economic disadvantage not only in one-parent families, by increasing income for custodial parents and by increasing income and thereby child-support payments from noncustodial parents, but also in two-parent families by increasing the earnings of both fathers and mothers.

Economic Support through Government Taxes and Transfers

A wide variety of public programs effectively transfer income from the government treasury to economically disadvantaged children by providing either cash payments or noncash benefits or services. Examples include Aid to Families with Dependent Children (AFDC), public assistance, Food Stamps, Child Nutrition, the Supplemental Food Program for Women, Infants, and Children (WIC), Public Housing and subsidized rent payments, Medicaid, Foster Care, Head Start, and the Earned Income Tax Credit (EITC).

Taken together, these cash and noncash benefits substantially reduce childhood poverty. By one accounting approach used by the U.S. Bureau of the Census (1995, P60-188, table 11), the percentage point reduction in the official poverty rate in 1993 for children under age eighteen was 1.2 percent for the EITC, 2.2 percent for nonmeans-tested government cash transfers, 1.5 percent for means-tested government cash transfers, 0.9 percent for additional means-tested government transfers excluding medical programs, and about 1.7 percent for Medicaid, for a total reduction in childhood poverty of about 7.5 percentage points. All told, then, government income transfers reduced official childhood poverty by about one-third in 1993, from about 26 percent to about 19 percent.

Nevertheless, using a poverty measure similar to the official poverty rate, Smeeding and Torrey (1996) find that the combined net effect of government taxes and transfers as of the mid-1980s was to reduce poverty for children under age six in the United States by only 2 percentage points, from 24 to 22 percent. This post-tax and transfer poverty rate was between two times and ten times greater than for other countries where the corresponding rates were 10, 4, 2, 4, and 8 percent, respectively, for Canada, Germany, Switzerland, France, and the United Kingdom.

Using a measure similar to the relative poverty rate discussed here (Hernandez, 1993a), estimates for the mid-1980s indicate that the net effect of government taxes and transfers taken together was to increase relative poverty among children under age 6 in the United States by about 2 percentage points from 29 to 31 percent (Smeeding and Torrey, 1996). These estimates show that before government taxes and transfers, the U.S. relative poverty rate of 29 percent for young children was less than the rate of 35 percent for the United Kingdom, and equal to the 29 percent for France, but substantially more than the rates for Canada, Germany, and Switzerland at 22, 11, and 12 percent, respectively (Smeeding and Torrey, 1996). Taking into account the effect of both government taxes and transfers, however, the poverty rate for children under age 6 in the United States was 31 percent, again much greater than the corresponding rates of 18, 9, 4, 10, and 15 percent, respectively, for Canada, Germany, Switzerland, France, and the United Kingdom (Smeeding and Torrey, 1996). In short, the net effect of government tax and transfer programs in the United States as of the mid-1980s was to increase relative poverty among young children, while these policies acted to reduce poverty among young children in these other countries by anywhere from 2 to 20 percentage points.

What accounts for these differences in poverty rates? Part of the difference occurs because fewer poor families with children in the United States receive government transfers. For example, around 1980, 73 percent of poor families in the United States received government transfers, 27 percent received none, while in Australia, the United Kingdom, Canada, West Germany, and Sweden, 99 to 100 percent of poor families with children received government transfers (Hobbs and Lippman, 1990).

Although many poor families with children in the United States do receive government transfers, most also are working-poor families with at least one family member who earned wage or salary income sometime during the year. For example, restricting the analysis to means-tested cash assistance in 1990, 52 percent of poor families with children received such assistance, at 26 percent for two-parent families, and 67 percent for one-parent families, but 60 percent of poor families with children were working-poor families who earned at least some wage or salary income, at 78 percent for two-parent families, and 49 percent for one-parent families. Hence, many poor children live in poverty despite parents' work, and many live in families who receive government assistance that is not generous enough, even when combined with income earned from work, to lift the family out of poverty.

Policies to Influence Racial and Ethnic Composition

As noted earlier, many nonwhite and Hispanic children may have educational needs (and related social needs) that differ from non-Hispanic white children, because of differences in poverty, language barriers, and cultural isolation. Population projections also indicate that because of trends in immigration and differential birth rates, the nonwhite and Hispanic proportion is likely to grow. Public policy discussion has not focused explicitly on reducing or slowing the increase in the racial and ethnic diversity of children, but there is substantial discussion about reducing the flow of immigrants into the United States, and in making certain public benefits unavailable to immigrant children.

If a policy to curtail immigration were adopted and effective, it would slow the increase in nonwhite and Hispanic children as a proportion of the total population during coming decades. But even if such immigration were somehow stopped immediately, it is important to reiterate that, as of 1990 nearly one-third of American children were nonwhite or Hispanic, and this proportion will continue to grow somewhat during coming years because of differential birth rates. For example, as of 1990 the number of children ever born per woman was 1.2 for whites, 1.4 for blacks, 1.6 for Native Americans, 1.1 for Asians, and 1.5 for those of Hispanic origin (Harrison and Bennett, 1995).

Although these fertility differentials may decline during the coming years, it does not seem likely that the fertility of most minority racial and ethnic groups will fall below that of the majority white non-Hispanic population. As long as this holds true, more than one-third of children in the United States will belong to racial and ethnic minorities, despite possible limits to immigration, and, in lieu of stricter immigration laws, racial and ethnic minorities will, together, account for about one-half of all children about thirty-five years from this writing.

Policies to Influence Family Composition and Parental Work

Educational needs may differ substantially between children in one-parent families, two-parent families with one worker, dual-earner families with both parents working standard weekday schedules, and dual families with parents working nights or weekends. The amount and timing of nonparental child care needed may also differ substantially depending on the number of parents in the home and their hours and days of work.

Public policies that might influence the number of parents in the home and the amount of time that they work have been discussed above, and need not be reviewed here. However, several additional consequences of such policies should be noted explicitly. First, insofar as public policies successfully encourage the formation or maintenance of two-parent families, these policies increase the potential availability of parents themselves to provide care for their children.

Second, insofar as public policies successfully encourage increased work outside the home, they increase the need for nonparental child care. Further, since nonstandard work schedules are especially common among low-paid jobs, increased work among parents of economically disadvantaged children may increase the need for nonparental care during evening, night, or early morning hours, or during weekends. If increased work leads to increased income, then additional resources will be available to pay for childcare, but unless increased income is greater than increased childcare costs, overall economic resources available for non-child care expenses will not increase, and increased work will simply shift child care from parents to nonparental care givers. Also, if the overall package of public policies (including government transfers) leads to increased parental work but to decreased family income, the overall effect on family economic resources will be deleterious.

One additional public policy, not yet mentioned, merits attention, parental leave from work for parents to care for newborn and young children. Although the amount of parental leave available to mothers and fathers does not directly effect family composition, it does influence the amount of time that parents can spend with newborn children. Many European countries have parental leave policies that are generous both in the time they allow parents to spend with young children and in the economic resources available to families of young children. Parental leave policy in the United States is quite limited in both regards.

Child-Care Policy and Research

Short of enormous—and quite unlikely—direct government transfers made available to families only if one parent remains out of the labor force to care for the children, none of the demographic and economic policies discussed thus far will substantially reduce the need for most parents to work to support their families, and in fact many of these policies would explicitly encourage increased parental work outside the home. Further, none of these policies is likely to substantially alter diversity in family living arrangements or racial and ethnic composition of children, and public policies are likely to reduce economic disadvantage only if substantially increased government transfers directly provide additional income to children in poor families and/or major government policies lead to increased work and/or earnings among poor parents.

In other words, public policies are not likely to reduce the need and demand for nonparental child care, but instead are more likely to increase this need and demand. Similarly, public policies are not likely to reduce most, if any, of the sources of demographic diversity of children, except for economic disadvantage, which is an area where public policy may be equally likely to increase the diversity experienced by children.

Hence, there is an increasing need for research on the educational needs of diverse children and the consequences for children of alternative approaches to child-care, and there is an increasing potential for public child care policy to influence the well being and developmental outcomes of children. The first child-care revolution was mandated and paid for by governments as a social good in the public interest (Hernandez, 1993a). This schooling was essential and integral to the viability of the emerging modern economy (Qvortrup, 1987, 1994). Free public education through elementary school and, subsequently, through high school led to revolutionary increases in educational attainments and in the knowledge and skills of both children and workers. These advances contributed greatly to the historic economic expansion associated with the Industrial Revolution, and hence to the multiplication of family income levels.

Today, with new productive technologies and increased global competition, there is a growing need for workers who are still more highly trained and educated, if the economic standard of living in the United States is to be maintained compared to other countries. As global economic competition becomes an increasing concern, we are in the midst of a second child-care revolution—one affecting children under age six whose parent or parents work. From this perspective, one can see child care as valuable, even essential, to society at large. It facilitates the work of mothers and their contribution both to their family income and to the economy, although little use has been made of the new tax payments created by rising mothers' employment to replace the resource (mothers' time) no longer available to young children (Jensen, 1994). The quality of child care also may influence the future international competitiveness of the U.S. economy by fostering the development of productive workers who will support the baby-boom generation as it reaches retirement. When high-quality child care leads to improved educational and developmental outcomes for children, it has value not only for the child and the parents, but also for the broader society (see especially chapters 1, 2, and 3 of this volume).

A recent National Academy of Sciences report (Phillips, 1995, pp. 20–25) summarizing the best available evidence indicates, however, that many children receive care of quite poor quality that is inadequate with regard to supervision, nurturance, and responsiveness of care givers, health and safety practices, and the availability of stimulating toys and other learning materials and opportunities. At least one in seven children, and perhaps a much larger proportion, receive poor-quality child care, and low-income children are especially likely to receive low-quality care, unless they are enrolled in subsidized high-quality arrangements. Low-income children also may be more vulnerable than higher-income children to negative developmental outcomes due to poor-quality child care.

Child care is expensive. Overall, families with a preschool child who pay for child care devote about 10 percent of their incomes to child care, but this ranges from only 6 percent for families with annual incomes of $50,000 or more to 23 percent for families with annual incomes under $15,000 (Hofferth, Brayfield, Deich, & Holcomb, 1991). High-quality care is particularly expensive, because it involves smaller group size, lower ratios of children to care givers, and higher levels of education and specialized training for care givers (Phillips, 1995, p. 26). The relative cost of child care as an expense necessitated by having a job is quite high for low-income families.

It is not surprising, then, that the enrollment rate in centers drops sharply with family income. For example, among children age four, the proportion enrolled in centers falls from 70 to 79 percent if family incomes are $35,000 or more, to 52 percent if family incomes are $25,000 to 34,999, to only 43 percent if family incomes are $15,000 to 24,999. This proportion rises substantially to 60 percent for children age four with family incomes less than $15,000, but only because 26 percent are enrolled in Head Start.

The question arises: Should the cost of that care be borne mainly or solely by parents, particularly since major public policies encourage or require parents to work outside the home?

Today, evolving economic conditions effectively require that an increasing proportion of mothers work. Recent welfare reforms mandate that additional mothers of young children find employment to support their families. Also, a highly educated and productive labor force is increasingly necessary to meet the challenge of global economic competition and to insure the retirement income of the baby-boom generation. In this context, it is important that new research inform the public policy debate about the kinds, the costs, and the quality of child care available to the youngest members of American society. Research about the value of child care to children, parents, and society at large may also help inform policy debate about the appropriate role of government in fostering and funding high-quality care for American children.

Conclusion: Priorities for Child-Care Policy and Research

What do the analyses and results presented in this chapter suggest for future child care policy and research, particularly for children living in poverty?

The highest research priority is for studies of how to design child-care programs that maximize the developmental outcomes of children who are disadvantaged by extremely limited economic resources, by having only one parent in the home, or by virtue of language barriers, cultural isolation, or other circumstances associated with minority racial or ethnic origin. This research should cast a wide net, addressing the educational, nutritional, health, and social needs of these children, for their educational needs and success cannot be divorced from other critical features of their development. In one such effort, a new National Academy of Sciences Committee on the Health and Adjustment of Immigrant Children and Families (for which the author serves as study director) will explore many of these issues for this particular population of children.

The second greatest research need, one that complements the first, is for international studies comparing child-care systems, programs, and pedagogical approaches across an array of countries. The research reviewed in chapters 2 and 9 of this volume shows that the developed countries differ substantially in the child care provided to their youngest members, and that these differences have important consequences for child well being and development. Further analysis of the advantages and disadvantages of the wide range of approaches used in various developed countries could increase knowledge about what constitutes child-effective and cost-effective care, and thereby increase the range of choices available to, and improve decisions of, the public and official policy makers in the United States.

Third, it is extremely important that the consequences of recent and projected changes in public welfare policies and programs for children's well being, development, and adult outcomes be carefully studied. Toward this end, the author has been leading an effort to develop a U.S. Bureau of the Census data collection system referred to as the Survey of Program Dynamics (SPD) with plans to collect panel data for all persons in a 20,000-household national sample on an annual basis for the period 1993 to 2002.

The aim of the SPD is to collect highly detailed data on the timing of and income received from participation in government welfare programs, on the timing of and income received from paid work by parents and other household members, on changes in family composition, and on a wide range of variables measuring child well being and development. Such panel data, which interview the same persons repeatedly over many years, provide an indispensable foundation for research to learn the consequences for children of major changes in public policy, including child care policy, that are now under debate.

Policy makers in Europe and elsewhere are also engaged in debates about the appropriate nature and magnitude of public policies for children and families. A final priority, then, is for such panel studies similar to those planned for the SPD to be implemented in other countries as well, so that policy decisions in the twenty-first century can benefit from the broadest possible knowledge about the consequences for children of alternative early childhood care and education systems.

Notes

The author is indebted to Arthur J. Norton for institutional leadership, scholarly counsel, and personal enthusiasm and encouragement, which created an indispensable and nurturing home in the U.S. Census Bureau for writing the book that provides the foundation for this chapter. Sarane Spence Boocock and W. Steven Barnett provided invaluable comments and suggestions on earlier drafts. Thanks are due also to Edith Reeves and Catherine O'Brien for statistical support, and to Stephanie Kennedy for secretarial support. The author bears sole responsibility for the results and opinions presented here.

1. This chapter draws especially on research reported in Hernandez (1993a), which used census and survey data for 1940, 1950, 1960, 1970, 1980, and 1989 in developing the first-ever statistics using children as the unit of analysis to chart a wide array of family and economic changes that affected children from the Great Depression through the 1800s. For a detailed description and analysis of reasons for these changes see Hernandez (1993a). For a summary of this research see Hernandez (1994).

For implications especially for young children and early childhood programs see Hernandez (1995). For extensions of this research see Hernandez (1996; 1997).

2. For recent studies of the effects for children of poverty and economic inequality, see Duncan and Brooks-Gunn (1997).

3. Sorensen (1995) estimates that 1.4 million people would be lifted out of poverty by a perfect child-support system. In personal communication, Sorensen provided an estimate that these people live in 0.4 million families. If there were one adult in each of these families, that is, 0.4 million adults, than the number of children in these families would be 1.0 million. Since some of these families have additional adults, typically because the mother has (re)married and a stepfather is in the home, the estimate of 1.0 million children lifted out of poverty is somewhat too high.

9

S. S. Gustafsson
F. P. Stafford

Equity-Efficiency Tradeoffs and Government Policy in the United States, the Netherlands, and Sweden

What are the child-development goals of parents and others in the adult community? How might these conflict with their own well being? To help answer these questions we consider differences among the United States, the Netherlands, and Sweden in the provision of child care and support for women's careers. We begin by identifying the diverse goals adults in advanced industrialized countries may have for the development of children and for themselves. The means to achieving

Adapted from Gustafsson, S. S., & Stafford, F. P. (1995). Links between early childhood programs and maternal employment in three countries. *The Future of Children* (Winter) 5(3):161–74, by permission of Center for the Future of Children, The David and Lucile Packard Foundation.

these goals, we will show, are very different from one country to the next and are path dependent, arising from historical differences.

In this chapter we discuss the tradeoffs parents and, more generally, an entire society faces in early-childhood care and education of children. In Section 1 of this chapter we set out a menu of choices facing parents and the larger adult society in caring for children. The main elements of choice relate to the allocation of time and money among children within and across families, and between the well being of the children versus the career of the parents. We also discuss the role of the larger society in transfering resources to the development of young children, given that (1) some parents will fail to act in an altruistic manner toward their children; (2) some parents will have insufficient resources to invest in their children; and (3) investment in children will have external effects, both negative from low levels (criminal behavior) and positive from high levels (the payoff from new technology created by the highly skilled [Stephan, 1996]). Section 2 organizes the material from section 1 in the form of economic models of altruisim, efficiency, and transfers, and section 3 discusses the ways in which the governments of the United States, the Netherlands, and Sweden have interceded in the provision of resources to young children, including those with learning impairments. A main finding is that these three highly industrialized societies have adopted very different policies relating to early childhood. Section 4 then examines some of the major empirical differences among these countries in child care of young children and labor market activity of mothers. A brief conclusion is set out in section 5.

1. Equity Efficiency and Externalities

Parents and policy makers would like to bring up children in an efficient (child development given the available resources) and equitable (fair) manner. This is generally not possible because the most efficient policy would often be at the expense of equity and because it is difficult to know "what works," since efficient child care is part of a large, complex set of choices. In Table 9-1 we present a summary of the conflicts between equity and efficiency in the design of systems of early childhood care and education (Barnett,1993). We distinguish between intrafamily and interfamily effects. The resulting four kinds of effects then become twelve by virtue of the need to distinguish between differences within the younger generation (child/child), across the generations (child/parent), and within the parental generation (parent/parent).

Table 9-1.
Equity-Efficiency Tradeoffs in Child Development

	Intrafamily		Interfamily	
	Equity	Efficiency	Equity	Efficiency
Child/Child	More able siblings vs. less able siblings Child with disabilities vs. "normal" siblings Male vs. female children	Human capital enhancement vs. monetary/financial transfers Efficiency costs of the intrafamily equity tax	Poor and working-class children vs. middle-class children Transfers to famillies of children with disabilities	Cost-effective child development Sufficient resources to children in poverty
Child/Parent	Parent's time input in child development vs. parent's need for child-free time (work and leisure) Resources for children vs. consumption of adults	Input of parent's time vs. inputs of experts in child development and education Opportunity costs of parent's time (work, investment in parent's human capital) vs. child development through parent's time	Transfers to single-parent families Subsidized child care Paid parental leaves	Optimal populatin growth Demand for parent's time outside home Returns to human capital investments of parents
Parent/Parent	Division of work between husband and wife Bargaining over time use and expenditure between husband and wife	Gains through investment in specialized human capital	Poor and working-class parents vs. middle-class parents Men vs. women: alimony, widow's pensions, displaced-homemakers insurance	Lost productivity from social stratification vs. human capital investment not passing cost-benefit test

To begin the discussion consider the child/child choices in row 1 of Table 9-1. The intrafamily resource allocation to children can be simultaneously egalitarian and efficient if the siblings are equally able to augment their capacities through investments in their human capital and parents invest sufficiently. But suppose one of two siblings has a serious disability, such as mental retardation (columns 1 and 2). If parents care about equal outcomes for the children they may invest more in the child with a disability. If so, siblings of children with disabilities may get less schooling and other resources than otherwise. We refer to this as an intrafamily "equity tax" on the more able sibling.

From the interfamily perspective (columns 3 and 4), suppose an equity goal is to offset the low well being of children in poor families. While this may be seen as purely an equity move, there are important efficiency aspects. The payoff to added resources beyond those of the family can be higher for children in poor families. One key question that arises is whether the transfer should be in the form of cash to the parents or resources in kind directly to the child. If the parents are informed altruists this choice may be unimportant. However, suppose all parents are informed about how to provide inputs to a child with disabilities, but some parents are selfish. An in-kind transfer will have the advantage that altruists will behave in the same way as if they received cash, but non-altruists will be constrained to do more than they otherwise would. Nondisabled siblings can also benefit from the transfer, so that sufficient resources to children in poverty will provide interfamily efficiency gains more as indicated in Table 9-1, column 4. Transfer of resources to the family via a social insurance mechanism will reduce the equity tax and provide more resources to this child, an illustration of how a policy with an equity motivation can have positive efficiency effects.

Parental transfers, particularly to children with disabilities are possibly more efficient in a form other than human investment, but many parents act and social programs are often designed to create more human wealth as the equity mechanism. As we will see in our inventory of programs below, there are strong differences across countries in this respect. In general, a system of family and social insurance with a very egalitarian view will deliver less resources to the more able and this might lead to underdevelopment of a country's research and development potential and at the same time support human investments beyond the range passing a cost-benefit test. To conclude our remarks on the child/child effects of Table 9-1, it is important to note that when some parents are poor, family reciprocal altruism across generations (as suggested by economic theory) may not be a viable mechanism to insure efficient investment across children of given ability in different families. In section 2 we will consider this issue again incorporating the role of liquidity contraints, uncertainty about the investment outcome, and the robustness of reverse transfers back to the parent.

The second type of equity-efficiency tradeoff is between the child and the parent, particularly the mother. One of the issues raised by feminists is the need for time away from young children, while traditional views have often emphasized the idea that the mother be available to meet the needs of the children twenty-four hours per day. The latter ideology has dominated the Netherlands until very recently, and Dutch feminists have spoken against this "duty of presence" assumption, although some Dutch feminists accept the duty of presence but (in the spirit of equity as much as efficiency!) want to share it with the father of the child in equal proportion (Droogleever Fortuijn, 1993, Pott-Buter, 1995). The debate over this involves issues of gender and child/parent equity[1] but also relates to often implicit beliefs about the productivity of mother's time relative to other caregivers. Specially, to what extent are trained care givers as effective or more effective in developing a child's capabilities?

All industrial countries have installed universal basic public education under the assumption that schoolteachers are needed for the development of childrens' skills. The question then becomes what mix of mother's time and expert's time is most efficient at different ages of the child? Economic logic says that this also depends on the opportunity cost of the mother's time in relation to the cost and productivity of specialized care givers. The former, in turn, depends on the wage rate and the marginal investment value of on-the-job training. The view taken by Swedish politicians has been that trained specialists are more effective than parents over a wide range of circumstances. It is clear from the writings of Alva Myrdal (Myrdal and Myrdal, 1934) that she believed experts to be more capable of contributing to child development than mothers beyond a very early age. This belief as well as its influence on Swedish politics over time has not been always positive according to Hirdman (1989). Also in Swedish politics since Myrdal there is a belief that some parents will not behave altruisitically, and equalization of developmental outcomes is more likely when the state intercedes.

The role of opportunity costs in the above choice is highlighted by situations of rising unemployment and declining demand for market labor. Under such conditions public debate and public policy initiatives tend to idealize the mother's parenting role (as during the Great Depression), while in situations of "labor shortage" (such as during World War II and the European postwar boom), there are proposals that more resources be made available for public child care. In the United States during the Great Depression, public funds for child care were made available to supply jobs for unemployed teachers, cooks, nurses, and nutritionists. (Getis & Vinovskis, 1992). However, when in 1939 to 1940, employment increased, child care funds from the Works Progress Administration were withdrawn. As the United States entered World War II there arose a new reason for subsidizing child care: mothers were needed in the war economy, and the Lanahan Act succeeded in enrolling large numbers of children, despite limited funds. In comparing recent Swedish and Dutch history, the "shortage" of labor in Sweden has made it easier to argue for public day care, whereas high unemployment in the Netherlands has fostered the common belief that increased female labor-force participation would only exacerbate the difficulty of finding work.

High opportunity costs of children should lead some women to choose voluntary childlessness or delay births to the point where biological factors limit fertility. Government policy then often centers on creating fertility incentives. Concerns over low fertility motivated Alva and Gunnar Myrdal (Myrdal and Myrdal, 1934) to argue for transfers to families with children as a way of decreasing the costs of children. To discourage fertility, policies have tried to provide incentives not to have children in developing countries and for low-wage populations in the United States by direct compensation (or reducing a preexisting level of child-dependent compensation such as AFDC) or by increasing the labor-market opportunites of young women. As discussed below, Sweden has a policy in which benefits depend on having children and working in the market jointly, which explains the high labor-force participation rates in conjunction with high fertility rates (Sundström and Stafford, 1992).

The fourth column in Table 9-1 highlights the external effects from children. Optimal population growth often depends on whether positive external or negative congestion effects result from denser population. Another external effect arises from antisocial behavior. In a simple consumer choice perspective, all benefits and costs of children go to the parents as buyers of a consumer durable in a stable family arrangement (Rosen, 1995), and governments will therefore cause deadweight losses through any policy affecting child care. In fact we know that parental investments in children and education have strong external effects (see Barnett chapter, this volume). The overwhelming majority of U.S. youth who end up in prison have less than a high-school education. An important example of positive external effects is in the role of a small number of very capable people in creating science and technology (Stephan, 1996) which, in turn, promotes economic growth in an only partially appropriable way (Romer, 1990).

Table 9-1 indicates possible equity and efficiency tradeoffs between men and women. We note that one question in this broad area is the potential efficiency gain from specialization between the husband and wife (Becker, 1981), which could lead to market activity by only one spouse (the husband?) while the other (the wife?) specializes in child care and other non market work. This result is modified by numerous factors, ranging from discrimination in the market to marriage matches between men and women with similar preferences for shared consumption (importantly including children and their development). Time-use panel research indicates some role for both division of labor (specialization) and family public goods (shared consumption). Stable marriages are more likely those where the husband and wife spend time in separate housework activites but more time together in leisure activities, ranging from active sports to socializing, and even to watching television together (Hill & Juster, 1985).

Recently, a great deal of work has explored the bargaining approach to marital relations and indicates that market income (Ott, 1992) and resources available to each spouse contingent upon separation shape the intrafamily division of resources between married couples. Under these conditions public child care creates a type of insurance for mothers as well as strengthening their bargaining position. This appears to be one of the reasons for more equal division of housework in Swedish families (Juster & Stafford, 1991; Flood and Gråsjö, 1995). An illustration of how child-care arrangements interrelate to other areas of family life, including government policies, is the abolition of widow pensions in Sweden (except for transitionary regulations applying to older women). Widows pensions were abolished because over 85 percent of adult women are in the labor force, a result of policies designed to encourage market work which we will highlight in sections 3 and 4.

2. Economic Models of Child-care and Career Choices of Adults

To evaluate the diverse and changing approaches to child development and labor-market activity of parents, particularly women, it is essential to have some analytical framework. In the past twenty years there has been extensive modeling of household choices of marriage, fertility, child care and altruism, market career dynamics, division of labor, and intrafamily bargaining and incentives. Much of this work was contributed by Becker (1981). We utilize this work to frame the issues from section 1 on equity and efficiency in the well being of parents and children and show how these connect to policies of different countries. The set of issues involving these questions is complex, and for this reason alone we would expect societies to have found quite different approaches to dealing with the same questions.

There is a substantial body of economic literature that investigates how families and other institutions operate to "produce" human capital and achieve some measure of equity in child development. It has been suggested that parents "try both to allocate resources equally between their children and to compensate, to some extent, for the handicaps of the children with lower natural endowments" (Griliches, 1979). It has also been argued that parents and children behave in a mutually altruistic manner (Becker, 1981). If this is so, the family is a central institution for the study of equity and efficiency. In this section we present two highly stylized models to illustrate these issues. In some instances, family altruism can create efficient outcome across families; in other instances, family behavior to achieve equity appears to be at odds with efficiency.

Intrafamily Allocation of Resources to Siblings and the "Equity Tax"

The first model is presented in Figure 9-1, which depicts parents choices for allocating resources between two siblings. Consider the simple linear relations for "production" of child development for two siblings:

$$(1) \; k_1 = a_{01} + a_{11}c_1$$
$$k_2 = a_{02} + a_{12}c_2$$

where total child development $K = k_1 + k_2$ is produced with resources to children $Z = c_1 + c_2$. The k_i represent the children's respective developmental outcomes and the c_i are the respective inputs of parental time and other developmental inputs. If one child is more able ($a_{01} > a_{02}$) and has greater ability to learn ($a_{11} > a_{12}$), then the production possibilities are represented in Figure 9-1. Suppose parents are concerned with maximizing total child development, K, irrespective of how it is shared between the two children of Figure 9-1. Then child development indifference contours are simply linear with a slope of −1 as with line BC' in Figure 9-1, and the chosen point would be B, where all resources go to the more able sibling. This is one point on the indifference curve BC' which can be reached along the production frontier BC. Of course one could use a more plausible production frontier (one which was "bowed out" and did not allow such extreme specialization of resources), but here we wish to motivate thinking on the subject and simply highlight differing parental choices between efficiency and equity.

Suppose in Figure 9-1 that the parents seek some form of equity for the siblings. One definition of equity is that there be equal inputs, which for the resource level Z implies an outcome at point D. Alternatively, equity can be defined as the parents' preference for equal outcomes. Such cases can be represented by indifference curves with a slope of −1 at the point where they cross the 45° line. As represented in Figure 9-1, we have the case where equal outcomes would obtain only if the slope of the opportunity set were $(-a_{11}/a_{12})$ −1 as well (point S).[2] When one child has learning limits relative to the other, families will only partly equalize outcomes. If we thought of successively smaller values of a_{12}, the choices would trace out a locus such as SS". Only if they are concerned with equity on an absolute basis (with fixed proportion indifference curves) would they fully equalize outcomes (SS' along the 45° line). In each of these three representations (at D, along SS' or along SS") we can think of the more able child as subject to an intersibling "equity tax": the more limited one sibling's ability or ability to learn, the less of a given amount of resources (Z) devoted to the other's development.

Resources to Children and Parents by Families and Through Social Insurance

The second model is presented in Figure 9-2. It represents the choices the parents face in using resources for the child or for themselves in acheiving different levels of their well being. To illustrate some of the conceptual issues as a prelude to understanding differences in social policy and family behavior, we begin with the notion of reciprocal altruism (Becker, 1981, p. 198) between parents and their children.[3] Reciprocal altruism implies a type of equity. In Figure 9-2 we have indifference curves between well being of the parent (P) and the child (C), which have a slope of −1 at the point where they cross the 45° line. Reciprocal altruists both prefer that the

Figure 9-1.
Intersibling Equity Tax

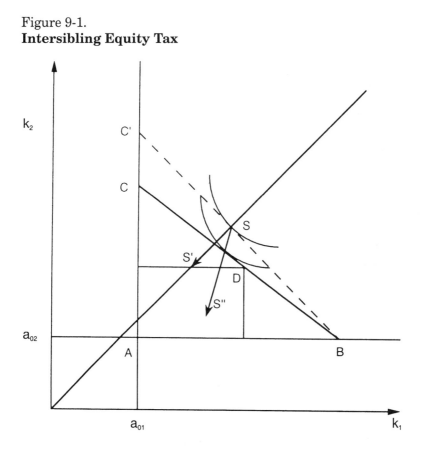

other be at the same level of well being and in our idealized world would not act opportunistically if getting to the 45° line (i.e., equality) required transfers between them and extended through time.

The investment of parental time and other resources in children involves a reduction in parental resources. In Figure 9-2, poorer parents are closer to the origin, and the richer the parent the greater the distance from the origin. Along the P-axis is the level of resources available to a parent. By investing in the human capital of the child, resources to the child rise, but at a decreasing rate, as represented by the curves rising to the northwest from the horizontal axis. At some point the parental transfer of resources to the child is more efficiently accomplished by nonhuman investment, as represented by the dashed lines with a slope of –1, suggesting a zero

Figure 9-2.
Child Development and the Distribution of Well Being over Children and Parents

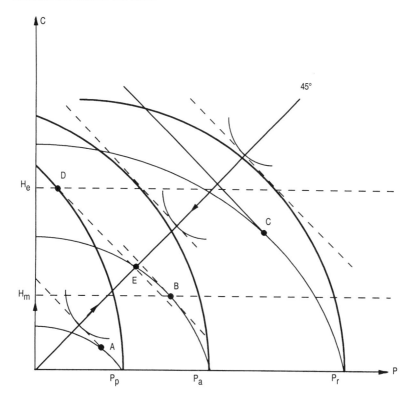

interest reference case, so that simple transfers and nonhuman investment can be represented jointly. In a rich family of reciprocal altruists (P_r, the parent would invest in the human capital of the child with own time or market inputs to the level H_e,[4] and beyond this would "give" resources to the child in the form of financial/ monetory investment (the point where the indifference curve is tangent to the 45° line).

Average-income (P_a) and poor (P_p) parents would (as drawn) invest in the human capital of a child of the same ability to the same extent, provided that reciprocal altruism exists (and that these rich and poor parents have equal parenting skills or can hire specialists such as school teachers to achieve equal effectiveness). In this case they would "sacrifice" to invest to the same level, H_e, with the expectation that the child would return the favor with a reciprocal transfer later in life. In the case of poor parents this reverse transfer would end up being quite large, namely DE, testing the limits of the system and occuring less commonly. An illustration of this is the sports star who transfers resources to the parents who made success possible.

If reciprocal altruism is sufficiently pervasive it has two elements to sustain it. First, as noted by Becker, families practicing reciprocal altruism could be expected to have stronger survival value in terms of influence, if not numbers. Second, from a social perspective there is efficiency in the conventional economic definition. Children of equal ability receive equal investment so that marginal returns on human investment across children are equal and equal the marginal return on financial/monetory investment.

We have seen that one type of equity, reciprocal altruism in the family, can be compatible with normal concepts of efficiency or social welfare. Does this extend more generally or is there a tradeoff between efficiency and equity under other conditions? Does the equity tax and efficiency loss in Figure 9-1 reappear in some other form? We argue that it does. Consider the case where some children have less developmental potential as represented by the thinner curves originating at P_r, P_a, and P_p. Efficiency requires a smaller investment in such children, and a rich parent would invest less in human capital and more in financial/monetary capital, as represented by the solid line with the slope of -1 from point C in Figure 9-2. Over some range this may be seen as "acceptable." Now consider the situation of a poor parent with a child with pronounced learning problems or physical disabilities. On their own, and under reciprocal altruism, the result raises two obvious equity concerns.

First, if the parents and children act as efficient reciprocal altruists, the equilibrium could be a child well being below some socially acceptable minimum, H_m,[5] and, the parents will be subject to a type of interfamily equity tax (relative to other parents) in their effort to improve their child's well being. Social insurance programs can be developed in an effort to boost the child's well being toward and beyond H_m. These use public funds to allow the parent to move in tandem with the child northwesterly along the 45° line. Important issues for the design of such social programs include whether parental earnings potential and child development skills are positively correlated and the extent to which specialists in child development and education can help children overcome developmental problems, particularly for children with the most disabilities. Where experts are perceived or known to be effective, publicly provided education (such as special-education programs or Head Start in the United States) provides both a more efficient production of human capital *and* a well-being transfer to parents of such children. Another possibility is to provide services intended to boost the parents' income, as with public programs for employment-related training for disadvantaged parents. In the United States as in the Netherlands there has been a growing belief that publicly sponsored jobs training for poor parents will allow the families (both parents and children) to improve their well being substantially.

The purpose of our highly stylized models in Figures 9-1 and 9-2 is to set out some of the main elements in the intergenerational production and distribution of well being. Clearly the approach is oversimplified, but it still characterizes some of the complex and conflicting elements in the overall picture. Some conflict between equity and efficiency seems inherent. As Tinbergen (1975, p. 133) suggests when maximizing social welfare subject to the constraint of equity—"every additional restriction will lead to lower social welfare."[6] In this context, the efficient altruist model above seems more likely to be the exception than the rule. Moreover, because of the system's complexity and the difficulty of knowing the "parameters" of the system, different industrialized countries are likely to "solve" the puzzle in ways consistent with more general beliefs or practices shaped by their own particular history and culture.

The potential for a positive contribution for social science is both to show logically and quantitatively how the system "works" and to show that certain relationships, while not governed by precisely known parameters, depend on some approximate values of parameters. To illustrate the point about uncertain system design, public and social scientists in Sweden generally believe that specialists can facilitate child development as well or better than parents of most children age two to four, while their counterparts in the Netherlands do not. Public policy discussion in the United States has centered on the role of family values, and has both implicitly assumed the effectiveness of family altruism and exhorted that it be more widely practiced. Knowledge of how family altruism operates and how effective it is should inform the debate.

3. Models of Government Behavior

Countries differ dramatically in the overall approach to preschool child care and other investments in the development of young children. In some, such as Britain and particularly the United States, the primary and nearly full responsibility is the parents'. In others, such as Sweden, government plays a much larger role. These differences have been characterized as different child-care regimes (Gustafsson & Stafford, 1994; Gustafsson, 1994; Esping-Andersen, 1990). According to Esping-Andersen (1990), welfare states can only be understood through their historical ideology, and the ideological legacy shapes the present-day actions of policy makers. He distinguishes three types or clusters of capitalist welfare states: the liberal or residualist, the conservative or corporatist, and the social democratic or institutional. We use Esping-Andersen's typology to explain some of the differences in child care provision and subsidization and the possible effects on labor supply of mothers with young children comparing Sweden, the Netherlands, and the United States. Whereas Esping-Andersen worked out his typology mainly for pensions, health security, and the creation of jobs in the public sector, it is in this chapter shown to perform as well in the domain of child care.

Three Different Policy Regimes

The three types of welfare states are not to be seen as clear cases but rather as a continuum, where one country has more elements of one of the three types of welfare states than of the other two types. Moreover, economic evaluation of specific elements of the systems sharpens the picture of the differences.

The *liberal welfare state* is characterized by a belief that the unfettered market brings welfare to the maximum number of citizens. Only if the market fails does the state intervene with welfare benefits, which are typically means tested and often carry a social stigma. This type of welfare state can therefore also be labeled the *residual* welfare state. The United States is the prototype of the liberal or residual welfare state, but Canada and Australia are also included in this category by Esping-Andersen (1990, p. 27).

The second cluster of welfare states are shaped by a *corporatist* statist legacy with a strong influence by the church. Welfare provisions are typically organized along occupational lines often with preferential treatment of civil servants. The family bread-winner is the welfare recipient often excluding married women from any right of their own to pensions or unemployment benefits. Esping-Andersen (1990, p. 27) mentions Austria, France, Germany, and Italy as belonging to this group, and his prototype country, which he analyzes in more detail, is Germany.

The third category is the social democratic or *institutional* welfare state. The most prototypical social democratic state is Sweden, but the other Nordic countries (Denmark, Norway, and Finland) are also included. Perhaps the most salient characteristic of the social democratic regime is its fusion of welfare and work. It is at once committed to a full-employment guarantee and entirely dependent on its attainment (Esping-Andersen, 1990, p. 28). In the social democratic welfare state, welfare provisions are institutional, seldom means tested, and more often apply to all citizens alike.

Sweden and the United States are the prototypes used by Esping-Andersen but the Netherlands, although included in his list of conservative, corporatist welfare states, may not fully match the idealized corporatist welfare state in Esping-Andersen's sense. An essential feature of this type of welfare state, besides its corporatist statist legacy, is the influence of the church. In analyzing the historical origins of the welfare state in the Netherlands, Dutch social scientists have emphasized the importance of 'pillarization' (*verzuiling*) (Stuurman, 1993). By this expression is meant a society organized along confessional lines where Roman Catholics and Calvinists made up the two most important pillars or columns, and later socialists formed a separate column of their own. The pillars created their own play schools, primary schools, secondary schools, universities, radio stations, newspapers, labor unions, and political parties. Because of pillarization a Roman Catholic seldom made friends with a fundamentalist Calvinist, and only at the very top level was there negotiation between groups. Rival churches have therefore shaped Dutch society and are primarily responsible for promoting the breadwinner ideology. This ideology is negative toward female labor-force participation, and its legacy still characterizes Dutch society to a great extent. Therborn (1989) contrasts the backgrounds of the Swedish and the Dutch welfare states by pointing to popular movements (*folkrörelser*) in Sweden and the pillarization (*verzuiling*) in the Netherlands. He also emphasizes the Roman Catholic influence in particular (pp. 210–11) and explains how a weak state was only "subsidiary" to the pillar led by a strong clergy in organizing welfare for members of their own pillar.

The Shaping of Different Early Childhood Policies

In Table 9-2 public policies in the area of early child development are summarized in an attempt to compare them across the countries on the topics of health care, parental leave, day care for preschool children, short-term extrafamily care, and school and after-school care for young school children. In this section we will compare the solutions to the equity/efficiency problems discussed in Figures 9-1 and 9-2 and Table 9-1 above that policy makers have attempted in the different countries. One of the problems addressed above is the potential equity tax that a sibling of a child with a disability may have to suffer from in the intra family resource allocation. This is one reason for identifying the needs that children with special problems may have and contrasting them to the needs that other children may have. With the help of Figure 9-2, it was shown that if children and parents were reciprocal altruists the parents would transfer resources to the child in early childhood and the child would transfer resources back to the parent in old age so that the outcome would be equity in the child/parent dimension seen over the entire lifetime.

In Figure 9-1 we showed the equity problem that parents with children of different abilities face. If they have a preference for equal outcomes between the siblings the more able child will be negatively affected since he/she will get less resources than other children and will be paying an "equity tax" to the less able sibling. Also the parent of a child with special needs may find it extremely difficult to get child-free time unless there is government-supported care available and will have to pay an individual "equity tax." Generally speaking, over the different policy areas that we consider in Table 9-2, the United States interferes the least in resource allocation of parents and children, whereas the Netherlands and Sweden interfere much more but with different intentions. Dutch policies intend to increase welfare of children but implicitly assume the alternative time use of mothers to be less important. In contrast, Swedish policies aim to bring all women and men into the labor force because this is seen as the only way of fully participating in society. To have a job in Sweden is a social right and, some have argued, a requirement.

In the United States, tax money is not used for health care of most preschool children, whereas such policies started to become available in the Netherlands as far back as the year 1900 and in the late 1930s gradually became available in Sweden. A purpose has been to discover health problems as early as possible as well as to check the living conditions of the newborn child and to monitor physical development. From an efficiency point of view, early discovery of problems may inhibit later and much more costly problems. The public Swedish health clinics also give health care to pregnant women, prepare them and their husbands for parenthood,

Table 9-2.
Public Programs for Young Children in the United States, the Netherlands, and Sweden

	United States		The Netherlands		Sweden	
	All children	Children with problems	All children	Children with problems	All children	Children with problems
Health care	Free vaccination Medicaid: 133% of poverty line	Head Start since 1965, 250,000 children Child Care Food Program Free education: 500,000 children with disabilities age three to five	Health clinics for children (*consultatiebureaus*): 98% of newborns, 75% of four year olds since 1990[a]	RIAGG Regional Institution for Ambulatory Mental Health Care; forty-two bureaus covering the whole country	Health clinics for children (*mödra-och barna vård centraler*) since 1930s	Interdisciplinary youth habilitation groups supplied by secondary communities[i]
Parental leave	Individual worker-employer agreements Unpaid dependent care	AFDC for poor single mothers since 1960 1996 welfare reform sets time limits on assistance SSI low-income children with disabilities Food stamps	Paid maternal leave sixteen weeks, 1990 Right for either parent to work part time six months since 1990		Paid parental leaves fifteen months before child is eight Occasional care max. 120 days until child is twelve Six-hour work day until child is eight	Paid parental leaves fifteen months occasional care until child is sixteen Six-hour work day until child is eight Both parents to instruction on child's disability[i]
Day care for preschool children	Child-care tax credit Parents deduct actual child-care expenses No subsidies for centers Some state and federal subsidies to poor preschool children	1990 child care bill for states subsidizes individual children[g] Title XX subsidizes individual children[g] 1996 consolidated programs into Child Care Development Fund	Day-care centers: 2% of children 0–4 in 1990[a] 268 centers in 1987[b] 614 centers in 1990[c]	110 medical day-care centers: 3,500 children Twenty-five centers for children with hearing problems Day care for children with motor disturbance: 1,200 children	Day-care centers (*daghem*): 34% of all children 0–6, 1990[d] Preschool teacher education required[e] Family day care: 14% of all children 0–6 in 1990[d]	Priority to day care, often with personal care for the handicapped child[i] Substitute care given in the child's home so that parents can attend to sibling's needs[i]

Table 9-2. *(continued)*
Public Programs for Young Children in the United States, the Netherlands, and Sweden

	United States		The Netherlands		Sweden	
	All children	Children with problems	All children	Children with problems	All children	Children with problems
Short-term, extra-family care			Play schools (*peuterpeelzalen*) two to three hours a day: one-third of two to three-year-old children covered in 1991[b] Personnel sometimes unpaid No special education required Toy libraries (*speelotheken*): educational bureaus offering coffee mornings for mothers, 1970s Special home training in how to play with child, from 1970s[b]	Home training for parents from ethnic minorities and for parents with mentally handicapped children[b] Play groups for disadvantaged children[b]	Part-day care groups (*deltidsförskola*): 8% of all children 0–6 in 1990[d] Open preschool (*öppna förskolar*) for children who do not have a space in a child-care center with preschool teachers[dc]	Special care during school vacations for handicapped children so that parents can continue working[i]
Young school children and after-school care	Universal public education age six, including lunch hour Universal kindergarten from age five, mostly half day	Medicaid up to poverty line	School starts at age four, not including lunch hour 12–2 and after-school care from 3 or 4 p.m.[b]	Several thousand children in training for language and speech problems in 1993[a] Children with visual problems: home-based guidance for a few hundred, 1993[a]	School starts at age seven, optionally at six, since 1993 All-day school day (*samman hållen skilday*) since 1974[d]	Priority to after-school care, often with personal care for the handicapped child[i] Pupils' homes (*elevhem*) for four youths in ordinary housing area[i]

Table 9-2. (*continued*)
Public Programs for Young Children in the United States, the Netherlands, and Sweden

United States		The Netherlands		Sweden	
All children	Children with problems	All children	Children with problems	All children	Children with problems
			Fifteen different parents' organizations for children with different handicaps[a]	Before- and after-school care centers (*fritidshem*) covering 35% of seven to nine year olds, plus 14% of seven to nine year olds in family after-school care, in 1990[d]	

Sources:
a. Hermanns, de Boer, & Kruidenier-Bron (1993)
b. Singer (1992)
c. Tijdens and Lieon (1993)
d. Knutsen (1991)

e. Knutsen (1992)
f. Gustafsson & Stafford (1994)
g. Lamb, Sternberg, & Ketterlinus (1992)
i. SOU (1991) no. 46

and give new mothers contraceptive advice. The Swedish mother and child health clinics are an outcome of the Myrdals' analysis and political activities in the 1930s for planned parenthood and improved child quality, including health of the children. All three countries have special health-care resources for children with problems, although in the United States access is largely dependent on parental income. In contrast, in the Netherlands and Sweden special health-care resources are made available to children who have specific identified handicaps regardless of family income. Among the most important of the U.S. programs is Head Start, which gives health care and early education to disadvantaged children.

The Head Start program originated in 1965 and departs from the U.S. norm in that in-kind support is given directly to children in the form of community-based provision of comprehensive educational, social and health services. About half a million families participate each year in the 1990s. The continued support for Head Start rests on several premises, based on our discussion above. First, the idea that specialists are more productive is supported by studies that show that early education alumni do better, by an amount passing the cost-benefit test (Barnett, 1993). Second, in line with our discussion in section 2, it is implicitly assumed that the parents would not (or could not, given their incomes) act altruistically to the point where simply transfering the same dollar resources to them would lead to nearly as much incremental spending on such child-development activities. In addition to the Head Start program, the Child Care Food program provides in-kind help by paying for the meals of low-income children, and other programs buy child-care slots for poor children.

The most prominent difference between the United States and the other two countries is that much less tax money is spent. There are a variety of programs—federal, state, and local—to aid poor families, but the idea of not using tax money to pay for people who are able to pay for themselves is present at all levels. Medicaid is a federal program that pays for all health care for children under age six and pregnant women up to 133 percent of the poverty line and for children aged six to twelve if family income is below the poverty line (to be extended to age twenty-one by the year 2001). Medicaid also provides early and period screening diagnosis and treatment services for low-income children. Under the Individuals with Disabilities Act (IDEA-Part B) all children with disabilities aged three to five are entitled to a free appropiate education (417,346 children in 1993). Although Head Start serves more children, this program is much more expensive. Also children with disabilities from birth to age three are entitled to therapies, and there is parent training. One consequence of the various entitlements is that disagreements emerge over who should pay for services that could be construed as either medical or education: should it be paid by private insurance, medicaid, some other government agency, or the public schools?

In both the Netherlands and Sweden health problems of children with disabilities are the responsibility of society as a whole, and the Dutch RIAGGs as well as the Swedish interdisciplinary youth habilitation groups are basically financed by tax money. The ambitious goals of Swedish policies toward children with disabilities are to permit both the children and their families to lead a normal life (SOU, 1991, no. 46). Parents, both mothers and fathers, are to be allowed to pursue their labor-market careers. The child, it is believed, must get the best possible specialist care with an individually tailored plan for medical and pedagogical advancement. The child is to be integrated into society, go to school like other children, and eventually be given suitable employment. Housing is to be in a normal housing area with a personal assistant (if so required) and all technical equipment that facilitates for the individual to lead a normal life—free of charge. A disability is determined relative to the damage or sickness in relation to the environment (SOU, 1991, no. 46, p. 22). If the goal of a normal life is successfully achieved, the equity tax of Figure 9-1 will be paid by the government and not by a sibling or the parents. Alternatively, these transfers to children with disabilities and their parents can be thought of as a form of social insurance (Varian, 1990), protecting the family against the losses associated with the birth of a child with disability. It is estimated that 1.5 percent of children and youth ages to nineteen years, about 30,000 individuals, have disabilities such that they can count on support according to the 1992 Act of Special Support and Service to Persons with Functioning Disabilities (SOU, 1991, no. 46, p. 145). Comparing Sweden and the Netherlands there is additionally substantial expert support free of charge for Dutch children with disabilities. The big difference between Sweden and the Netherlands is that there is no intention to substitute for the mother in caring for Dutch children.

Generally, Holland differs from Sweden in that the mother is assumed to be as much or more efficient than trained care givers in the case of children with normal learning abilities. In contrast to the public day-care programs of Sweden, where special training is required, it is still customary for some of the personnel in day-care centers to be unpaid voluntary workers (*vrijwilligerswerk*). In contrast to the case of normal children, the Dutch government spends a great deal on children with learning problems. To illustrate, there were 110 medical day-care centers in 1993 serving 3,850 children with disabilities (Hermanns, de Boer, and Kruidenier-Bron, 1993). Also persons of all ages with disabilities get devices such as wheelchairs and the like free of charge (as in Sweden). In the case of children with special needs the mother is expected to bring the child to the specialist or the specialist goes to her home to train her. The system has a wide array of specialists with a result that help for children with disabilities is fragmented, especially at the diagnostic stage where children and their mothers have to visit a large number of different experts who may offer widely differing opinions. One concern the Dutch have over this system is that 90 percent of state outlays for children with disabilities is spent on institutions rather than on educating the parents to be more effective (Hermans and Hol, 1992).

The ideology of mothering as a full-time job is very strong in the Netherlands. Even Dutch feminists (Droogleever Fortuijn 1993; Pott-Buter, 1995) have little understanding of the Swedish reliance on subsidized day care. Instead the goal is a symmetric, family-oriented model where both the mother and the father work part-time and take turns in the home. This complies with the enduring idea of parenting as a full-time job modernized to be carried out half the time by each parent. The U.S. view on the role of mothers in the early education of their children resembles the Dutch view in several respects. Head Start and early-childhood special-education programs are not designed to accomodate a working mother's needs, and the AFDC program (Aid for Parents with Dependent Children) gave a subsidy to single mothers, which is income tested. In 1996, the Personal Responsibility and Work Opportunity Reconciliation Act fundamentally altered policy toward single mothers, devolving authority to state governments, limiting recipient time, and offering training, retraining, child-care, and public work and help to find absent (nonaltruistic) fathers and make them contribute to the childrens' support.

The means by which Swedish parents are assumed to take an active role in and have an influence on their childrens' development and combine this with their social right/obligation to perform market work are given by the extensive rights to parental leaves for newborn children and occasional leaves for sickness and contact days. Contact days are meant for parents to have contact with the child's other care giver, visiting the day-care center or primary school two days a year. The legislation assumes that both parents of a child with a disability have careers and that without external support many would be forced to give up their careers. External support, as suggested in Table 9-2, should be extensive enough to facilitate dual careers and a high standard of family well being (SOU, 1991, no. 46, p. 157). Care during school vacations and substitute care given in the home of children with disabilities at times during night hours, are seen as allowing parents to devote time to siblings who otherwise often will not get enough attention from parents (SOU, 1991, no. 46, p. 176). These policies both offset the equity tax, which would otherwise be borne by the sibling (as explained in Figure 9-1), and represent a solution to the child/child- equity problem laid out in Table 9-1. This policy also reflects the premise that professional care givers are effective as substitutes for mothers.

The Dutch view that parenting is a full-time job and the Swedish view that both parents have equal responsibilities in care and a right to a market job are visible in the different ways the two countries have organized public efforts in the education of young children. Until recently there has been virtually no extrafamily full day-care in the Netherlands, but public support has gone into part-day play schools. Also, primary school (which is universal from age four) does not include the lunch hours, and school hours are determined individually by each school. The result is that if two siblings go to different schools there may be eight trips a day for the mother to bring children in the morning, take them home for lunch, bring them to school in the afternoon and take them home after school. To solve this mother-as-a-chauffeur problem, Sweden decided on the continuous school day (*sammanhållen skoldag*) in 1974. Practically, this means that all children go to school all weekdays at 8 o'clock and that schools have obligations to supply activities for the children during breaks in the regular instruction. All schoolwork including individual work (or what would be homework in U.S. schools) should take place at school, particularly for younger children.

As a consequence of the Swedish view that productivity in caring for all children can be enhanced by expertise, there have long been educational requirements for personnel who have jobs in day-care centers. Knutsen (1991, p. 77) cites a government report from 1943 where the requirement of a two-year training program for day-care workers was formulated. Ambitious pedagogical goals for children in daycare were formulated in a 1972 government report that was used in the instruction of preschool teachers and child-minders, the two types of personnel employed in Swedish day-care (Knutsen, 1991). By way of contrast, Singer (1992) reports that as late as 1984, two-fifths of the day-care centers in the Netherlands relied to some extent on unpaid workers. Moreover, no specialized education or expertise was required to become a day-care worker. It is still quite common to hear Dutch people express the view that caring for children does not require any specialized education because any mother can do the job.

4. Patterns of Child Care and Employment of Mothers

Hours of market work for mothers of preschool children show distinctly different patterns among the three countries. In Table 9-3 data for Sweden (1984), the Netherlands (1988), and the United States (1988) are presented, using the same definitions—to the extent possible. In the Netherlands the normal pattern is that mothers care for their preschool children themselves at home. Around three-quarters of all mothers do not work at all, and if they do work it is only a few hours in the week, less than half time. In the United States it is more common than in Sweden not to participate in the paid-labor force. Almost half of the U.S. mothers are full-time homemakers compared to less than a third of the Swedish pre-school mothers. From the second year of the child's life the pro-portion of Swedish mothers who are full-time homemakers is only 20 to 25 percent in Sweden as compared to around 40 to 45 percent in the United States. However, the proportion of full-time workers is by far the largest in the United States, where from the second year of life of the child as many as one-third of the mothers work thirty-five hours or more per week. In Sweden the proportion of mothers who are full-time workers never exceeds 26.7 percent during the child's first five years of age, whereas in the United States it increases to 41.2 percent when the child is four to five years old.[7] Full-time working mothers are virtually nonexistant in the Nether-lands, increasing only to 6.8 percent by the time the youngest child reaches four to five years.

A peculiarity of Swedish mothers is that they work twenty to thirty-four hours per week, or "long part-time" rather than no work at all or full-time market work. Working long part time is very uncommon in the Netherlands, and it is also rather uncommon in the United States. The particular work pattern of Swedish mothers is facilitated by public policies, including fifteen months of paid parental leaves, subsidized, community-run day-care centers covering more than half the children two to six years old, and the right to work a six-hour work day until the child is eight years old.

Paid parental leaves in 1988 (Statistics Sweden, 1989) allowed

Table 9-3.
Mothers' Hours per Week of Market Work by Age of Child

Age of youngest child	United States				The Netherlands				Sweden			
	None	1–19	20–34	35+	None	1–19	20–34	35+	None	1–19	20–34	35+
under 1	57.6	8.5	8.5	25.4	74.4	18.2	4.0	3.5	58.8	1.5	17.7	22.1
1	45.1	10.6	10.9	33.3	78.0	16.1	4.3	2.6	20.4	26.5	42.9	10.2
2–3	44.5	5.8	11.2	38.6	73.2	21.2	1.4	4.2	23.9	19.5	39.9	16.8
4–5	36.9	9.7	12.1	41.2	62.1	28.1	2.9	6.8	25.0	13.3	35.0	26.7
0–5	48.4	8.3	10.2	32.9	72.6	20.3	3.2	5.8	31.7	15.4	34.2	18.7

Source: Gustafsson and Stafford (1994). The date are based on our analyses of: National Longitudinal Surveys of Young Women, Age 23–30 as of 1988 (n=2650) for the United States; OSA Survey of Women, Age 18–65 as of 1988 (n=1079) for the Netherlands; and HUS Survey of Women, Age 18–64 as of 1984 (n=379) for Sweden.

around 90 percent of Swedish parents, father or mother, to care for their child until the child is one year old. This contrasts to the situation in the United States where almost one-third of first-time mothers were at work three months after their first child was born (Leibowitz et. al., 1992). The situation regarding child-care for mothers with market work can be summarized as follows in the three countries. In Sweden subsidized, quality, public child-care is virtually universally available, and mothers have jobs. In the United States, there is a market for child-care and mothers to a large extent have jobs. In the Netherlands until recently there has been neither a market nor subsidized child-care, and mothers rarely have had jobs. However the number of mothers with small children who work in the market has been increasing. By 1992, almost 43 percent of mothers of preschool children were labor-force participants (Maassen van den Brink, 1994).

The Childcare Stimulation Act of 1991 in the Netherlands is the first government action that explicitly caters to the needs of the working mother rather than assigning priority to children's educational needs. The 1991 act subsidizes child-care centers and family day-care homes, but excludes (the part-day) play schools from subsidies because they are not meant for the working mother. The new subsidies will increase the proportion of children who are in subsidized child-care from 2 percent to 4 percent. The act has subsequently been extended to 1997 (Tijdens and Lieon, 1993).

Contemporary U.S. policy discussion on day care has focused on market-based expansions of child care with emphasis on family need. The Childcare and Development Block Grant passed by Congress in 1990 authorized new grants to states to fund childcare assistance to low- and moderate-income families, expansion of existing tax credits for low-income parents, and added funding for Head Start (Golonka & Ooms, 1991, cited by Hofferth and Wissoker, 1992). This set of new initiatives can be classified as price reductions, income increases, and subsidies for quality of child care. Consistent with long-standing traditions, these initiatives target low-income families, and the actual services are purchased through the market and not from government providers. For most parents the current U.S. child-care system is a highly diverse market and family-based system. Of employed women with preschool-age children, 30 percent are cared for primarily by a parent, 26 percent in a center, 19 percent in family day care, and 18 percent by relatives other than parents (Hofferth et. al., 1991).

The organization of child care in the United States neatly fits Esping-Andersen's (1990, p. 26) characterization of the liberal welfare state: "Means-tested assistance, modest universal transfers or modest social-insurance plans. Benefits cater mainly to a clientele of low-income, usually working-class, state dependents. In this model, the progress of social reform has been severely circumscribed by traditional, liberal work-ethic norms: it is one where the limits of welfare equal the marginal propensity to opt for welfare instead of work. Entitlement rules are therefore strict and often associated with stigma; benefits are typically modest. In turn, the state encourages the market, either passively—by guaranteeing only a minimum—or actively—by subsidizing private welfare schemes." In the United States there is a market for child care. You get the child care you pay for, and the types and costs of child care as well as its quality differ between families according to their incomes.

The Swedish child-care system fits Esping-Andersen's defining properties of the social democratic welfare state. Child care is universal, at least ideally, though there is rationing of spaces in some communities (Gustafsson and Stafford, 1992). It is used both by the middle class and by the working class, and it is of high quality. Access is not means tested, but parental fees are usually progressive with family income, with parents currently paying, on average, about 12 to 13 percent of total costs. The Swedish day-care system is organized to accomodate the needs of the working mother. To get a place at the child-care center, both parents (or the single parent), must be working or studying at least twenty hours per week. This is an important factor in child-care subsidies' effect on labor supply. Municipalities organize and run the day-care system with funds from the central state and their own income taxation to support day care.

Thus, the Swedish system fuses welfare and market work. It alleviates the financial problems of single motherhood that haunt the United States since virtually every divorced or never-married woman has a job and day care is available for her child. Recent trends, however, threaten to undermine the child-care system. The Social Democrats were out of power from 1991 to 1994, and in 1992 and 1993 Sweden was hit by the most severe economic contraction since the 1930s with open unemployment increasing to 7 percent and an additional 5 percent of the labor force in active labor-market programs in 1995. The municipal monopoly in receiving state subsididies for child-care provision has been abolished, and private organizations now can organize day care and receive a state subsidy. The moderate government of 1991 to 1994 introduced a care allowance and extended a subsidy to nonworking mothers. This was abolished in the fall of 1994 when the Social Democrats regained power. If full employment is not achieved again (and forecasts are gloomy about this), the Swedish welfare state and the provision of day care for all children may be threatened, although there is strong political concensus in favor of public day care.

Although the organization of child care is so different between the United States and Sweden, the patterns of extrafamily day care in the two countries (Table 9-4) show some strong similarities. (Parallel data for the Netherlands were not available to us.) First, the proportion of children for whom no extrafamily care is used decreases with age of child from 43 to 44 percent of the one year olds to 29 to 32 percent of the six year olds. The main difference between the two countries is in the first year of the child's life, when the paid parental leave induces Swedish parents to care for the children themselves at home. In contrast, 49.8 percent of the U.S. children less than one year old are cared for outside the family. Another similarily is in the choice parents from both countries make between a schoollike center versus a more family-like "sitter" case. The proportion in center care increases with age up to 31.2 percent of the six-year-old children in the United States and 40.5 percent in Sweden. It is also clear that the older preschool children in Sweden have a greater chance of getting a space in the subsidized public day care than do younger children, based on the queuing practices when spaces are rationed.

The differences in child-care policy are related to fertility outcomes (Hoem, 1993). The pronatalist elements in the Swedish system have been tied into market work by women. To illustrate, parental leave benefits are strongly related to preleave earnings in the labor market (Sundström and Stafford, 1992). Consequently there are incentives to postpone child bearing until a market career has been established. It is the case that total fertility has been almost as high, and in the 1990s higher, in Sweden than in the United States, but in Sweden the teenage birthrate is low compared to that of older women, the exact opposite of the United States. In the Netherlands total fertility has been low and teenage fertility the lowest in a multicountry comparison (Jones et. al., 1986). Recent research on Swedish fertility shows that the probability of having a child is much higher for more-educated than for less-educated women, controlling for cohort, social background, marital status, and age at first birth (Olah, 1995). Similar results hold for the likelihood of a third birth (Hoem, 1994).

Table 9-4.
Child-Care Mode According to Age of Youngest Child, if Less Than Seven (column percentages)

	Age of Child							
	0 years	1 year	2 years	3 years	4 years	5 years	6 years	all
Sweden								
No child care	90.5	43.3	36.2	36.2	31.2	29.7	32.3	41.8
Private child-care center	1.9	4.9	3.3	2.5	3.2	3.5	3.8	3.4
Private child-care sitter	3.6	10.6	7.0	6.1	6.1	5.6	5.8	6.5
Public child-care center	1.7	22.9	33.2	35.5	39.0	41.8	36.7	30.6
Public child-care sitter	2.2	18.1	20.2	19.6	20.3	19.2	21.3	17.6
TOTAL	100	100	100	100	100	100	100	100
United States								
No child care	49.8	44.0	34.7	31.8	31.9	26.7	29.1	36.3
Private child-care center	5.2	8.8	15.1	24.5	24.8	32.4	31.2	18.7
Private child-care sitter	45.0	47.3	50.3	43.7	43.3	40.9	39.7	45.1
TOTAL	100	100	100	100	100	100	100	100
NUMBERS OF OBSERVATIONS	251	423	372	327	254	225	189	2041

Sources. Sweden: Statistics Sweden (1989); primary source, a special analysis of the 1988 Childcare Survey (Statistics Sweden).
United States: Calculations from NLS-Y, 1988.

5. Conclusion

Child Care in a Changing Economy

The parental generation is assumed to care about the well being and development of the children. Household-level economic models help us understand the important elements of parent behavior and how public policy interacts with parent behavior and the well being of parents and children. First, cognitive and physical skills of children need to be developed. In that development parents face critical questions dealing with efficiency versus equity. Children of the same parents differ in their developmental potential. Parents work to discover particular affinities and abilities of their individual children. One motivation for such a search is to focus resources in a direction where a higher payoff is expected, or an efficiency motivation. Another motivation for such a search is to realize a type of fairness: each child can be regarded as successful in some realm. However, what if one child has a large overall developmental deficit compared to the siblings?

In terms of economic theory one might postulate that the parents could compensate this child by transfer of resources in the form of physical capital or wealth rather than in the form of individual skill or human capital. Perhaps capital transfer is used to some extent and may be important in some cases. We do know that equity appears to be a substantial motivation in many cases. A dramatic example of equity effects occurs when a child has Down Syndrome. Time inputs to child care by parents of children to age three with Down Syndrome is on the order of 26.2 hours of primary child-care time per week compared to 10.1 hours per week for the U.S. national average (Stafford, 1991). Analysis also suggests that the normal siblings receive *less* parental time than they otherwise would.

An important element in child development is the extent to which the family or the state is seen as the key sponsor or provider of developmental resources. The role of the nuclear family is particularly central in the United States, with differences among different subcultures and through time, while in other industrial countries a larger share of responsibility is placed on other institutions, including publicly provided child care as in Sweden and other Scandinavian countries. Another question in comparing countries is: How similar are the goals of parents? Certainly countries vary in the extent to which equity and perceived efficiency of outcome by gender is regarded as important to the parents.

Perhaps there will be convergence among countries in these goals as the cultures become more aware of one another through time. Are there common economic and social circumstances that accelerate a trend toward similarity across the countries?

During the past twenty-five years there have been two major changes in the U.S. labor market and, to varying degrees, in other advanced industrialized countries. First, the job market has continued to shift in favor of skilled workers, with strong returns to human capital in the form of education (Murphy & Welch, 1993) and work experience. This occurred despite increases in the relative supply of skilled workers. Second, the growth of women's labor-force participation has increased the supply of skilled workers but placed new challenges on the family and other institutions responsible for the early development and training of young children. All industrial countries have incentives for better production and utilization of human capital. Whether a primarily market regime (U.S.) or governmentally shaped regime (Sweden) is employed, seems to matter. The Swedish system subsidizes child care and disproportionately so for educated parents. While this can be claimed to create dead-weight losses from overinvestment in children (Rosen, 1995), it does shape behavior. More educated and older parents, who can be argued to be better able to deal with child problems (Maassen van den Brink, 1994), have more children in Sweden (Hoem, 1993; Walker, 1995; Olah, 1995). In the United States the goverment has played a much smaller role and has operated through the market, via tax policies, to reduce the cost of privately purchased child care. The overall fertility rate is not higher than in Sweden but is more concentrated among younger persons, including teenagers (Jones et al., 1986) and those with less education.

The period from 1939 to 1960 was characterized by rapid growth in the United States (even net of the adjustment for the Great Depression) and by wage compression (Goldin and Margo, 1992). From the late 1960s to the present time there has been a puzzling slowdown in the growth of average wages but with favorable wage developments for skilled workers, particularly women (Olsen, 1994). One explanation of high levels of labor-force activity, even in the presence of young children, is the life-cycle career payoff to work experience in the United States compared to earlier times and to other industrialized countries such as Sweden (Sundström, 1994) and the Netherlands (Gustafsson and Stafford, 1994). Parenting practices and time management during the early career when young children are present is critical to understanding the means of facilitating market work by young women. Given the high fertility rates of young minority women in the United States, the way in which they accomplish the joint responsibilities of home care and market work has large effects on their lifetime labor- market prospects.

As early as the mid-1970s it was apparent from time use data that educated women in the United States had departed from their earlier practice of reducing labor supply when preschool children were in the household. To accomodate both child-care time and market work, educated women in the United States became subject to a "time squeeze" with a sacrifice of sleep and leisure (Hill and Stafford, 1985). Less-educated women also maintain high levels of labor-market activity when young children are present (Leibowitz et al., 1992). This may be motivated by limited income from sources other than their own earnings, and gives rise to questions about time allocation for them during this key life-cycle juncture. In sharp contrast to the United States, free time of young Swedish women *rises* during the preschool period (Flood and Klevmarken, 1992). This appears to be the result of greater sharing of child-care responsibilities and parental leave policies in Sweden. It is also possible to interpret the greater sharing of child-care respon- sibilities by Swedish men as the result of public policy that creates an intrafamily bargaining environment more favorable to women (Manser and Brown, 1980).

Research Needs

Time allocations by women to their children and the job market affects not only their careers but the eventual well being and capabilities of their children as adults. Based on a small panel sample from the Time Use Survey (U.S) over the period 1975/76 to 1981/82, it was found that subsequent teacher ratings of an array of school performance measures were positively related to prior preschool time inputs by the mother, but were negatively related to market work time of the mother (Stafford, 1987). Early home environment has been shown to relate to parenting styles (Baker et al., 1993; Mott, 1993). A more complete assessment requires studies of the *quantity* of care time of various types, as well. This needs to be studied in a longitudinal design beginning with children at an early age. This is because equity is a strong influence on parental behavior over time. When parents receive feedback of poor school performance, a typical response is to intercede with more resources for children in difficulty (Natali, 1976; Stafford, 1991). Another reason for use of a longitudinal study is that parents appear to acquire parenting skills and are far better at coping with behavioral and physical problems of young children as a function of their age and prior parenting experience (Maassen van den Brink, 1994). Moreover, family formation and dissolution rates are high, and children may experience different home environments through time and in comparison with their siblings (Hofferth et al., 1991).

Juster and Stafford (1991) have established the practicality of obtaining time-diary data for children as young as age three (with the care-giving adult as correspondent), as well as for their parents. Such data provide detailed descriptions of children's activities in the home and their interactions with parents. With some methodological work it should be possible to extend the time-diary method from a home interview to account for activities away from home, including a *school diary* in which the day-care provider or teacher records diary entries during the "school day." Collection of national data, including time diaries, parenting practices, and developmental measures, will be carried out in 1997 for the United States (Hofferth & Stafford, 1995). Possibly parallel data will be collected for other industrialized countries, including the Netherlands and Sweden. This will permit a much better understanding of how the differing child-care regimes and policies of industrial countries actually shape early-childhood environments and development.

Notes

1. An early Swedish government document (SOU 1938 No. 20 cited by Knutsen, 1991:74) argued that one reason for support of kindergarten was to give the housewives a few hours of leisure time.

2. Note that here the endowed difference, $a_{01} > a_{02}$, is fully offset so long as $a_{11} = a_{12}$.

3. Recent tests of altruism in the transfer of *income* among extended family members suggest a weak role for reciprocal altruism (Altonji, Hayashi and Kotlikoff, 1992). However, parental resources for young children is a very different and more important matter in our opinion. Parents may transfer resources at a generous rate until at some point the children are "on their own."

4. The actual effectiveness of own time versus market inputs is of major significance. If parent's (mother's) own time is valuable over a wide interval then the market work by the mother would be lower. If the market wage of women rises and market purchased or other nonfamily inputs are seen as productive of child development, then extensive market careers

with on-the-job training of mothers become more efficient for altruistic families.

5. There may be a strong parental and social concern about the *form* of the child's capital. Simply transfering nonhuman wealth may not be seen as equitable. It may be that substantial weight is placed on human capital, as illustrated by the strong effort by parents of children with Down Syndrome to achieve some level of personal functioning of the child. Societies appear to differ substantially in this regard, with disability programs in the United States placing greater relative weight on *total* transfer rather than on the form of the transfer.

6. As noted in a somewhat different context, the cost of delivering equity in an insurance setting has a greater dead-weight cost when outcomes depend on productive behavior and effort rather than on luck (Varian, 1990).

7. In Table 9-3 the proportion working fulltime of Swedish mothers with a child less than one is unexpectedly high since there is paid parental leaves for twelve months in 1984. In principle the paid leave should not be included because the survey question is "Did you work for pay last week?" and "How many hours?" Some mothers may have misunderstood the question and included themselves if they were on leave from a full-time job. The father may have been on leave, in which case the mother must be working, otherwise he does not get his 90 percent of income compensated.

10

A. Zervigon-Hakes

Culture
Clash

Translating Research Findings into Public Policy

The chapters in this volume review large bodies of research illustrating the benefits of early-childhood programs in promoting positive outcomes such as school readiness and school achievement and in preventing negative outcomes such as criminal behavior, adolescent pregnancy, or school failure. Translating that research, or any other research findings, into policy and practice, however, is a formidable task. On the one hand, researchers with an interest in public policy may feel stymied when their studies

Adapted from Zervigon-Hakes, A. M. (1995). Translating research findings into large-scale public programs and policy. *The Future of Children* (Winter) 5(3):175–91, by permission of Center for the Future of Children, The David and Lucile Packard Foundation.

do not lead to immediate policy shifts. On the other hand, policy makers may be frustrated by researchers who do not seem to understand which questions are important to study and cannot seem to present their findings without lapsing into technical jargon, qualified by endless caveats.

This chapter compares policy makers (elected and appointed officials as well as career bureaucrats) and researchers to explore the different constituencies, styles, and interests of each group, and the ways in which the media and other institutions can facilitate communication among the two groups and the public. Understanding the differences between policy makers and researchers in the ways they gather and use information can help ensure better cooperation when the research and policy communities do work together.

Florida introduced many initiatives for young children and their families in the early 1990s and employed state-funded research to help plan and monitor some of those initiatives. The third-party longitudinal evaluation of Florida's prekindergarten program and the research and public-policy collaborative work that led to Florida's decision to entitle disabled infants and toddlers to early-intervention services is presented as an example of how researchers and policy makers can collaborate successfully to transform early-childhood policy and practice. The chapter concludes with the lessons distilled from these experiences, presented as recommendations to help the research and policy communities work together.

The Different Worlds of Researchers and Policy Makers

Many researchers and policy makers share an interest in improving outcomes for young children. Each group searches for what will work, and in that search, each group can make its own unique contribution. Policy makers can provide new dollars or shift allocations of existing dollars among programs, and they can influence the effectiveness of programs by setting outcome expectations and procedural requirements. Researchers can assess the needs for new services, the quality and outcomes of existing services, and the reasons why implemented programs succeed or fail. A partnership between the two groups would seem mutually beneficial, but such partnerships rarely emerge, perhaps because each group operates in a different culture with different demands, communication styles, and measures of success (see Table 10-1).

Policy Makers

Policy makers are not a monolithic group. There are important distinctions among elected officials, appointed staff working for elected officials, and career staff.

Elected Officials

Elected officials (from the president to senators, congressional representatives, governors, mayors, and city council members) are responsible for proposing and approving the creation, continuation, and expansion of all publicly funded programs that serve young children and families. They set the stage for program quality by establishing program goals and funding levels, which largely determine service intensity and duration and the number of children and families who can be served.

Elected officials are driven by the interests of their constituents who elected them to represent their interests. This means, for example, that they seek programs or activities that will produce visible payoffs within election cycles that range from two to six years and within budget cycles that are typically annual. They may therefore try to create new programs or change current programs dramatically before an upcoming election because major changes are newsworthy and the mere fact that these new programs exist can be portrayed as a success. Producing visible results often means being a master of the immediate, understanding how to seize opportune moments for achieving consensus with peer law makers for a particular goal. Utilizing long-term measured strategies to accomplish a goal has few cultural rewards for the elected policy maker.

With an eye toward reelection, elected officials tend to be pragmatic. Many seek to avoid controversy because embracing any side in a controversial matter can alienate a sizable part of the electorate. In addition, even the image of controversy surrounding a political figure can make the public uneasy and can create the feeling that the official is unable to manage the affairs of government. Consequently, elected officials are most likely to choose controversial issues very cautiously supporting changes and addressing issues that will please more than 50 percent of the voting population.

Seeking dramatic change while avoiding controversy is a dilemma often faced by elected officials. To resolve the dilemma, elected officials sometimes propose controversial changes immediately after an election, when the next election is still years away.

Table 10-1.
Public Policy Makers and Researchers: Their Roles, Communication Styles, and Interests

Areas of Comparison	Elected Public Official	Appointed Policy Maker	Career Policy Maker	Researcher
Policy Maker Type (executive & legislative branch)	Federal: President, members of Congress State: Governor and some agency heads, legislators Local: Mayor, city council member	Cabinet secretaries and assistant secretaries Legislative staff aids or assistants	Non-appointed government program chiefs/directors and staff	University professors "Think tank" employees Consultant contractors Government agency career research employees
Role	To represent the interests of multiple, often divergent, constituencies in the public policy-making arena To monitor the activities of government in meeting the long- and short-term needs of all its citizens	To represent, manage, and implement the governmental agenda of an administration or legislator To develop expertise in their appointed content area To provide advice in their area of responsibility for the elected official	To administer and monitor publicly funded or regulated programs	To study and describe phenomena in a systematic manner, providing objective information on findings To serve as an expert in a particular field
Public's Perception of This Role	More concerned with reelection and special interests than good public policy and programs	Leader with influence Responsive to elected official's agenda Provider of information about current and future public policy direction	Bureaucratic	Knowledgeable Information is credible Sometimes impractical
Communication Media	Newspaper Television One- or two-page issue briefs Large public events	Newspaper, television One- to five-page issue briefs Executive summaries of program reports Conferences Public events	Newspaper Television Governmental program reports Conferences	Technical journals Technical books Governmental program reports Academic conferences

Areas of Comparison	Electic Public Official	Appointed Policy Maker	Career Policy Maker	Researcher
Communication Style	Friendly, people-oriented communicator with all literacy levels Brief, hurried interactions Few acronyms Does not like to say "no" Often optimistic about change	Often similar to elected official, but serves as a translator of information and often displays more technical knowledge in specific areas	Uses agency acronyms and technical language Must say "no" often Briefs elected or appointed staff Cautious about new policy redirection	Difficulty expressing information briefly Uses technical language Critical questioner
Usual Range of Research Interest	Interdisciplinary; related to committee responsibility Economic consequences Population trends Constituent problems Current public interest issues Electoral promise issues	Program or content area of responsibility Economic consequences Population trends Constituent problems Staff and program successes Elected officials' concerns	Program-specific interdisciplinary and discipline-specific research relevant to program	Discipline specific; usually concentrates on one branch of a field
Timing	Expects quick response Has short time span to accomplish objectives Likely to become disinterested when controversial, or not supported by constituency Most interested in dramatic change when first elected	Expects quick response Has short time span to accomplish objectives Most receptive to new research when first appointed and learning job	Expects quick response Has short time span to accomplish objectives	Needs time to conduct quality research and is often unable to speed the process

This may be especially true in nonpresidential election years when fewer people vote and the influence of single-issue voters is greatest. The officials elected in these off-year elections often have a specific agenda. Their concern for one particular issue may lead them to address that issue as soon as possible. After a few attempts to create change, they begin to encounter the intense lobbying of groups who may be hurt by their agendas; they thereby gain a broader appreciation of how their actions may affect the broad electorate they represent, and they begin to moderate their initiatives.

Elected officials want to make government work for their constituents and to help individuals. They are responsive to publicly presented information and, indeed, the elected official's interest in creating or changing public policy is more often prompted by anecdotal data offered by a concerned constituent, rather than research findings. Elected officials typically learn about programs by listening to testimony from a constituent or the media or through site visits. Consequently, they are most often interested in and knowledgeable about the broad brush strokes of a program rather than the detailed, complex components on which the program's quality may hinge. Elected officials are forced to deal with multiple, current, and visible crises, which also limits the extent to which they can learn complex details about any one program.

For the elected official, reality is the public's perception of an issue or problem. Elected officials thus look for activities that will generate favorable stories in the press. A favorable news story gives policy makers an instant and inexpensive feedback loop to their constituencies about the job they are doing and can help shape the public perception of an issue. It also means that officials will try to respond quickly to constituent requests or concerns so as to forestall possible bad publicity.

Elected policy makers need to know which groups will support or oppose an issue and whether that issue is a defining one for them. Single issue constituencies who are organized can be very powerful in advocating for or against a proposal. Elected officials and their appointees must be adept at anticipating and responding to the expected questions from all groups who may oppose a new proposal.

How, then, do elected officials encounter and use research? It is unlikely that they will read research directly in an academic journal. Rather, they are likely to learn about a new study from the media, a constituent, or an advocacy group. Learning about it from one of those sources may actually convince an elected official that the topic is important.

Sometimes, when the elected official's interest in a particular topic has already been established, the official may seek out a researcher in that field. The researcher can then use the opportunity to provide information to the policy maker, but the researcher should remember that elected officials will be most interested in the broad picture, not the details.

Because elected officials tend to shy away from controversy, it is precisely at those times when controversy is unavoidable that elected officials may be most open to data and research to help them make up their minds or to help bolster the positions they may want to take. Such research can be studies that provide information about constituent opinion (polls), studies that tend to support the positions that the officials have taken or—perhaps most important—studies that indicate that the new policies will lead to beneficial change for a number of groups. For elected policy makers, it is not enough to prove that a proposed change will benefit a single group, because such change can nevertheless have deleterious effects on other groups. Officials may also seek out researchers to help them present the objective arguments for controversial proposals to the public.

Appointed Legislative and Executive Branch Staff Members

The elected executive branch official appoints staff to implement the administration's goals and priorities and to manage the implementation of public programs in the specific area for which they are appointed. Examples of such staff include cabinet secretaries and their appointed bureau chiefs, at the federal level, or their equivalents at the state level. Similarly, state and federal legislators have appointed staff who seek to help the legislator achieve his or her goals.

Appointed officials usually arrive with a new administration and are responsible for supervising career staff who may have been in an agency long before the appointee arrived and will likely remain long after the appointee has gone. To succeed, appointees must therefore garner the energy and support of the career staff they supervise. Career staff have detailed program knowledge and a relationship with constituent, provider-advocate groups, which can be invaluable to a new administration as it weighs policy alternatives. An appointed official with good management skills will develop a new vision with career staff, engaging them in designing the proposed changes a new administration may desire. Without career staff support, appointed officials may find themselves surrounded by controversy and unfavorable news leaks. This dynamic tension often serves to moderate the actions of an administration seeking broad change.

Appointed staff owe their allegiance to the policy maker who appointed them. They are responsive to the official's electoral constituencies and are therefore driven to accomplish their tasks within the same short budget and electoral time frames as are elected officials. Appointed staff, also, therefore may seek to establish new programs or make the same dramatic sorts of changes that elected officials value.

In contrast with elected officials, however, most appointed staff specialize in a content area. They are expected to provide the elected official, when asked, with prompt, concise information briefs. These are often stressful jobs requiring individuals to be instant experts. Consequently, newly appointed staff must work quickly to absorb information and to learn their area.

Appointed and elected officials are the most visible representatives of an administration. Both groups, therefore, are equally motivated to avoid controversy, to seek positive press coverage, and to undertake activities that will result in quick, positive outcomes.

Given their greater needs for details and their greater focus on specific areas, appointed officials want and use more information about their areas of concern than do elected officials. They especially want to know how to implement new programs and how to improve those older programs that are consonant with the focus of their administration. Often enthusiastic about research findings, they want to know which programs work, but, like elected officials, they appreciate most those researchers who can summarize the policy implications of their research briefly.

Career Policy Makers

Usually associated with an agency, career policy makers typically function in a monitoring or technical assistance role for publicly funded programs. At the federal level, preschool career policy makers generally oversee block grants to states (for example, child care) or direct grants (for example, Head Start) administered by local grantees. Career staff are responsible for drafting the rules and regulations that govern the programs administered by that agency. They also oversee the publicly funded evaluation research mandated by Congress. Similarly the state-level career staff monitor regulates and enforces the regulation of local programs as well as oversees publicly funded research.

Career policy makers are "civil servants" whose role is to protect and preserve the ongoing performance of government to meet citizen needs as defined by law. Unless their program is eliminated, they do not lose their jobs when an administration changes.

In contrast with the two other groups, many career bureaucrats are leery of change, even though they may actually have the power to interpret policies and make high-impact changes. Their skittishness is partly because they realize that they must live with the long-term consequences of change. They know that any change can have unintended, negative consequences for other individuals or programs. In addition, career staff have watched administrations come and go and seen fellow bureaucrats lose jobs or status after strongly supporting a previous administration's new program.

Invested in existing programs that define their job tasks, career staff are unlikely to desire rapid, massive shifts in those programs. In fact, it is in the career officials' interest to garner more funds and more interest in the programs they oversee. A program perceived as beneficial is less likely to be attacked or eliminated, so any research that indicates the effectiveness of a program administered by the career official will be well received, while reports of new programs that conflict or compete for funds with their program may be met with less interest.

In contrast with the other two groups of policy makers, career staff are more attuned to the specialized rules and regulations that define the broad outlines of legislatively funded programs. Career staff are the policy makers who will read and understand fairly detailed research.

Sandwiched between the appointed staff and the programs they oversee, career staff are interested in research that evaluates program effectiveness or is designed to help improve program quality. They may be especially interested in longitudinal studies and replication research that focuses on their programs and helps identify factors needed to translate pilot projects to large-scale community programs (De Lone, 1990).

Researchers

Researchers are also not a monolithic entity. Some choose to work as professors in universities or colleges, others work in the public sector as program evaluators, monitors and collectors of program and population statistics, and still others work as employees of "think tanks," or as contractors.

University-based Researchers

University-based researchers are the most visible group and are normally hired to teach and conduct research in their field. Since they enjoy protection, through tenure, from political pressure they are often considered the most likely research group to provide unbiased studies . Those professors that are not reliant on grants for funding possess the greatest independence in choosing research topics and publishing research results.

Researchers in "Think Tanks" and Contractors

Researchers in "think tanks" or contractors have skills similar to the university-based researcher, but there are important differences. These firms generally employ individuals from the public policy arena as well as researchers. This collaborative partnership gives firms access to the former policy makers' practical experience, grants, and colleagues in agencies. Researchers in these firms are relied upon to design and conduct technically sound studies. Findings from think tank firms are often found in public policy reports as well as in peer review journals.

Think tanks that employ former policy makers are thought to be more likely to produce documents that answer questions of importance to the policy maker and to be sensitive to the policy makers' need for brief, timely reports. They may also be perceived to be less independent due to the role of former policy makers in either obtaining grant funds or participating in research design and development.

Researchers in Agencies

Agency researchers play an important role in monitoring agency accomplishments or assessing current trends affecting the agencies mission. For this reason, they are more likely to conduct short-term studies utilizing large agency data bases, to conduct quality-assurance studies, and to produce descriptive statistics on trends for their agencies. They are less likely to conduct studies with clinical trials and longitudinal studies that explore interventions. Yet, they may get this experience when monitoring studies funded by their agency. Because agency researchers are answerable to policy makers, they are more likely to gain an understanding of the importance of having information that is readily available. Agency researchers are the least likely to be perceived as independent, but they serve an important function as translators and evaluators of outside research to agency policy makers.

Researchers, particularly those in universities, are most likely to advance in their professions if they publish their work in recognized academic journals and/or regularly win grants and contracts to conduct new research projects. In many ways, the skills and qualities that lead to success in publishing and winning grants are precisely the opposite of the skills that lead to success for policy makers.

For example, to publish frequently or to garner research funds, researchers typically must become ever more specialized over time. This contrasts with the need of policy makers to handle a broad, multidisciplinary range of issues. Publishing in academic journals requires that researchers must communicate their relatively esoteric knowledge using a technical language that is seldom understood by any but their peers. Few researchers write for newspapers or the television broadcasts that are the daily staples for policy makers. Moreover, in most academic disciplines theoretical research has higher prestige than practical research so that university researchers tend to address questions of theory that are interesting to other academics rather than more mundane questions of policy and practice.

Academic arguments require attention to detail and an ability to be extremely critical about the content and process of research studies. These analytical skills result in communications that are quite a contrast with the typical statements by policy makers. For example, researchers, in an attempt to be specific and scientifically accurate, are likely to detail all the possible problems with their findings, the findings of other researchers, or even with the assumptions of the policy makers. To the researcher, this is good research; to the policy maker, it is likely to appear, at worst, cynical and rude, and, at best, wishy-washy or irrelevant.

Researchers and policy makers also differ in what they consider to be good research. In evaluating studies researchers focus on technical quality, while policy makers focus on usefulness. Researchers want to control as many aspects of the environment as possible through research design so as to strengthen the basis for drawing firm conclusions. Conducting studies in more natural settings such as one or more communities with services delivered by community agencies, rather than university staff, greatly reduces the researchers' control and opens a study to a considerable number of potential problems. (See Barnett, this volume, for a discussion of research methods.) In addition, preschool researchers often strive to follow families and children over time because they know that some of the most significant changes that occur as a result of exposure to a service program may be observed many years after services have ceased. Researchers may take a long view in which they see certain policy issues as permanent or recurring even if current interest in an issue fades away.

In contrast, public officials must make the leap of faith from a few pilot studies to support a broad-based new program. They must make their decisions long before longitudinal studies are complete. They recognize that opportunities for action and public interest in a topic can fade quickly and that they may not have another opportunity for successful action. In fact, by the time most such studies are complete, the public and policy makers, driven by a new election or budget cycle, have moved on to other issues.

Researchers, particularly university-based researchers, differ from policy makers in the typical audiences to whom they speak, with those differences compounding the drive for specificity on the part of the researcher and generality on the part of the policy maker. The university-based researcher, as a teacher of young adults, typically delivers field-specific information in a classroom where he or she is the seldom challenged expert shaping the discussion and evaluating the audience. More critical, for the researcher, are audiences of peer researchers who are also specialists in the chosen field and in research procedures. Criticism, in these instances, is often detailed in nature focusing on the assumptions, procedures, and processes the researcher used to conduct his or her research. In contrast, the policy maker speaks with and is often interrogated by audiences with multiple agendas about information that is of broad scope and multidisciplinary in nature.

Despite these many differences in skills and styles, policy makers still seek to wrap themselves in the legitimacy provided by researchers who have employed objective scientific methods to arrive at conclusions that the public, the media, and policy makers all credit as impartial and trustworthy. Researchers continue to conduct studies to impact decision making about public policy and program practices. Because researchers and policy makers can use each others' considerable talents to improve programs and child outcomes, there is a need to balance the concerns of each. While there are likely to be tradeoffs for each profession, there are additional communications that researchers could make that would improve their access to public policy makers. For instance, researchers who have learned to articulate research and findings in formats useful to the media and policy makers often find themselves called on to provide advice to policy makers.

Institutions That Bridge the Gap between
Research and Public Policy

Policy makers can only use research if they know about it. A variety of groups, such as the media, local program administrators, advocacy groups, and foundations, help interpret research findings and bring them to the attention of policy makers.

Media

Newspaper, radio, and television are important information conduits. The individuals who produce the news therefore play an important role in providing policy makers and the public with information. Like policy makers, they are interested in the meaning of research, not the process, and are adept at using everyday language to communicate (Bailar, 1995).

Elected policy makers use the media to present issues of importance to their constituency, and they read or watch the news to be responsive to electorate concerns. Indeed, reading daily newspaper clips is an important part of a policy maker's job.

Researchers who effectively present their findings to the media will find it easier to convince policy makers of the importance of their work. In addition, publicly elected officials often use the occasion of a newly released research study to suggest a particular approach, issue, or program. Good news stories may also provide the publicly elected official, supportive of the program, with corroborating evidence that can be communicated back to their constituency.

Local Program Administrators

Program administrators, often directors of community-based nonprofit organizations (e.g., preschool or Head Start program directors), can legitimize programmatic research findings by confirming that their experiences match the results reported by the researchers, by translating technical jargon into everyday language, and by urging adoption of researchers' recommendations. Elected, appointed, and career policy makers are likely to ask program administrators (who may be constituents in a legislator's district) for a reaction to research findings before deciding to support change.

Program administrators are likely to be consumers of research. For instance, preschool administrators read technical journals and attend conferences to keep up with the technology of their profession. They utilize studies to determine best practices, to train staff, to learn about new effective services, and to advocate for additional funds for their own programs.

Advocacy and Professional Organizations

Policy makers also listen to advocacy and professional organizations because they represent a defined part of the electorate. While advocacy and professional groups sometimes may be perceived as self-serving or single focused, officials still like to know how these organized groups and the voters they represent will respond to a new initiative or policy proposal.

The most sophisticated of children's advocacy groups (e.g., the Children's Defense Fund) or professional associations (e.g., the American Academy of Pediatrics or the National Association for the Education of Young Children) frequently conduct and summarize selected research to validate their calls for more funding or different regulations for a particular program. Advocacy groups are particularly adept at using the media. They may also have lobbyists on their payrolls to try to influence the policy-making process.

Researchers do not always think about using advocacy groups to disseminate their work, but these groups are an excellent avenue for that sort of activity. Researchers who are concerned about children's policy, for example, sometimes write up their study results in a issue brief, and send the brief to an advocacy group that can then convey the research message to policy makers.

Foundations

The more than 30,000 foundations in America are important funders, communicators, distributors, and legitimizers of quality research. In addition, foundations can convene meetings of research and policy teams to discuss specific issues of concern. They are often governed by well-known business and civic leaders, and the larger foundations are frequently staffed by individuals with technical research expertise.

Given grant budgets that are much more limited than those controlled by public policy makers, foundations usually see their role as helping to initiate new programs, but then hoping that other funding sources will step in to continue the program. In 1992, it was estimated that Foundations award grants of approximately $10 billion a year (Renz and Lawrence, 1994). This is contrasted to total government budgets totaling about $2.5 trillion annually (U.S. Department of Commerce, 1994). Foundations may therefore require outcome evaluations of the programs they support with the belief that positive evaluations will make it more likely that other public or private funders will continue to support the project.

Because such evaluation research was undertaken to be useful to policy makers, research emerging from foundation-supported projects often is presented in brief and well-written reports and distributed widely to technical journals, media, and policy makers.

Case Study
A Research and Policy Partnership in Florida

Researchers and policy makers have different time tables, needs, and styles, but they can work together. The two following case studies describe examples in which research changed the landscape of early-childhood policy and programs in Florida.

During the 1980s, Florida's population increased dramatically, especially its population of families with young children living in poverty. The state of Florida, under the leadership of both Republican and Democratic governors, consequently increased funding for established programs and initiated a number of new statewide programs for very young children and their families. Among the many new initiatives was a state-funded, center-based preschool program for low-income children (prekindegarten) and the implementation of a federal voluntary entitlement of early-intervention services for very young children with disabilities. The latter program was initiated only after a major state-funded research and evaluation study and years of work by researchers, policy makers, families, child advocates, the media, and foundations. Florida's Cost Implementation Study for Public Law 99-457, Part H (Zervigon-Hakes, 1991) and the evaluation of Florida's prekindegarten (King, Rohani, & Cappellini, 1993) preschool initiative are therefore examples of how research helped change the policy landscape.

Third-Party Evaluations of
Early-Childhood Programs
Translating Research Findings for Large-Scale,
Established Public Programs

Evaluations of Florida's prekindergarten program were conducted each year from 1991 to 1994 using a sample of 641 children who began prekindergarten in its first year of large-scale implementation, September of 1988 (King, Rohani, and Cappellini, 1993). Children were followed through second grade. Because the prekindergarten program is a large-scale, statewide, public program, from the policy-maker viewpoint, the evaluation could provide important information on the value of large-scale early-intervention efforts to Florida's low-income children at risk for school failure. Although the legislators and staff who mandated the evaluation wanted the demonstration project to be evaluated, they did not have expertise in research design. Therefore evaluators and service providers did not work together in setting up the program and the research design did not have the potential for drawing firm conclusions as in a carefully controlled research demonstration project.

Six hundred and forty-one children who participated in the prekindergarten program in the 1988–1989 school year were compared with a similar size group who did not receive any publicly funded preschool services and were in the 1989–1990 kindergarten class. The comparison group was similar in sex, race, age, and eligibility for free or reduced-cost lunch. Approximately 55 percent of the children were African American, five percent were Hispanic and 40 percent were white.

Numerous problems typical of policy maker-directed studies existed for the researchers. The elected policy-maker interest is highest when starting a new program. Consequently, more attention to research is paid in the first year of a program. This is, however, probably the worst time to measure a program because staff, materials, sites, and equipment are often not consistently available. Moreover, in this case evaluators were forced to use a retrospective design since the legislature mandated five-year findings for a group that was already being served. This type of research does not allow definitive statements about differences in outcomes because groups cannot be chosen randomly prior to the treatment. In addition, there is some evidence that because Florida did not have a statewide program for young children with disabilities in place, school officials selected children who were most at risk—those likely to develop a disability.

Other limitations occur when studying programs in a natural environment where it is impossible to control for differences in staff, environments, assessment instruments, data collection, and input. Yet, because the study was commissioned by the state, researchers were able to choose large samples for each comparison group and to freely utilize school district data. Researchers attempted to overcome many of the limitations imposed upon the study by using numerous statistical measures to evaluate the same outcome. The research team used meta-analysis procedures for calculating significance for measures that could not be combined due to differences in instruments (Glass, McGaw, & Smith, 1981). Statistical significance was declared for combined school district scores if effect sizes were different from 0 by a probability of 0.05. A test of "educational significance" was required of combined effect sizes of (0.25) one-quarter of a standard deviation or more (Tallmadge, 1997).

Data on children were gathered from program reports, children's records, site observations, and surveys of administrators, teachers, and parents. The study team looked annually for short-term and long-term effects (through second grade). Findings are similar to demonstration studies in that short-term effects were found, but few significant differences are found for first and second grade. Other demonstration studies begin to show effects by fourth grade (Lazar, Darlington, Murray, Royce, and Snipper, 1982; Schweinhart and Weikart, 1982).

Strong, short-term, cognitive effects were found using two methods of analysis (value-added analysis [Cook and Campbell, 1979] and age-cohort analysis [Byrk, Strenio, & Weisberg, 1980]). Because data for comparison groups were not available for the 1988–1989 school year when the children were in the prekindergarten program, these two methods were used. Value-added analysis estimated pre- and post-test differences due to the preschool experience above that expected from maturation. Age-cohort analysis allowed assumption that pretest age scores of older prekindergarten children would be the same as post-test scores of younger prekindergarten children (who were the same age at the time of testing). A significant difference between the two would be the result of program effects.

Longer-term effects analyzed through second grade were school attendance, exceptional-student education placement, retention, and academic progress. Reading and math achievement test differences for the program group were found to be significant for kindergarten but not for first or second grade. No significant effects were found for reading or math grades. Researchers hope that a further measure in later grades will be taken since earlier longitudinal studies show stronger differences in later years for reading and math achievement (Lazar, Darlington, Murray, Royce, and Snipper, 1982) and grades for girls beginning in grade seven or eight (Lally, Mangione, and Honig, 1988). Significant program effects for reduced retention were reported for the preschool group in kindergarten, but the comparison group had significantly fewer retentions in first grade; in second grade, there were no effects. Anecdotal data and record reviews revealed improved record keeping by school districts and positive descriptions of improved emotional and social skills of children.

It was the State Coordinating Council for Early Childhood Services and consumers (not the researchers) who made the prekindergarten program an issue for legislators. Researchers provided important data and information that council members and consumers used with their anecdotal stories to affect policy-maker decisions. Though the longitudinal study funded by the legislature produced important and interesting trends between groups, it is unfortunate that a randomized prospective study was not funded. The third-party evaluation of Florida's prekindergarten program provides a good example of how longitudinal research efforts can inform career staff on how to improve current programs just by imposing an interchange between researchers, program staff, and policy makers. Program changes that may not have occurred without researcher involvement included the requiring of school principals to receive training on child development, the establishment of training and curricula for programs, the improvement of equipment and playgrounds, the improvement in use of developmental measures to assess child needs, and the development of competencies and certification for staff.

Florida's Cost-Implementation Study for Infants and Toddlers
Translating Research Findings for Establishing a New Large-Scale Public Program

In 1986, Public Law 99-457, Part H of the federal Individuals with Disabilities Education Act (IDEA) offered all states and territories of the United States planning dollars and a timeline of five years to develop and implement a statewide, comprehensive, coordinated, multidisciplinary early-intervention system for infants and toddlers. Because the new legislation was an entitlement program, entering into it could be very onerous for a state with a burgeoning population such as Florida. Under an entitlement program, a state must provide sufficient funds annually for services to all eligible individuals regardless of whether federal dollars earmarked for the program increase over time. States with growing populations are especially pressed by entitlement programs because the demands of such programs can squeeze funds from other deserving programs and groups. Given these financial concerns, deciding whether to participate in Part H was a difficult choice for Florida lawmakers.

By 1989, the Florida Interagency Coordinating Council for Infants and Toddlers, the oversight Board for Florida's Part H award, decided that a single group should be selected to coordinate the planning process and conduct the studies needed to determine whether Florida should participate in Part H, and, if so, design the new system of services.

In early 1990, retired U.S. Senator Lawton Chiles, who was then director of the Collins Center for Public Policy at Florida State University, was asked to oversee the research project. Chiles brought commitment and considerable skills to the task: he had a personal interest in young children with risk conditions (his grandson was born with low birth weight), he could anticipate the policy questions that were likely to be asked, and, once the studies were completed, he could provide the leadership with elected policy makers that could help pass whatever implementing legislation the research suggested.

Four study teams, composed of researchers and advisory groups (which included program directors, advocacy groups, career and appointed policy makers) were assembled in March 1990 to formulate key research questions. The questions that were investigated over the course of the two-year study included: identification of the eligible population, description of services, estimation of costs, and the legal and systems-level changes necessary to create the proposed new system (Zervigon-Hakes, 1991). The next sections briefly describe the results.

The Prevalence Team: Who should be served?

One of the most important policy questions in the study was to define who should be served by the proposed new program because that would then determine the cost for the program. The prevalence team decided to study not just infants with existing disabilities but also children who were affected by risk conditions that were likely to lead to a disability or other poor outcome (for example, very low birthweight or failure to thrive).

Several methods were employed to describe and count infants at risk for disabilities, including case studies, literature reviews, expert panels, interviews, population surveys, and agency service utilization studies. The most important source of information was a survey of health providers in Palm Beach County, a large, ethnically and economically diverse county, to determine the prevalence of at-risk infants in the county. The survey was supplemented by indepth case studies of a sample of families to determine how service needs varied as a function of varying family and child characteristics.

Researchers used statistical techniques to extrapolate from this one county to other counties and to the state the number of children who would be at risk for disabilities, adjusting for population growth, birth rates, ethnic and racial differences, and family income.

Around 28 percent of infants and toddlers were estimated to have one or more established conditions, biological or environmental risk conditions (Foster, Mandolang, Ellzey, Weller, & Terrie, 1991). Many infants and toddlers with disabilities and their families were found to also be experiencing stressful events associated with poor outcomes. Children who had risk conditions were more likely to have moved or immigrated in the past year, experienced a death in the home, or lived with a family member who was seriously ill, retarded, or incarcerated. A surprising number of infants were found to be in homes where family members had been the victim of a serious crime.

The Service Delivery Team:
What services should be offered?

A service delivery team used the numbers gathered by the prevalence team to calculate estimates of current and future service needs of identified children for later use by the cost team. Members of the service delivery team used literature reviews, provider and parent interviews, expert advisory groups, surveys, site visits, and simulations of family service planning procedures to create their recommended system of services. As depicted in Figure 10-1, the team concluded that the federally required therapeutic and educational services were not the only services needed by high-risk infants and toddlers and their families, but that families needed assistance in meeting basic survival needs as well (Stone, Graham, Duwa, Strousse, & Fanin, 1991).

The Cost Team: What will early intervention cost?

The cost team worked to create a new method of accounting and costing services that would encourage the blending of funds across state agencies and the allocating of resources to meet unique, individual family and child needs (Hall, Walsh, & Walby, 1991; Hall, Stone, Walsh, Wager, Zervigon-Hakes, & Graham, 1993). The goal was to provide a budgeting tool for state leaders that would encourage the state to move away from program-bound budgets based on categorical labels and instead generate budgets based on estimates of child- and family-centered services.

State Administering System Team:
What overarching system is needed?

Essentially a steering committee, this unique team, led by the study director, consisted of the heads of each study team, career and appointed policy makers from various bureaus, representatives of

Figure 10-1.
Services Required by Part H; and Services Not Required, But Needed by Vulnerable Infants, Toddlers, and Their Families

P.L. 99-457, Part H, Required Services

- ☐ Audiology
- ☐ Psychology
- ☐ Family Training, Home Visits, and Counseling
- ☐ Health
- ☐ Nutrition
- ☐ Child Find (screening and identification)

- ☐ Speech/Language Pathology
- ☐ Physical Therapy
- ☐ Social Work
- ☐ Medical (only diagnostic, and as needed for participation in early intervention)
- ☐ Multidisciplinary Evaluation
- ☐ Family Support Planning Process

- ☐ Occupational Therapy
- ☐ Nursing
- ☐ Transportation
- ☐ Special Instruction
- ☐ Assistive Technology
- ☐ Vision
- ☐ A Lead Service Coordinator

Services Not Required by Part H That Were Found to Be Needed

Developmental Child Care
Medical Child Care
Medical Foster Care
Therapeutic Foster Care/Shelter Care
Other Health Services
Family Support (respite, homemaker, parent-to-parent)
Housing
Educational Opportunities

Vocational Training
Family Planning
Family Therapy
Family Unification Services
Comprehensive Drug Treatment
Medications
Dental Services
After-School Care
Legal Services

Source: A. Zervigon-Hakes (1991). *Florida's Cost/Implementation Study for Public Law 99-457, Part H, Infants and Toddlers—Phase II Findings: Executive Summary.* Florida Department of Education. Tallahassee, Fla., pp. 11, 12.

parents of disabled children, the medical community, and legal staff. The team coordinated the work of the other research team, maintained policy-maker involvement, developed implementation options, and generated the study's overall policy options (Zervigon-Hakes, 1991).

The team's most important job was to translate research into pragmatic policy decisions. Legal staff researched state laws pertaining to each proposed service, such as center-based preschools or case management, to determine changes that might be required or desired. The team then spent many hours in meetings, weighing different policy options and their economic implications to reach consensus. In subsequent years, the researchers and policy makers in this team were called upon to inform legislative bodies, facilitate agency decision making, and to help with implementation decisions.

From Research to Practice

The study's findings clearly had important implications for policy makers. For the first time, data were available that local policy makers could use to estimate the number of families and children who might be at risk for disabilities in their counties. The study documented the environmental stressors faced by families of children with disabilities and the multiple service needs of families, which suggested that the medical and social services communities should work together in a family- and child-focused approach. Funds currently being expended on the population and additional costs that might be incurred if Florida were to implement Part H were estimated. The laws that would need to be changed were listed. Finally, the study provided descriptive data about individual children, which helped policy makers understand the families their decisions would affect.

The First Battle

Based on the data, the study team concluded that Florida should participate in Part H. Nevertheless, the findings had to be transmitted to policy makers, and both policy makers and the public had to be persuaded. This turned out to be a difficult process.

For example, despite the research findings, two major Florida agency heads, the Secretary of the Department of Health and Rehabilitative Services and the Commissioner of Education, and a host of child-advocacy groups initially opposed adopting the federal entitlement, largely because of fears about the financial implications. Lawton Chiles, by then governor of the state, while in sympathy with the study findings, supported the recommendations of his staff and the advocates not to apply for the federal entitlement.

However, families of young children with disabilities supported the study's recommendations. Policy makers, eager to avoid controversy, and desiring to meet the needs of a vocal constituency group, proposed a new initiative based on the study findings. A statewide system of comprehensive preschool and family services for young children with high-risk conditions was proposed as recommended by the study, but whose services would not be entitled. The new initiative was supported by most children's advocacy groups, but only grudgingly by disappointed families of disabled children. They continued to press for the entitlement.

The study languished for a year, but researchers and families kept the issue alive. One of the researchers received grants to gather data on the potential cost savings that would result if early-intervention programs were implemented statewide (Zervigon-Hakes & Lochenbach, 1991) and to present the Part H study and new data to the public in a series of statewide forums (Zervigon-Hakes, Nabors, & Harris, 1991). Over 2,000 policy makers, consumers, and local providers attended the forums and developed recommendations based on study findings and their own local concerns. These recommendations were published and used by advocates to brief newspaper editorial boards around the state.

The Second Battle

In 1992, Congress appropriated additional funds to enable states to implement Part H. The research team seized the opportunity of new funds to reopen the issue. In November 1992 the researchers sent an advisory on the increase of funds to key state-level agency staff and then issued another report, again recommending that Florida participate in Part H (Zervigon-Hakes, Graham, & Hall, 1993).

Researchers presented their report to legislative and agency staff as well as parent and preschool advocacy groups in December 1992. Researchers and advocates met with the governor and key staff in January 1993.

Within one month, the governor and the Commissioner of Education endorsed the entitlement, but the secretary of the Florida Department of Health and Rehabilitative Services (DHRS), who would have to take responsibility for P.L. 99-457, still did not. The governor directed his appointed secretary of DHRS to take another look at the issue. Appointed bureau chiefs and career staff in both departments were privately split and worked within their agencies to consolidate support for their respective positions. A critical juncture occurred when one bureau chief, who had participated in the study, openly supported the placement of the early-intervention program within his jurisdiction. The Secretary of DHRS then gave support.

Many advocacy groups who had not supported the entitlement earlier now supported it because they were convinced that the additional federal funds would be sufficient to prevent a raid on other children's services. Advocates presented an important united front to legislators who had to appropriate funds and assign agency responsibility.

Researchers briefed reporters from Florida's radio and television stations and newspapers at a March 1993 press conference. Findings were presented in easy-to-understand briefing articles that focused on the questions legislators and the public were likely to ask, and, in subsequent months, the researchers made themselves available to legislators and their fiscal staff for additional questions.

Advocates rhetorically piqued legislator and media interest by asking, Can Florida afford to ignore seven-and-one-half million federal dollars for at-risk and disabled infants and toddlers? They briefed editorial boards in Florida's eleven major media markets on research findings. Parents brought news clips to their legislators. The media kept the story alive.

In the waning days of the 1993 legislative session, the legislature granted the Department of Health and Rehabilitative Services a one-year trial to implement the entitlement. Annual review by the legislature of the costs and benefits was an important compromise that gave legislators a measure of comfort with the entitlement. The program continued beyond the trial period due to parents and providers who mobilized each legislative session to protect it. The researchers continue to be asked for information.

Conclusions and Recommendations

Researchers who worked on the Part H project clearly had moved beyond the traditional role of researcher. They worked with policy makers to formulate studies that would answer questions of interest to policy makers and then made sure the results of those studies were accessible and understandable by the media, advocates, and elected officials. The policy makers, for their part, listened both to what their constituents wanted and to what the research studies demonstrated. Both groups were powerfully influenced by the media and advocacy groups who used the research findings to keep attention focused on the needs of very young children with disabilities and their families.

Researchers nevertheless remained researchers, not advocates. They involved policy makers of all party affiliations in their work and presented findings objectively as one of many policy options. Researchers made a single presentation of the findings to each major policy-making audience and the media. After that, they made presentations only when invited. Advocates were the individuals who reminded policy makers about the findings and continued to press for policy change. Advocates lobbied for the policy option they liked; researchers provided information on the pros and cons of various options.

Based on the experiences in Florida, recommendations for researchers and policy makers who are interested in working together to generate change are listed in Tables 10-2 and 10-3. As indicated in the tables, researchers should involve policy makers in all stages of their research. Collaboration is important during initial formulation of questions to be researched, during ongoing review of interim findings, and before presentation of final results. Findings should be presented at the level of detail that is appropriate for the intended audience: detailed and technical for academic audiences, more general but focused on programmatic concerns and without technical jargon for the career and appointed policy maker, and very general for the public, the media, and elected policy makers. In all instances, findings should be presented clearly and as briefly as possible. Researchers should understand that changing policy takes time, just as good research does.

Policy makers who are interested in working with researchers must understand the need of those researchers to scour every research forest for trees with methodologically weakened limbs. They must understand that need for rigor but still remain clear when dealing with researchers about what key policy questions must be answered. They should understand, however, that to answer some of those key questions with precision may take more resources and more time than they had planned to commit.

Policy makers are driven by budgetary and election cycles, but they should realize that some ideas and proposals will come up again and again. Newly implemented demonstration programs represent natural experiments that should be viewed as chances to learn, and, given the long-term benefits of early-childhood programs, research concerning such programs should be longitudinal in nature.

Table 10-2.
**Recommendations for Researchers
Who Seek to Influence Policy Makers**

1. When designing a study, involve career staff and appointed policy makers in ongoing reviews of study progress, and in reviews of final results.

2. Conduct research that can answer practical implementation questions, such as: Who should be served? What services are needed? How much will they cost? How can they be funded? What agency should oversee the services? What legal issues are involved?

3. Communicate findings in easily read brief reports and papers.

4. Provide findings about the details of programs to career and appointed program staff, not elected policy makers.

5. Communicate information through various media. Meet with newspaper, television, and radio representatives, provide press releases, hold press conferences to publicize results, and provide newspapers with short briefings on research findings.

6. Put a "face" on research findings. Use anecdotal and case data to describe the importance of findings, and include constituents familiar with the subject when meeting with elected legislators.

7. Network with advocates, program administrators, and career and appointed staff to establish an identity as a person with expertise in a specific content area.

8. When communicating with elected officials or their staff, recognize that some segment of the population may disagree vehemently with the research findings. Be willing to consider options and alternatives and to commit time to disseminate research findings. Researchers may have to review laws, draft legislation, provide information for responses to constituent concerns, and discuss practical options with policy makers.

9. Provide timely reports within appropriate election and legislative cycles.

10. Work with an interdisciplinary group of researchers to design and think through the implications of research findings before formulating policy recommendations.

11. Be patient but persistent and ready to brief policy makers on important findings. Issues of importance are cyclical in the political world.

Table 10-3.
Recommendations for Policy Makers
Who Seek to Benefit from Research

---

1. Involve researchers in interdisciplinary "think tank" sessions to frame the questions of greatest concern to policy makers.

2. Require publicly funded research projects to provide brief one- or two-page synopses of findings to elected legislative and administrative policy makers as well as the reports that are sent to career staff.

3. Fund interdisciplinary research that brings program, consumer, and economic specialists together with policy makers.

4. Provide researchers with the time and the resources to produce high-quality work. Good longitudinal research on early-childhood programs requires time for children to grow up. A significant investment is required for well-designed studies with randomized treatments and controls.

5. Evaluate new programs after they have had time to become established. If data on program effectiveness in multiple natural settings is important, it is critical that programs not be measured in the first year when start-up is occurring.

6. Be clear with researchers about your needs for brief, jargon-free reports.

The research and policy communities are different in many ways, but they are often united by a common desire to help children and families. With an understanding of the needs and styles of each community, the two groups can work together to ensure that the most creative, economical, and effective services are offered to America's families.

References

Introduction

Barnett, W. S. (1993). New wine in old bottles: Increasing the coherence of early-childhood care and education policy. *Early Childhood Research Quarterly* 8:519–58.

Hernandez, D. J. (1993). *America's children: Resources from family, government, and the economy*. New York: Russell Sage Foundation.

West, J., Hausken, E., & Collins, M. (1993). *Profile of children's child-care and early-education program participation*. (Statistical Analysis Report NCES 93–133). Washington, D.C.: U.S. Department of Education, National Center for Education Statistics.

1. Long-Term Effects on Cognitive Development and School Success

Abelson, W. D. (1974). Head Start graduates in school: Studies in New Haven, Connecticut. In S. Ryan (Ed.), *A report on longitudinal evaluations of preschool programs*. Vol. 1 Washington, D.C.: U.S. Department of Health Education, and Welfare, pp. 1–14.

Abelson, W. D., Zigler, E., & DeBlasi, C. L. (1974). Effects of a four-year follow-through program on economically disadvantaged children. *Journal of Educational Psychology* 66(5):756–71.

Advisory Committee on Head Start Quality and Expansion. (1993). Creating a twenty-first-century Head Start. Final Report to the committee. Washington, D.C.: U.S. Department of Health and Human Services.

Allington, R. L., & Walmsley, S. A. (1995). *No quick fix: Rethinking literacy programs in America's elementary schools*. New York: Teachers College Press.

Andrews, S., Blumenthal, J., Johnson, D., Kahn, A., Ferguson, C., Lasater, T., Malone, P., & Wallace, D. (1982). The skills of mothering: A study of parent-child development centers. *Monographs of the Society for Research in Child Development* 46(6). Serial No. 198.

Barnett, W. S. (1992). Benefits of compensatory preschool education. *Journal of Human Resources* 27(2):279–312.

Barnett, W. S. (1993). Benefit-cost analysis of preschool education: Findings from a twenty-five year follow up. *American Journal of Orthopsychiatry* 63(4):500–8.

Barnett, W. S. (1996a). Economics of school reform: Three promising models. In H. F. Ladd (Ed.), *Holding schools accountable: Performance-based reform in education*. Washington, D.C.: Brookings, pp. 299–326.

Barnett, W. S. (1996b). *Lives in the balance: Benefit-cost analysis of the High/Scope Perry Preschool program through age twenty-seven*. Monographs of the High/Scope Educational Research Foundation. Ypsilanti, Mich.: High/Scope Press.

Barnett, W. S., & Camilli, G. (1997). *Definite results from loose data: A response to "Does Head Start make a difference?"* Updated version of paper presented at the Seminar on Labor and Industrial Relations, Princeton University. Mimeo. New Brunswick, N.J.: Rutgers University, Graduate School of Education.

Barnett, W. S., Frede, E. C., Mobasher, H., & Mohr, P. (1987). The efficacy of public preschool programs and the relationship of program quality to efficacy. *Educational Evaluation and Policy Analysis* 10(1):37–49.

Baydar, N., & Brooks-Gunn, J. (1991). Effects of maternal employment and child-care arrangement on preschoolers' cognitive and behavioral outcomes: Evidence from the children of the National Logitudinal Survey of youth, *Developmental Psychology* 27:932–45.

Beller, K. (1983). The Philadelphia Study: The impact of preschool on intellectual and socio-emotional development. In Consortium for Longitudinal Studies (Ed.), *As the twig is bent . . . lasting effects of preschool programs*. Hillsdale, N.J.: Erlbaum, pp. 133–70.

Boutte, G. S. (1992). *The effects of home intervention on rural children's home environments, academic self-esteem, and achievement scores—A longitudinal study*. Unpublished Dissertation, UMI Dissertation Services.

Brooks-Gunn, J., McCormick, M. C., Shapiro, S., Benasich, A. A., & Black, G. W. (1994). The effects of early-education intervention on maternal employment, public assistance, and health insurance: The Infant Health and Development Program. *American Journal of Public Health* 84(6):924–30.

Burchinal, M., Lee, M., & Ramey, C. (1989). Type of day care and intellectual development in disadvantaged children. *Child Development* 60:128–37.

Caldwell, B. M. (1987) Sustaining intervention effects: Putting malleability to the test. In J. J. Gallagher and C. T. Ramey, *The malleability of children*. Baltimore, Md.: Brookes, pp. 115–26.

Campbell, D. T. (1991). Quasi-experimental research designs in compensatory education. Paper presented at OECD Conference on Evaluating Intervention Strategies for Children and Youth and Risk. Washington, D.C., May 6–7, 1991.

Campbell, F. A. (1994). Unpublished analyses of Abecedarian data on IQ and achievement by group and gender. Chapel Hill: University of North Carolina.

Campbell, F. A., Breitmayer, B., & Ramey, C. T. (1986). Disadvantaged single teenaged mothers and their children: Consequences of free educational day care. *Family Relations* 35:63–68.

Campbell, F. A., & Ramey, C. T. (1993). Mid-adolescent outcomes for high-risk students: An examination of the continuing effects of early intervention. Paper presented at the biennial meeting of the Society for Research in Child Development, March 26. New Orleans.

Campbell, F. A., & Ramey, C. T. (1994). Effects of early intervention on intellectual and academic achievement: A follow-up study of children from low-income families. *Child Development* 65:684–98.

Caughy, M. O., DiPietro, J., & Stobino, M. (1994). Day-care participation as a protective factor in the cognitive development of low-income children. *Child Development* 65:457–71.

Ceci, S. J. (1991). How much does schooling influence general intelligence and its cognitive components? A reassessment of the evidence. *Developmental Psychology* 27:703–22.

Chugani, H. T., and Phelps, M. E. (1986). Maturational changes in cerebral function in infants determined by 18FDG positron emission tomography. *Science* 231:840–43.

Chugani, H. T., Phelps, M. E., & Mazziotta, J. C. (1987). Positron emission tomography study of human brain functional development. *Annals of Neurology* 22(4):487–97.

Clark, C. M. (1979). Effects of the project Head Start and Title I preschool programs on vocabulary and reading achievement measured at the kindergarten and fourth-grade levels. Unpublished doctoral dissertation cited by McKey and colleagues 1985. Wayne State University.

Consortium for Longitudinal Studies (Ed.). (1983). *As the twig is bent . . . lasting effects of preschool programs*. Hillsdale, N.J.: Erlbaum.

Cook, T. (1991). Clarifying the warrant for generalized causal inferences in quasi-experiments. In M. W. McLaughlin and D. Phillips (Eds.), *Evaluation and education at quarter century*. NSSE Yearbook 1991.

Copple, C. E., Cline, M. G., & Smith, A. N. (1987). Path to the future: Long-term effects of Head Start in the Philadelphia School District. Washington, D.C.: U.S. Department of Health and Human Services.

Currie, J., & Thomas, D. (1995). Does Head Start make a difference? *American Economic Review* 85(3):341–64.

Datta, L. (1983). Epilogue: We never promised you a rose garden, but one may have grown anyway. In Consortium for Longitudinal Studies (Ed.), *As the twig is bent . . . lasting effects of preschool programs*. Hillsdale, N.J.: Erlbaum, pp. 467–80.

Desai, S., Chase-Lansdale, P. L., & Michael, R. T. (1989). Mother or market? Effects of maternal employment on the intellectual ability of four-year-old children. *Demography* 26:545–61.

Deutsch, M., Deutsch, C. P., Jordan, T. J., & Grallo, R. (1983). The IDS Program: An experiment in early and sustained enrichment. In Consortium for Longitudinal Studies (Ed.), *As the twig is bent . . . lasting effects of preschool programs*. Hillsdale, N.J.: Erlbaum, pp. 377–410.

Eckroade, G., Salehi, S., & Carter, J. W. (1988). An analysis of the midterm effects of the extended elementary education prekindergarten program. Baltimore: Maryland State Department of Education.

Eckroade, G., Salehi, S., & Wode, J. (1991). An analysis of the long-term effect of the extended elementary education prekindergarten program. A paper presented at the annual meeting of The American Educational Research Association, Chicago, Ill.

Educational Testing Service. (1976). *Stability and change in family status, situational, and process variables and their relationship to children's cognitive performance*. (Disadvantaged Children and Their First School Experiences: ETS-Head Start Longitudinal Study). Princeton, N.J.: ETS.

Ekstron, R., Goertz, M., & Rock, D. A. (1988). *Education and American youth*. Philadelphia: Falmer Press.

Entwisle, D. R. (1995). The role of schools in sustaining early-childhood program benefits. *The Future of Children* 5(3):133–44.

Evans, E. (1985). Longitudinal follow-up assessment of differential preschool experience for low-income minority-group children. *Journal of Educational Research* 78(4):197–202.

Fuerst, J. S., & Fuerst, D. (1993). Chicago experience with an early-childhood program: The special case of the Child Parent Center Program. *Urban Education* 28:69–96.

Gallagher, J. J., & Ramey, C. T. (Eds.). (1987). The malleability of children. Baltimore, Md.: Brookes.

Garber, H. L. (1988). The Milwaukee Project: Prevention of mental retardation in children at risk. Washington, D.C.: American Association on Mental Retardation.

Gardner, H. (1983). *Frames of mind: The theory of multiple intelligences.* New York: Basic Books.

Goodstein, H. A. (1975). The prediction of elementary school failure among high-risk children. Unpublished paper cited by McKey and colleagues 1985. Connecticut University.

Gray, S. W., Ramsey, B., & Klaus, R. (1982). *From three to twenty: The Early Training Project.* Baltimore, Md.: University Park Press.

Gray, S., Ramsey, B., & Klaus, R. (1983). The Early Training Project, 1962–1980. In Consortium for Longitudinal Studies (Ed.), *As the twig is bent . . . lasting effects of preschool programs.* Hillsdale, N.J.: Erlbaum, pp. 33–70.

Haskins, R. (1989). Beyond metaphor: The efficacy of early-childhood education. *American Psychologist* 44:274–82.

Haynes, N. M., & Comer, J. P. (1993). The Yale School Development Program: Process, outcomes, and policy implications. *Urban Education* 28(2):166–99.

Hebbeler, K. (1985). An old and a new question on the effects of early education for children from low-income families. *Educational Evaluation and Policy Analysis* 7(3):207–16.

Helburn, S., & Culkin, M. L. (1995). Cost, quality, and child outcomes in child-care centers: Executive summary. Denver: University of Colorado at Denver, Economics Department.

Herzog, E., Newcomb, C. H., & Cisin, I. H. (1974). Double deprivation: The less they have, the less they learn. In S. Ryan (Ed.), *A Report on longitudinal evaluations of preschool programs.* Vol. 1. Washington, D.C.: U.S. Department of Health, Education, and Welfare.

Husen, T., & Tuijnman, A. (1991). The contribution of formal schooling to the increase in intellectual capital. *Educational Researcher* 20(7):17–25.

Infant Health and Development Program (IHDP). (1990). Enhancing the outcomes of low-birth-weight premature infants. *Journal of the American Medical Assoication* 263(22):3035–42.

Jester, R. E., & Guinagh, B. J. (1983). The Gordon Parent Education Infant and Toddler Program. In Consortium for Longitudinal Studies (Ed.), *As the twig is bent . . . lasting effects of preschool programs.* Hillsdale, N.J.: Erlbaum, pp. 103–32.

Johnson, D., & Walker, T. (1991). A follow-up evaluation of the Houston Parent Child Development Center: School performance. *Journal of Early Intervention* 15(3):226–36.

Kagitcibasi, C. (1996). *Family and human development across cultures: A view from the other side.* Mahwah, N.J.: Erlbaum.

Kanawha County Board of Education. (1978). Kanawha Couty Head Start evaluation study. Unpublished report.

Karnes, M. B., Schwedel, A. M., & Williams. M. B. (1983). A comparison of five approaches for educating young children from low-income homes. In Consortium for Longitudinal Studies (Ed.), *As the twig is bent . . . lasting effects of preschool programs.* Hillsdale, N.J.: Erlbaum, pp. 133–70.

King, F. J., Cappellini, C. H., & Gravens, L. (1995). *A longitudinal study of the Florida Prekindergarten Early Intervention Program, Part III.* Tallahassee: Florida State University, Educational Services Program.

King, F. J., Cappellini, C. H., & Rohani, F. (1995). *A longitudinal study of the Florida Prekindergarten Early Intervention Program, Part IV.* Tallahassee: Florida State University, Educational Services Program.

King, F. J., Rohani, F., & Cappellini, C. H. (1995). A ten-year study of a prekindergarten program in Florida. Tallahassee: Florida State University, Educational Services Program.

Kolb, B. (1989). Brain development, plasticity, and behavior. *American Psychologist* 44(9):1203–12.

Lally, J. R., Mangione, P., & Honig, A. (1988). The Syracuse University Family Development Program: Long-range impact of an early intervention with low-income children and their families. In D. Powell (Ed.), *Parent education as early-childhood intervention: Emerging directions theory research and practice.* Norwood, N.J.: Ablex, pp. 79–104.

Lamb, M., & Sternberg, K. (1990). Do we really know how day care affects children? *Journal of Applied Development Psychology* 11:351–79.

Lazar, I., Darlington, R., Murray, H., Royce, J., & Snipper, A. (1982). Lasting effects of early education: A report from the Consortium for Longitudinal Studies. *Monographs of the Society for Research in Child Development* 47(2–3). Series No. 195.

Lee, V. E., Brooks-Gunn, J., Schnur, E., & Liaw, F. R. (1990). Are Head Start effects sustained? A longitudinal follow-up comparison of disadvantaged children attending Head Start, no preschool, and other preschool programs. *Child Development* 61:495–507.

Levenstein, P., O'Hara, J., & Madden J. (1983). The Mother-Child Home Program of the Verbal Interaction Project. In Consortium for Longitudinal Studies (Ed.), *As the twig is bent . . . lasting effects of preschool programs.* Hillsdale, N.J.: Erlbaum, pp. 237–63.

Levin, H. M. (1987). Accelerated schools for disadvantaged students. *Educational Leadership* 44(6):19–21.

Locurto, C. (1991). Beyond IQ in preschool programs? *Intelligence* 15:295–312.

Marcon, R. A. (1990). *Early learning and early identification: Final report of the three-year longitudinal study.* Washington, D.C.: District of Columbia Public Schools.

Marcon, R. A. (1993). *Early learning and early identification follow-up study: Transition from the early to the later childhood grades 1990–93.* Washington, D.C.: District of Columbia Public Schools, Center for Systemic Change.

Marcon, R. A. (1994). Doing the right thing for children: Linking research and policy reform in the District of Columbia Public Schools. *Young Children* 50(1):8–20.

McCarton, C., Brooks-Gunn, J., Wallace, I., Bauer, C., Bennett, F., Bernbaum, J., Broyles, S., Casey, P., McCormick, M., Scott, D., Tyson, J., Tonascia, J., & Meinert, C. (1997). Results at age 8 years of early intervention for low-birth-weight premature infants. *Journal of the American Medical Association* 277:126–32.

McDonald, M. S., & Monroe, E. (1981). A follow-up study of the 1966 Head Start program, Rome City Schools. Unpublished paper.

McGill-Franzen, A., & Allington, R. L. (1993). Flunk 'em or get them classified: The contamination of primary grade accountability data. *Educational Researcher* 22(1):19–22.

McKey, R., Condelli, L., Ganson, H., et al. (1985). *The impact of Head Start on children, families, and communities.* Final report of the Head Start Evaluation, Synthesis, and Utilization Project. Washington, D.C.: U.S. Department of Health and Human Services.

Miller, L. B., & Bizzell, R. P. (1983). The Louisville Experiment: A comparison of four programs. In Consortium for Longitudinal Studies (Ed.), *As the twig is bent . . . lasting effects of preschool programs.* Hillsdale, N.J.: Erlbaum, pp. 171–200.

Miller, L. B., & Bizzell, R. P. (1984). Long-term effects of four preschool programs: Ninth- and tenth-grade results. *Child Development* 55(6):1570–87.

Natriello, G., McDill, E. L., & Pallas, A. (1987). Schooling disadvantaged children: *Racing against catastrophe.* New York: Teachers College Press.

Neisser, U., Boodoo, G., Bouchard, T. J., et al. (1995). Intelligence: Knowns and unknowns. Report of a Task Force established by the Board of Scientific Affairs of the American Psychological Association. Washington, D.C.: American Psychological Association.

NICHD Early Child Care Research Network. (1996). Child care and the family: An opportunity to study development in context. *SRCD Newsletter* (Spring):4–7.

Nieman, R. H., & Gastright, J. F. (1981). *The long-term effects of ESEA Title I preschool and all-day kindergarten: An eight-year follow-up.* Cincinnati, Ohio: Cincinnati Public Schools.

Olds, D., & Kitzman, H. (1993). Review of resarch on home visiting for pregnant women and parents of young children. *The Future of Children* 3(3):53–92.

O'Piela, J. M. (1976). Evaluation of the Detroit Public Schools Head Start program. 1975–1976. Detroit, Mich.: Detroit Public Schools.

Palmer, F. (1983). The Harlem Study: Effects by type of training, age of training, and social class. In Consortium for Longitudinal Studies (Ed.), *As the twig is bent . . . lasting effects of preschool programs.* Hillsdale, N.J.: Erlbaum, pp. 201–36.

Phillips, D. A. (Ed.). (1987). *Quality in child care: What does research tell us?* Washington, D.C.: National Association for the Education of Young Children.

Phillips, D. A., McCartney, K., & Scarr, S. (1987). Child-care quality and children's social development. *Developmental Psychology* 23:537–43.

Pinkleton, N. B. (1976). A comparison of referred Head Start, non-referred Head Start and non-Head Start groups of primary school children on achievement, language processing, and classroom behavior. Unpublished doctoral dissertation cited by McKey and colleagues (1985). University of Cincinnati.

Purkey, S. C., & Smith, M. S. (1983). Effective schools: A review. *Elementary School Journal* 83:427–54.

Ramey, C. T., Bryant, D. M., & Suarez, T. M. (1985). Preschool compensatory education and the modifiability of intelligence: A critical review. In D. Detterman (Ed.), *Current topics in human intelligence.* Norwood, N.J.: Ablex, pp. 247–96.

Reedy, Y. B. (1991). A comparison of long-range effects of participation in Project Head Start and the impact of three differing delivery models. Unpublished paper for the graduate program in school psychology, Pennsylvania State University.

Reynolds, A. J. (1993). One year of preschool intervention or two: Does it matter? *Early Childhood Research Quarterly* 10:1–33.

Reynolds, A. J. (1994a). Effects of a preschool plus follow-on intervention for children at risk. *Developmental Psychology* 30:787–804.

Reynolds, A. J. (1994b). *Longer-term effects of the Child Parent Center and Expansion Program.* Paper presented at the annual meeting of the Chicago Association for the Education of Young Children, February 4.

Roberts, J., Rabinowitch, S., Bryant, D. M., Burchinal, M., Koch, M., & Ramey, C. T. (1989). Language skills of children with different preschool experiences. *Journal of Speech and Hearing Research*, 32:773–86.

Roderick, M. (1994). Grade retention and school dropout: Investigating the association. *American Educational Research Journal* 31(4):729–59.

Ross, S. M., Smith, L. J., Casey, J., & Slavin, R. E. (1995). Increasing the academic success of disadvantaged children: An examination of alternative early-intervention programs. *American Educational Research Journal* 32(4):773–800.

Royce, J. M., Darlington, R. B., & Murray, H. W. (1983). Pooled analyses: Findings across studies. In Consortium for Longitudinal Studies (Ed.), *As the twig is bent . . . lasting effects of preschool programs.* Hillsdale, N.J.: Erlbaum.

Scarr, S., & McCartney, K. (1988). Far from home: An experimental evaluation of the Mother-Child Home Program in Bermuda. *Child Development* 59:531–43.

Schweinhart, L. J., Barnes, H. V., Weikart, D. P., Barnett, W. S., & Epstein, A. S. (1993). *Significant benefits: The High/Scope Perry Preschool study through age 27.* Monographs of the High/Scope Educational Research Foundation, No. 10. Ypsilanti, Mich.: High/Scope Educational Research Foundation.

Seitz, V. (1990). Intervention programs for impoverished children: A comparison of educational and family support models. *Annals of Child Development* 7:73–104.

Seitz, V., & Apfel, N. H. (1994). Parent-focused intervention: Diffusion effects on siblings. *Child Development* 65:677–83.

Seitz, V., Rosenbaum, L. K., & Apfel, N. H. (1985). Effects of family support intervention: A ten-year follow-up. *Child Development* 56:376–91.

Shipman, V. C. (1970). Disdavantaged children and their first school experiences: ETS-Head Start Longitudinal Study. *Preliminary description of the initial sample prior to school enrollment.* ETS Technical Report Series, PR-70–20. Princeton, N.J.: Educational Testing Service.

Shipman V. C. (1976). *Stability and change in family status, situational, and process variables and their relationship to children's cognitive performance.* Princton, N.J.: Educational Testing Services.

Slaughter, D. T., Washington, V., Oyemade, U. J., & Lindsey, R. W. (1988). Head Start: A backward and forward look. *Social Policy Report* 3(2):1–19.

Slavin, R. E., Karweit, N. L., & Wasik, B. A. (1994). *Preventing early school failure: Research, policy, and practice.* Boston: Allyn & Bacon.

Spitz, H. H. (1986). *The raising of intelligence: A selected history of attempts to raise retarded intelligence.* Hillsdale, N.J.: Erlbaum.

Spitz, H. H. (1991). Commentary on Locurto's "Beyond IQ in Preschool Programs?" *Intelligence* 15:327–33.

State Education Department, University of the State of New York. (1982). *Evaluation of the New York State experimental prekindergarten program: Final report.* ERIC Document Reproduction Service No. Ed 219 123. Albany: New York State Education Department.

Sternberg, R., & Detterman, D. (Eds.). (1986). *What is intelligence?* Norwood, N.J.: Ablex.

St. Pierre, R., & Lopez, M. (1994). The comprehensive child-development program. Presentation to the National Research Council, Board on Children and Families, December 16. Washington, D.C.

St. Pierre, R., Swartz, J., Murray, S., Deck, D., & Nickel, P. (1993). *National evaluation of the Even Start Family Literacy Program: Report on effectiveness*. U.S. Department of Education, Office of Policy and Planning.

Van de Reit, V. & Resnick, M. B. (1973). Learning to learn: An effective model for early childhood education. Gainesville: University of Florida Press.

Wasik, B. H., Ramey, C. T., Bryant, D. M., & Sparling, J. J. (1990). A longitudinal study of two early-intervention strategies: Project CARE. *Child Development* 61:1682–96.

Weikart, D. P., Bond, J. T., & McNeil, J. T. (1978). *The Ypsilanti Perry Preschool Project: Preschool years and longitudinal results through fourth grade*. Ypsilanti, Mich.: High/Scope Press.

Westinghouse Learning Corporation and Ohio University. (1969). *The impact of Head Start: An evaluation of the effects of Head Start on children's cognitive and affective development*. Vols. 1 and 2. Report to the Office of Economic Opportunity. Athens: Westinghouse Learning Corporation and Ohio University.

White, K., & Casto, G. (1985). An integrative review of early-intervention efficacy studies with at-risk children: Implications for the handicapped. *Analysis and Intervention in Developmental Disabilities* 5:7–31.

Willer, B., Hofferth, S. L., Kisker, E. E., et al. (1991). *The demand and supply of child care in 1990*. Washington, D.C.: National Association for the Education of Young Children.

Woodhead, M. (1988). When psychology informs public policy: The case of early-childhood intervention. *American Psychologist* 43:443–54.

Zaslow, M. (1991). Variation in child-care quality and its implications for children. *Journal of Social Issues* 47(2):125–39.

Zigler, E., & Muenchow, S. (1992). Head Start: The inside story of America's most successful educational experiment. New York: Basic Books.

Zigler, E., & Styfco, S. J. (1993). Using policy research and theory to justify and inform Head Start expansion. *Social Policy Report* 8(2).

2. Long-Term Outcomes in Other Nations

Andersson, B. E. (1989). Effects of public day care—A longitudinal study. *Child Development* 60:857–67.

Andersson, B. E. (1992). Effects of day care on cognitive and socio-emotional competence in thirteen-year-old Swedish school children. *Child Development* 63:20–36.

Bairrao, J., & Tietze, W. (1993). *Early-childhood services in the European Community*. A report submitted to the Commission of the European Community, Task Force Human Resources, Education, Training, and Youth.

Boocock, S. S. (1991). The Japanese preschool system. In E. R. Beauchamp (Ed.), *Windows on Japanese education*. New York: Greenwood Press, pp. 97–125.

Bracey, G. W. (1996). International comparisons and the condition of American research. *Educational Researcher* 25 (1):5–1.

Braithwaite, John. (1983). *Explorations in early-childhood education*. Hawthorn, Victoria: Australian Council for Educational Research.

Broberg, A., Hwang, C. P., Lamb, M. E., & Ketterlinus, R. D. (1989). Child-care effects on socioemotional and intellectual competence in Swedish preschoolers. In J. S. Lande, S. Scarr, & N. Gunzenhauser (Eds.), *Caring for children: Challenge to America*. Hillsdale, N.J.: Erlbaum, 1989, pp. 49–76.

Bronfenbrenner, U. (1970). *Two worlds of childhood: U.S. and U.S.S.R.* New York: Russell Sage Foundation.

Bruner, J. (1980). *Under five in Britain: The Oxford preschool research project*. London: Grant McIntype.

Carlson, H. L., & Stenmalm, L. (1989). Professional and parent views of early-childhood programs: A cross-cultural study. *Early Childhood Development and Care* 50:51–64.

Chandler, A. M. K., Walker, S. P., Connolly, K., & Grantham-McGregor, S. M. (1995). School breakfast improves verbal fluency in under-nourished Jamaican children. *Community and international nutrition* (no volume number): 894–900.

Child and Youth Research Center. (1988). The impact evaluation of Early Childhood Enrichment Program, 1983–1987. Quezon City, Philippines: CYRC.

Clark, M. M. (1988). *Children under five: Educational research and evidence*. New York: Gordon and Breach Science Publishers.

Cochran, M. M. (1993). *International handbook of child-care policies and programs*. Westport, Conn.: Greenwood.

Cochran, M. M. (1996). Fitting early care and development to sociocultural characteristics and societal needs. Paper presented at conference on Early Child Development: Investing in the Future, Atlanta, Ga., April 8–9.

Cochran, M. M., & Gunnarsson, L. (1985). A follow-up study of group day care and family-based childrearing patterns. *Journal of Marriage and the Family* 47:297–309.

Curtis, A. (1992). Early-childhood education in Great Britain. In G. A. Woodill, J. Bernhard, & L. Prochner (Eds), *International handbook of early-childhood education*. New York: Garland, pp. 231–49.

Edwards, C., Gandini, L., & Forman, G. (Eds.). (1993). *The hundred languages of children: The Reggio Emilia approach to early-childhood education*. Norwood, N.J.: Ablex.

Feeney, S. (Ed.). (1992). *Early childhood in Asia and the Pacific: A source book*. New York: Garland.

Goelman, H., & Pence, A. (1987). Effects of child care, family, and individual characteristics on children's language development: The Victoria Day Care Research Project. In D. A. Phillips (Ed.), *Quality in child care: What does research tell us?* Washington, D.C.: National Association for the Education of Young Children, pp. 89–104.

Grantham-McGregor, S., Powell, C., Walker, S., Chang, S., & Fletcher, P. (1994). The long-term follow-up of severely malnourished children who participated in an intervention program. *Child Development* 65:428–39.

Gunnarsson, L. (1993). Sweden. In M. M. Cochran (Ed.), *International handbook of child-care policies and programs*. Westport, Conn.: Greenwood, pp. 491–514.

Gurkan, T. (1992). Early-childhood education and care in Turkey. In G. A. Woodill, J. Bernhard, & L. Prochner (Eds.), *International handbook of early-childhood education*. New York: Garland, pp. 481–89.

Helburn, S. W. (Ed.) (1995). *Cost, quality, and child outcomes in child-care centers*. Report prepared for seven supporting foundations. Denver: University of Colorado.

Ispa, J. (1994). *Child care in Russia in transition*. London: Bergin & Garvey.

Kagitcibasi, C. (1991). *The early-enrichment project in Turkey*. Paris: UNESCO-UNICEF-WFP.

Kagitcibasi, C. (1995). *Family and human development across cultures: A view from the other side*. Mahwah, N.J.: Erlbaum.

Kagitcibasi, C. (1996). Parent education and child development. Paper presented at conference on Early Child Development: Investing in the Future, Atlanta, Ga., April 8–9.

Kamerman, S. B., & Kahn, A. (1981). *Child care, family benefits and working parents*. New York: Columbia University Press.

Kaul, V. (1992). Early-childhood education in India. In Woodill, Bernar, & Prochner, pp. 275–92.

Kellaghan, T., & Greaney, B. J. (1993). The educational development of students following participation in a preschool programme in a disadvantaged area. Dublin: St. Patrick's College, Educational Research Centre.

Lamb, M. E., Hwang, C. P., & Broberg, A. (1991). Swedish child-care research. In E. Melhuish & P. Moss (Eds.), *Day care for young children: International perspectives*. London: Tavistock/Routledge, pp. 102–20.

Lombard, A. D. (1994). *Success begins at home*, 2nd ed. Guilford, Conn.: Dushkin.

Lomperis, A. M. T. (1991). Teaching mothers to read: Evidence from Columbia on the key role of maternal education in preschool child nutritional health. *Journal of Developing Areas* 26(1):25–51.

McKay, A., & McKay, H. (1983). Primary school progress after preschool experience: Troublesome issues in the conduct of follow-up research and findings from the Cali, Columbia study. In K. King and R. Myers (Eds.), *Preventing school failure*. Ottawa, Ont.: International Development Research Center, pp. 36–41.

McKay, H., Sinisterra, L., McKay A., Gomez, H., & Lloreda, P. (1978). Improving cognitive ability in chronically deprived children. *Science* 200:270–78.

McLean, S. V., Piscitelli, B., Halliwell, G., & Ashby, G. F. (1992). Australian early-childhood education. In G. A. Woodill, J. Bernhard, & L. Prochner (Eds.), *International handbook of early-childhood education*. New York: Garland, pp. 49–73.

McMahan, I. D. (1992). Public preschool from the age of two: The *ecole maternalle* in France. *Young Children* 47(5):22–28.

Moss, P. (1990). Childcare in the European Community. *Women of Europe*, Supplement No. 31. Brussels: European Commission Childcare Network.

Myers, R. G. (1992). *The twelve who survive: Strengthening programs of early childhood*. New York: Routledge, in cooperation with UNESCO.

New, R. S. (1990). Excellent early education: A town in Italy has it! *Young Children* 45(6):4–10.

Nitta, N., & Nagano, S. (1975). The effects of pre-school education. *Research Bulletin of the National Institute for Educational Research* 13:17–19.

Ochiltree, G., & Edgar, D. (1990). The effects of non-maternal care in the first twelve months of life on children in the first year of school: Preliminary findings from a two-stage study (The Australian Early Childhood Study). Melbourne: Australian Institute of Family Studies.

OECD (Organization for Economic Cooperation and Development). (1993). *Education at a glance: OECD Indicators 1993*. Paris: Centre for Educational Research and Innovation.

Olmsted, P. P. (1989). A look at early-childhood education in the United States from a global perspective. Paper commissioned by the National Center for Educational Statistics.

Olmsted, P. P. (1992). A cross-national perspective on the demand for and supply of early-childhood services. In A. Booth (Ed.), *Child care in the 1990s*. Hillsdale, N.J.: Erlbaum, pp. 33–41.

Olmsted, P. P., & Weikart, D. P. (Eds.). (1989). *How nations serve young children*. Ypsilanti, Mich.: High/Scope Press.

Olmsted, P. P., & Weikart, D. P. (Eds.). (1994). *Families speak: Early-childhood care and education in eleven countries*. Ypsilanti, Mich.: High/Scope Press.

Opper, S. (1989). Child care and early education in Hong Kong. In P. P. Olmsted & D. P. Weikart (Eds.), *How nations serve young children: Profiles of child care and education in fourteen countries*. Ypsilanti, Mich.: High/Scope Press, pp. 119–42.

Osborn, A. F., & Milbank, J. E. (1987). *The effects of early education. A report from the Child Health and Education Study*. Oxford: Clarendon Press.

Palti, H., Adler, B., & Baras, M. (1987). Early educational intervention in the maternal and child health services—long-term evaluation of program effectiveness. *Early Child Development and Care* 27:555–70.

Perez-Escamilla, R., & Pollitt, E. (1995). Growth improvements in children above three years of age: The Cali study. *Community and International Nutrition* (no volume number): 885–93.

Philp, H. S., with Chetley, A. (1988). *A small awakening: The work of the Bernard van Leer Foundation: 1965–1986*. The Hague: Bernard van Leer Foundation.

Podmore, V. N. (1993). *Education and care: A review of international studies of the outcomes of early-childhood experiences*. Wellington: New Zealand Council for Educational Research.

Pollitt, E., et al. (1993). *Early supplementary feeding and cognition. Monographs of the Society for Research in Child Development* 58(7, Serial No. 235).

Prochner, L. (1992). Themes in late twentieth-century child care: A cross-national analysis. In G. A. Woodill, J. Bernhard, & L. Prochner (Eds.), *International handbook of early-childhood education*. New York: Garland, pp. 11–19.

Raudenbush, S. W., Kidchanapanish, S., & Sang Jin Kang. (1991). The effects of pre-primary access and quality on educational achievement in Thailand. *Comparative Education Review* 35(2):255–73.

Rhee, U., & Lee, K. (1983). A study on the effectiveness of four different early childhood education program models. *Journal of Educational Research* 21(2):83–104.

Rhee, U., & Lee, K. (1987). The effectiveness of four early-childhood program models: Follow-up at fourth grade. *Journal of Educational Research* 25(2):119–37.

Rhee, U., & Lee, K. (1990). The effectiveness of four early-childhood program models: Follow-up at middle school. *Journal of Educational Research* 28(3):147–62.

Sharpe, P. (1991). Parental involvement in preschools: Parents' and teachers' perceptions of their roles. *Early Child Development and Care* 71:53–62.

Sim, K. P., & Kam, H. W. (Eds.). (1992). *Growing up in Singapore: The preschool years*. Singapore: Longman Singapore.

Sjolund, A. (1973). *Daycare institutions and children's development*. Westmead, U.K.: Saxon House.

Smith, A. B. (1992). Early-childhood education in New Zealand: The winds of change. In G. A. Woodill, J. Bernhard, & L. Prochner (Eds.), *International handbook of early-childhood education*. New York: Garland, pp. 49–73.

Stevenson, H. W., & Stigler, J. W. (1994). *The learning gap*. New York: Summit Books.

Tietze, W. (1987). A structural model for the evaluation of preschool effects. *Early Childhood Research Quarterly* 2(2):133–53.

Tobin, J., Wu, D. Y. H., & Davidson, D. H. (1989). *Preschool in three cultures: Japan, China and the United States*. New Haven, Conn.: Yale University Press.

UNESCO. (1993). *World education report 1993*. Paris: UNESCO.

Van Ilzendoorn, M. H., & van Vliet-Visser, S. (1988). Attachment and intelligence. The relationship between quality of attachment in infancy and IQ in kindergarten. *Journal of Genetic Psychology* 149:23–28.

Woodill, G. A., Bernhard, J., & Prochner, L. (Eds.). (1992). *International handbook of early-childhood education*. New York: Garland.

Woodward, M. (1977). *Intervening in disadvantage: A challenge for nursery education*. A review of British research into preschool education for disadvantaged children, prepared for the National Foundation for Educational Research (NFER), London.

Wylie, C. (1994). *What research on early-childhood education / care outcomes can and can't tell policy makers*. Wellington: New Zealand Council for Educational Research.

Yeoh, B. S. A., & Huang, S. (1995). Childcare in Singapore: Negotiating choices and constraints in a multicultural society. *Women's Studies International Forum* 18(4):445–61.

Young, M. E. (1996). *Early-child development: Investing in the future*. Washington, D.C.: World Bank.

Zaveri, S. (1994). *India village preschool study*. Report prepared for Aga Khan Education Service, Centre for Research and Development, India.

Zimmerman, S. L., Antonov, A. I., Johnson, M., & Borisov, V. A. (1994). Social policy and families. In J. W. Maddock, M. J. Hogan, A. I. Antonov, & M. S. Matskovsky (Eds.), *Families before and after Perestroika: Russian and U.S. perspectives*. New York: Guilford Press, pp. 186–219.

3. Preschool Program Quality in Programs for Children in Poverty

Arnett, J. (1986). Caregivers in day care settings: Does training matter? Unpublished doctoral dissertation, University of Virginia.

Barnett, W. S. (1995). Long-term effects of early childhood programs on cognitive and school outcomes. *The Future of Children* (5):25–50.

Barnett, W. S., Frede, E. C., Mobasher, H., & Mohr, P. (1987). The efficacy of public preschool programs and the relationship of program quality to efficacy. *Educational Evaluation and Policy Analysis* 10(1):37–49.

GOVERNORS STATE UNIVERSITY
UNIVERSITY PARK
IL 60466

Belsky, J. (1984). Two waves of day-care research: Developmental effects and conditions of quality. In R. Ainslie (Ed.), *The child and the day-care setting: Qualitative variations and development*. New York: Praeger, pp. 1–34.

Bereiter, C. (1986). Does direct instruction cause delinquency? *Early Childhood Research Quarterly* 1(3):289–92.

Bereiter, C., & Englemann, S. (1966). *Teaching the disadvantaged child in the preschool*. Englewood Cliffs, N.J.: Prentice-Hall.

Berk, L. (1985). Relationship of educational attainment, child-oriented attitudes, job satisfaction, and career commitment to caregivers' behavior toward children. *Child Care Quarterly* 14:103–29.

Berk, L. (1996). *Infants, children, and adolescents*. Needham Heights, Mass.: Simon & Schuster.

Bredekamp, S. (Ed.). (1987). *Developmentally appropriate practices in early-childhood programs serving children from birth through age eight*. Washington, D.C.: National Association for the Education of Young Children.

Bredekamp, S., & Rosegrant, T. (Eds.). (1992). *Reaching potentials: Appropriate curriculum and assessment for young children*. Washington, D.C.: National Association for the Education of Young Children.

Bronfenbenner, U. (1974). Is early intervention effective? *A report on longitudinal programs*, vol. 2. (DHEW Publication Number OHD74-24). Washington, D.C.: U.S. Government Printing Office.

Bruner, J. (1962). Introduction. In L. Vygotsky, *Thought & language*. Cambridge, Mass.: MIT Press.

Brush, L., Gaidurgis, A., & Best, C. (1993). *Indices of Head Start program quality*. Report prepared for the Administration of Children, Youth, and Families, Head Start Bureau. Washington, D.C.: Pelavin.

Bryant, D. M., Burchinal, M., Lau, L., & Sparling, J. J. (1994). Family and classroom: Correlates of Head Start children's developmental outcomes. *Early Childhood Research Quarterly* 9:289–309.

Bryant, D. M., Peisner, E. S., & Clifford, R. M. (1993). *Evaluation of public preschool programs in North Carolina*. Chapel Hill, N.C.: Frank Porter Graham Child Development Center.

Charlesworth, R., Hart, C., Burts, D., & DeWolf, M. (1993). The LSU studies: Building a research base for developmentally appropriate practice. *Advances in Early Education and Day Care* 5:3–28.

Child Care Employee Project. (1991). *What states can do to secure a skilled and stable child-care work force: Strategies to use the new federal funds for child-care quality*. Oakland, Calif.: Child Care Employee Project.

Chubrich, R. E., & Kelley, M. F. (1994). Head Start Expansion in the 1990s: A critique. *Association of Childhood Education International's Focus on Early Childhood* 6:1–3.

Clarke-Stewart, A., & Gruber, C. (1984). Day care forms and features. In R. C. Ainslie (Ed.), *Quality variations in dare care*. New York: Praeger, pp. 67–96.

Cole, M. Gay, J., Glick, J. A., & Sharp, D. W. (1971). *The cultural context of learning and thinking*. New York: Basic Books.

Cost and Quality Team, The. (1995). *Cost, quality, and child outcomes in child-care centers*. Executive summary. Denver: University of Colorado at Denver.

Datta, L. (1976). The impact of the Westinghouse/Ohio evaluation on the development of Project Head Start. In C. Abt (Ed.), *The evaluation of social programs*. Beverly Hills, Calif.: Sage.

Farran, D. C. (1990). Effects of intervention with disadvantaged and disabled children: A decade review. In S. J. Meisels & J. P. Schenkott (Eds)., *Handbook of early intervention*. Cambridge: Cambridge University Press, pp. 501–35.

Feeney, S., & Chur, R. (1985). Effective teachers of young children. *Young Children* 47:52.

Fenichel, F. (Ed.). (1992). *Learning through supervision and mentorship to support the development of infants, toddlers and their families: A source book*. Washington, D.C.: Zero to Three/National Center for Clinical Infant Program.

Fraiberg, S. (1975). Intervention in infancy: A program for blind infants. In B. Z. Friedlander, G. M. Steritt, and G. E. Kirk (Eds.), *Exceptional infant* (vol. 1). New York: Bruner/Mazel, pp. 103–36.

Frede, E. C., Austin, A. B., & Lindauer, S. K. (1993). The relationship of specific developmentally appropriate teaching practices to children's skills in first grade. *Advances in Early Education and Child Care* 5:95–111.

Frede, E. C., & Barnett, W. S. (1992). Developmentally appropriate public school preschool: A study of implementation of the High/Scope curriculum and its effects on disadvantaged children's skills at first grade. *Early Childhood Research Quarterly* 7:483–99.

Garber, H. L. (1988). *The Milwaukee Project*. Washington, D.C.: American Association for Mental Retardation.

General Accounting Office. (1990). *Early-childhood programs: What are the costs of high-quality programs?* Wasington, D.C.: U.S. GAO.

Gersten, R. (1986). Response to consequences of three preschool curriculum models through age fifteen. *Early Childhood Research Quarterly* 1 (3):293–302.

Goffin, S. G. (1994). *Curriculum models and early-childhood education: Appraising the relationship*. New York: Merrill.

Gray, S. W., Ramsey, B. K., & Klaus, R. A. (1982). *From three to twenty: The Early Training Project*. Baltimore, Md.: University Park Press.

Hale-Benson, J. (1990). Visions for children: African-American early childhood education programs. *Early Childhood Research Quarterly* 5:199–213.

Harms, T. & Clifford, R. M. (1980). *Early childhood environment rating scale.* New York: Teachers College Press.

Haskins, R. (1989). The efficacy of early-childhood education. *American Psychologist* 44(2):274–82.

Hayes, C., Palmer, J., & Zaslow, M. (Eds.). (1990). *Who cares for America's children? Child-care policy for the 1990s.* Washington, D.C., National Academy Press.

Holloway, S. D., & Reichart-Erickson, M. (1988). The relationship of day-care quality to children's free-play behavior and social problem-solving skills. *Early Childhood Research Quarterly* 3:39–54.

Howes, C. (1983). Caregiver behavior in center and family day care. *Journal of Applied Developmental Psychology* 4:99–107.

Howes, C., Smith, E., & Galinsky, E. (1995). *The Florida child-care quality improvement study: Interim report.* New York: Families and Work Institute.

Hunt, J. M. V. (1961). *Intelligence & experience.* New York: Ronald Press.

Hyson, M. D., Hirsh-Pasek, K., & Rescorla, L. (1990). The Classroom Practices Inventory: An observation instrument based on NAEYC's guidelines for developmentally appropriate practices for four- and five-year-old children. *Early Childhood Research Quarterly* 5:475–594.

Jipson, J. (1991). Developmentally appropriate practice: Culture, curriculum, connections. *Early Education and Development* 2:120–36.

Jorde-Bloom, P. (1988). *A great place to work: Improving conditions for staff in young children's programs.* Washington, D.C.: National Association for the Education of Young Children.

Kamii, C. (Ed.). (1990). *Achievement testing in the early grades: Games grown-ups play.* Washington, D.C.: National Association for the Education of Young Children.

Karnes, M. B., Schwedel, A. M., & Williams, M. B. (1983). A comparison of five approaches for educating young children from low-income homes. In Consortium for Longitudinal Studies (Ed.), *As the twig is bent . . . lasting effects of preschool programs.* Hillsdale, N.J.: Erlbaum, pp. 133–70.

Karnes, R., Zehrbach, R., & Teska, J. (1972). An ameliorative approach in the development of curriculum. In R. K. Parker (Ed.), *The preschool in action: Exploring early-childhood programs.* Boston: Allyn & Bacon, pp. 353–81.

Karnes, M., Zehrbach, R., & Teska, J. (1977). Conceptualization of GOAL (Games Oriented Activities for Learning). In M. D. Day & R. D. Parker (Eds.), *The preschool in action: Exploring early childhood programs.* Boston: Allyn and Bacon, pp. 174–94.

Lally, J. R., & Honig, A. S. (1977). The Family Development Research Program: A program for prenatal, infant, and early-childhood enrichment. In M. D. Day and R. D. Parker (Eds.), *The preschool in action: Exploring early-childhood programs*. Boston: Allyn and Bacon, pp. 149–74.

Lally, R., Mangione, P., & Honig, A. (1987). *Long-range impact of an early intervention with low-income children and their families*. San Francisco: Far West Laboratories.

Lazar, I. (1983). Discussion and implications of the findings. In Consortium for Longitudinal Studies (Ed.), *As the twig is bent . . . lasting effects of preschool programs*. Hillsdale, N.J.: Erlbaum, p. 464

Love, J. M., Ryer, P., Faddis, B. (1992). Caring environments: Program quality in California's publicly funded child-development programs. A report on the legislatively mandated 1990–91 Staff/Child Ratio Study.

Marcon, R. A. (1994). Early learning and early identification follow-up study: Transition from the early to the later grades. A report prepared for the District of Columbia Public Schools. Washington, D.C.: District of Columbia Public Schools.

McCartney, K. (1984). The effect of quality day-care environment upon children's language development. *Developmental Psychology* 20:244–60.

Meisels, S. J., Dorfman, A., Steele, D. (n.d.). Equity and excellence in group-administered and performance-based assessments. Unpublished paper.

Mehan, H. (1979). What time is it, Denise? Asking known information questions in classroom discourse. *Theory into Practice* 18:285–94.

Miller, L. B. (1984). Long-term effects of four preschool programs: Ninth- and tenth-grade results. *Child Development* 55:1570–87

Miller, L. B., & Bizzell, R. P. (1983). The Louisville Experiment: A comparison of four programs. In Consortium for Longitudinal Studies (Ed.), *As the twig is bent . . . lasting effects of preschool programs*. Hillsdale, N.J.: Erlbaum, pp. 171–200.

Miller, L. B., & Dyer, J. L. (1975). Four preschool programs. Their dimensions and effects. *Monographs for the Society of Research in Child Development* 40:5–6.

Morgan, G., Azer, S., & Costley, J. (1993). *Making a career of it: The state of the states report on career development in early care and education*. Boston: Center for Career Development in Early Care and Education at Wheelock College.

Neilson, L. (1990). Research comes home. *The Reading Teacher* 44:248–50.

Nelson, K. (1981). Social cognition in a script framework. In J. Flavell & L. Ross (Eds.). *Social cognitive development*. Cambridge: Cambridge University Press.

Nelson, K. (1986). *Event knowledge: Structure and function in development*. Hillsdale, N.J.: Erlbaum.

Palmer, F. H. (1972). Minimal intervention at age two and three and subsequent intellective changes. In R. K. Parker (Ed.), *The preschool in action: Exploring early childhood programs*. Boston: Allyn & Bacon.

Phillips, D., Howes, C., & Whitebook, M. (1992). The social policy context of child care: Effects on quality. *American Journal of Community Psychology* 20(1):25–51.

Phillips, D., Scarr, S., & McCartney, K. (1987). Child-care quality and children's social development. *Developmental Psychology* 23:537–43.

Ramey, C., & Campbell, F. (1991). In A. C. Huston (Ed.), *Children in poverty: Child development and public policy*. New York: Cambridge University Press, pp. 190–221.

Ramey, C. T., McGinness, G. D., Cross, L., Collier, A. M., & Barrie-Blackey, S. (1982). The Abecedarian approach to social competence. Cognitive and linguistic intervention for disadvantaged preschoolers. In K. M. Borman (Ed.), *The social life of children in a changing society*. Hillsdale, N.J.: Erlbaum, pp. 145–74.

Richardson, V. (1994). Conducting research on practice. *Educational Researcher* 23(5):5–10.

Royce, J., Darlington, R., & Murray, H. (1983). In Consortium for Longitudinal Studies (Ed.), *As the twig is bent . . . lasting effects of preschool programs*. Hillsdale, N.J.: Erlbaum, p. 442.

Ruopp, R., Travers, J. Glantz, F. M., & Coelen, C. (1979). Children at the center: Summary findings and their implications. *Final report of the National Day Care Study*, vol. 1. Cambridge, Mass.: Abt.

Schweinhart, L. J., Barnes, H. V., & Weikart, D. P. (1994). *Significant benefits: The High/Scope Perry preschool study through age 27*. Ypsilanti, Mich.: High/Scope Press.

Schweinhart, L. J., Weikart, D. P., & Larner, M. B. (1986). Consequences of three preschool curriculum models through age fifteen. *Early Childhood Research Quarterly* 1(1):15–46.

Seppanen, P. S., Godon, K. W., & Metzger, J. L. (1993). Final report, vol. 2. *Observational study of Chapter 1-funded early-childhood programs*. Washington, D.C.: U.S. Department of Education.

Siegler, R. S. (1976). Three aspects of cognitive development. *Cognitive Development* 8:481–520.

Sonquist, H. D., & Kamii, C. K. (1967). Applying some Piagetian concepts in the classoom for the disadvantaged. In D. P. Weikart (Ed.), *Preschool intervention: A preliminary report of the Perry Preschool Project*. Ann Arbor, Mich.: Campus, pp. 89–104.

Spodek, B. (1991). Early-childhood curriculum and cultural knowledge. In B. Spodek & O. Saracho (Eds.), *Issues in early-childhood curriculum, yearbook in early-childhood education*, vol. 2. New York: Teachers College Press.

Swadener, B. B., & Kessler, S. A. (1991). Introduction to the special issue: Reconceptualizing early-childhood education. *Early Education and Development* 2:85–94.

Tobin, J. J., Wu, D. Y. H., & Davidson, D. H. (1989). *Preschool in three cultures: Japan, China and the United States*. New Haven, Conn.: Yale University Press.

U.S. General Accounting Office. (1994). *Early-childhood programs: Local perspectives on barriers to providing Head Start services*. GAO/HEHS-95-8. Washington, D.C.: GAO, December 21.

U.S. General Accounting Office. (1995). *Early childhood centers: Services to prepare children for school often limited*. GAO/HEHS-95-21. Washington, D.C.: GAO, March.

Vandell, D. L., Henderson, V. K., & Powers, C. P. (1989). A longitudinal study of children with day-care experiences of varying quality. *Child Development* 59:1286–92.

Vygotsky, L. S. (1978). *Mind in society*. Cambridge, Mass.: Harvard University Press.

Wagner, D. A. (1978). Memories of Morocco: The influence of age, schooling, and environment on memory. *Cognitive Psychology* 10:1–28.

Wagner, R. K., & Sternberg, R. J. (1985). Practical intelligence in real-world pursuits: The role of tacit knowledge. *Journal of Personality and Social Psychology* 49:436–58.

Walsh, D. J. (1991). Extending the discourse on developmental appropriateness: A developmental perspective. *Early Education and Development* 2:109–19.

Weikart, D. P. (Ed.). (1967). *Preschool intervention: A preliminary report of the Perry Preschool Project*. Ann Arbor, Mich.: Campus.

Weikart, D. P. (1972). A traditional nursery program revisited. In R. K. Parker (Ed.), *The preschool in action: Exploring early childhood programs*. Boston: Allyn & Bacon, pp. 189–215.

Weikart, D. P., Epstein, A. S., Schweinhart, L. J., & Bond, J. T. (1978). *The Ypsilanti Preschool Curriculum Demonstration Project: Preschool years and longitudinal results*. Ypsilanti, Mich.: High/Scope Press.

Weikart, D. P., Kamii, C. K., & Radin, N. L. (1967). Perry Preschool Project progress report. In D. P. Weikart (ed.), *Preschool intervention: A preliminary report of the Perry Preschool Project*. Ann Arbor, Mich.: Campus, pp. 1–88.

Westinghouse Learning Corporation. (1969). *The impact of Head Start: An evaluation of the effects of Head Start on children's cognitive and affective development*. EDO 36321. Washington, D.C., Westinghouse Corporation.

Whitebook, M., Howes, C., & Phillips, D. (1989). Who cares? Child-care teachers and the quality of care in America. *Final report of the*

National Child Care Staffing Study. Oakland, Calif.: Child-Care Employee Project.

Woodhead, M. (1988). When psychology informs public policy: The case of early-childhood intervention. *American Psychologist* 43(6):443–54.

Zigler, E., & Styfco, S. J. (1994). Is the Perry preschool better than Head Start? Yes and no. *Early Childhood Research Quarterly* 9:269–87.

4. Regenerating Two-Generation Programs

Burghardt, J., & Gordon, A. (1990). *More jobs and higher pay: How an integrated program compares with traditional programs*. New York: Rockefeller Foundation.

Cameron, S., & Heckman, J. (1993). Nonequivalence of high school equivalents. *The Journal of Labor Economics*, 11:1–47.

Carnegie Task Force on Meeting the Needs of Young Children. (April 1994). *Starting points: Meeting the needs of our youngest children*. New York: Carnegie Corporation.

Development Associates, Inc. (1994). National evaluation of adult-education programs: Draft final report. Arlington, Va.: Development Associates.

Duncan, G. J. (1991). The economic environment of childhood. In A. C. Huston (Ed.), *Children in poverty: Child development and public policy*. New York: Cambridge University Press, pp. 23–50.

Gueron, J., & Pauly, E. (1991). *From welfare to work*. New York: Russell Sage.

Huston, A. C., McLoyd, V. C., & Garcia Coll, C. (1994). Children and poverty: Issues in contemporary research. *Child Development* 65:275–82.

IHDP (Infant Health and Development Program). (1990). Enhancing the outcomes of low-birth-weight, premature infants. *Journal of the American Medical Association* 263(22):3035–42.

Johnson, D., & Walker, T. (1991). Final report of an evaluation of the Avance parent education and family support program. Report submitted to the Carnegie Corporation. San Antonio, Tex.: Avance.

Karweit, N. L. (1994). Can preschool alone prevent early learning failure? In R. E. Slavin, N. L. Karweit, & B. A. Wasik (Eds.), *Preventing early school failure: Research, policy, and practice*. Boston: Allyn and Bacon.

Maynard, R. (1993). *Building self-sufficiency among welfare-dependent teenage parents: Lessons from the Teenage Parent Demonstration*. Princeton, N.J.: Mathematica Policy Research.

Quint, J. C., Polit, D. F., Bos, H., & Cave, G. (1994). *New Chance: Interim findings on a comprehensive program for disadvantaged young mothers and their children*. New York: Manpower Demonstration Research.

Ramey, C. T., Ramey, S. L., Gaines, R., & Blair, C. (1994). Two-generation early interventions: A child-development perspective. In S. Smith (Ed.), *Two-generation programs for families in poverty: A new intervention strategy*. Norwood, N.J.: Ablex.

Ramey, C. T., & Ramey, S. L. (1992). Early educational intervention with disadvantaged children—To what end? *Applied and Preventive Psychology* 1:130–40.

Riccio, J., Friedlander, D., & Freedman, S. (1994). GAIN: *Benefits, costs, and three-year impacts of a welfare-to-work program*. New York: Manpower Demonstration Research.

Schorr, L. (1988). *Within our reach: Breaking the cycle of disadvantage*. New York: Doubleday.

Smith, S. (1991). Two-generation program models: A new intervention strategy. Social Policy Report, vol. 5 (1), Society for Research in Child Development, Ann Arbor, Mich.

St. Pierre, R., Goodson, B., Layzer, J., & Bernstein, L. (1994). National Evaluation of the Comprehensive Child Development Program: Report to Congress. Cambridge, Mass.: Abt.

St. Pierre, R., Swartz, J., Gamse, B., Murray, S., Deck, D., & Nickel, P. (1995). National evaluation of Even Start Family Literacy Program: Final Report. Cambridge, Mass.: Abt.

Swartz, J., Smith, C., Berghauer, G., Bernstein, L., & Gardine, J. (1994). Evaluation of the Head Start Family Service Center Demonstration Projects: First-year evaluation results. Cambridge, Mass.: Abt.

Travers, J., Nauta, M., & Irwin, N. (1982). *The effects of a social program: Final report of the Child and Family Resource Program's Infant-Toddler Component*. Cambridge, Mass.: Abt.

5. The Effects of Welfare Reform on Teenage Parents and Their Children

Aber, J. L., Berlin, L., Brooks-Gunn, J., & Carcagno, G. (1995). The "Interactions and Developmental Processes" study of the Teenage Parent Demonstration Project: Final report. Princeton, N.J.: Mathematica Policy Research.

Bachrach, C. A., Clogg, C. C., & Carver, K. (1993). Outcomes of early childbearing: Summary of a conference. *Journal of Research on Adolescence* 3(4):337–48.

Baydar, N., Brooks-Gunn, J., & Furstenberg, F. F., Jr. (1993). Antecedents of literacy in disadvantaged youth. *Child Development* 64:815–29.

Baldwin, W., & Cain, V. S. (1980). The children of teenage parents. *Family Planning Perspectives* 12(17), 34–43.

Bane, M. J., & Ellwood, D. T. (1989). One fifth of the nation's children: Why are they poor? *Science* 24b:1047–53.

Bloom, D., Kopp, H., Long, D., & Polit, D. (1991). LEAP: *Implementing a welfare initiative to improve school attendance among teenage parents.* New York: Manpower Demonstration Research.

Bloom, H., Orr, L., Cave, G., Bell, S., Doolitle, F., & Lin, W. (1994). *The National JTPA Study: Overview of the impacts, benefits, and costs of Title II-A.* Cambridge, Mass.: Abt.

Brooks-Gunn, J., & Chase-Lansdale, P. L. (1995). Adolescent parents. In M. Bornstein (Ed.), *Handbook of parenting.* Hillsdale, N.J.: Erlbaum.

Brooks-Gunn, J., & Furstenberg, F. F., Jr. (1986). Antecedents and consequences of parenting: The case of adolescent motherhood. In A. Fogel and G. Melson (Eds.), *Origins of Nurturance.* Hillsdale, N.J.: Erlbaum, pp. 233–58.

Brooks-Gunn, J., & Furstenberg, F. F., Jr. (1987). Continuity and change in the context of poverty: Adolescent mothers and their children. In J. J. Gallagher and C. T. Ramey (Eds.), *The malleability of children.* Baltimore, Md.: Brookes, pp. 171–88..

Brooks-Gunn, J., Guo, G., & Furstenberg, F. F., Jr. (1993). Who drops out of and who continues beyond high school? A twenty-year follow-up of black urban youth. *Journal of Research on Adolescence* 3(3):271–94.

Chase-Lansdale, P. L., Brooks-Gunn, J., & Paikoff, R. L. (1991). Research and programs for adolescent mothers: Missing links and future promises. *Family Relations* 40(4):396–404.

Chase-Lansdale, P. L., & Vinovskis, M. A. (1995). Whose responsibility? A historical analysis of the changing roles of mother, fathers, and society in assuming responsibility for poor U.S. children. In P. L. Chase-Lansdale & J. Brooks-Gunn (Eds.), *Escape from poverty: What makes a difference for children?* New York: Cambridge University Press.

Cherlin, A. J. (1995). Child care and the Family Support Act: Policy issues. In L. Chase-Lansdale and J. Brooks-Gunn (Eds.), *Escape from poverty: What makes a difference for children?* New York: Cambridge University Press.

Clewell, B. C., Brooks-Gunn, J., & Benasich, A. A. (1989). Evaluating child-related outcomes of teenage parenting programs. *Family Relations* 38:201–9.

Cohen, E., Golonka, S., Maynard, R., Ooms, T., & Owen, T. (1994). *Welfare reform and literacy: Are we making the connection?* Washington, D.C.: Family Impact Seminar and National Center on Adult Literacy.

Congressional Research Service. (1994). *Welfare proposal in the contract with America.* CRS Report 94-909 EPW. Washington, D.C.: U.S. Library of Congress.

Congressional Research Service. (1995a). *AFDC reform: Why again?* CRS Report 95-63 EPW. Washington, D.C.: U.S. Library of Congress.

Congressional Research Service. (1995b). *Time-limited welfare proposals.* CRS Issue Brief. Washington, D.C.: U.S. Library of Congress.

Ellwood, D. (1986). *Targeting strategies for welfare recipients.* Princeton, N.J.: Mathematica Policy Research.

Friedlander, D., Freedman, S., & Riccio, J (1993). *GAIN: Two-year impacts in six counties.* New York: Manpower Demonstration Research Corporation.

Furstenberg, F. F. (1976). *Unplanned parenthood: The social consequences of teenage childbearing.* New York: Free Press.

Furstenberg, F. F., Jr., Brooks-Gunn, J., & Morgan, P. (1987). *Adolescent mothers in later life.* New York: Cambridge University Press.

Furstenberg, F. F., Jr., Brooks-Gunn, J., & Chase-Lansdale, L. (1989). Adolescent fertility and public policy. *American Psychologist* 44(2):313–20.

Galinsky, E., Howes, C., Kontos, S., & Shinn, M. (1994). *The study of children in family child care and relative care: Highlights of findings.* New York: Families and Work Institute.

Gueron, J., & Pauly, E. (1991). *From welfare to work.* New York: Russell Sage.

Hagen, J., & Lurie, I. (1993). *Implementing JOBS: The initial design and structure of local programs.* Albany, N.Y.: Nelson A. Rockefeller Institute of Government.

Hayes, C. D. (1987). *Risking the future: Adolescent sexuality, pregnancy and childbearing.* Final Report of the National Research Council's Panel on Adolescent Pregnancy and Childbearing, vol. 1. Washington, D.C.: National Academy Press.

Hershey, A. (1991a). *Case management for teenage parents: Lessons from the Teenage Parent Demonstration.* Princeton, N.J.: Mathematica Policy Research.

Hershey, A. (1991b). *Enrolling teenage AFDC parents in mandatory education and training programs: Lessons from the Teenage Parent Demonstration.* Princeton, N.J.: Mathematica Policy Research.

Hershey, A., & Maynard, R. (1992). *Designing and implementing services for welfare dependent teenage parents: Lessons from the DHHS/OFA-sponsored Teenage Parent Demonstration.* Written statement for the Committee on Ways and Means, March 6. Princeton, N.J.: Mathematica Policy Research.

Hershey, A., & Nagatoshi, C. (1989). *Implementing services for welfare-dependent teenage parents: Experiences in the DHHS/OFA Teenage Parent Demonstration.* Princeton, N.J.: Mathematica Policy Research.

Hershey, A., & Rangarajan, A. (1993). *Delivering education and employment services to teenage parents: Lessons from the Teenage Parent Demonstration.* Princeton, N.J.: Mathematica Policy Research.

Hershey, A., & Silverberg, M. (1993). *Costs of mandatory education and training programs for teenage parents on welfare: Lessons from the*

Teenage Parent Demonstration. Princeton, N.J.: Mathematica Policy Research.

Hill, S., Greenberg, M., & Levin-Epstein, J. (1991). *Babies on buses: Lessons from initial implementation of the JOBS teenage parents provisions.* Washington, D.C.: Center for Law and Social Policy.

Kisker, E., Maynard, R., Gordon, A., & Strain, M. (1989). *The child-care challenge: What parents need and what is available in three metropolitan areas.* Princeton, N.J.: Mathematica Policy Research.

Kisker, E., and Silverberg, M. (1991). Child-care utilization by disadvantaged teenage mothers. *Journal of Social Issues* 47(2):159–78.

Klebanov, P. K., Brooks-Gunn, J., & Duncan, G. J. (1994). Does neighborhood and family poverty affect mothers' parenting, mental health, and social support? *Journal of Marriage and the Family* 56(2):441–55.

Larner, M. (1994). *In the neighborhood: Programs that strengthen family day care for low-income families.* New York: National Center for Children in Poverty.

Levin-Epstein, J., & Greenberg, M. (1991). *Teenage parents and JOBS: Early state statistics.* Washington, D.C.: Center for Law and Social Policy.

Martinson, K., & Friedlander, D. (1994). *GAIN: Basic education in a welfare-to-work program.* New York: Manpower Demonstration Research.

Maynard, R. (1994). Subsidized employment and non-labor market alternatives to welfare. In D. Nightengale and R. Haveman (Eds.), *The work alternative: Welfare and the realities of the job market.* Washington, D.C.: Urban Institute Press.

Maynard, R., Nicholson, W., & Rangarajan, A. (1993). *Breaking the cycle of poverty: The effectiveness of mandatory services for welfare dependent teenage parents.* Princeton, N.J.: Mathematica Policy Research.

Maynard, R., & Rangarajan, A. (1994). Contraceptive use and repeat pregnancies among welfare-dependent teenage mothers. *Family Planning Perspectives* 26(5):198–205.

Polit, D. (1992). *Barriers to self-sufficiency and avenues to success among teenage mothers.* Princeton, N.J.: Mathematica Policy Research.

Polit, D., & White, C. (1988). *The lives of young, disadvantaged mothers: Five-year follow-up of the Project Redirection sample.* Saratoga Springs, N.Y.: Humanalysis.

Quint, J., Polit, D., Bos, H., & Cave, G. (1994). *New Chance: Interim findings on a comprehensive program for disadvantaged young mothers and their children.* New York: Manpower Demonstration Research.

Quint, J., & Riccio, J. (1985). *The challenge of serving pregnant and parenting teens: Lessons from Project Redirection.* New York: Manpower Demonstration Research.

Schochet, P. Z., & Kisker, E. E. (1992). *Meeting the child-care needs of disadvantaged teenage mothers: Lessons from the Teenage Parent Demonstration.* Princeton, N.J.: Mathematica Policy Research.

Smith, S. (1995). Two-generational programs: A new intervention strategy and directions for future research. In L. Chase-Lansdale and J. Brooks-Gunn (Eds.), *Escape from poverty: What makes a difference for children?* New York: Cambridge University Press.

Smith, S., & Zaslow, M. (1995). Two-generational programs research and theory. In S. Smith (Ed.), *Two-generation programs for families in poverty.* Norwood, N.J.: Ablex.

Strain, M., & Kisker, E. (1989). *Literacy and the disadvantaged: Analysis of data from the national assessment of educational progress.* Princeton, N.J.: Mathematica Policy Research.

Upchurch, D., & McCarthy, J. (1989). Adolescent childbearing and high school completion in the 1980s: Have things changed? *Family Planning Perspectives* 21:199–202.

U.S. General Accounting Office. (1994). *Welfare to work: Current AFDC program not sufficiently focused on employment.* Washington, D.C.: U.S. General Accounting Office, Report 12/19/94, GAO/HEHS-95-28.

U.S. General Accounting Office. (1994). *Families on welfare: Teenage mothers least likely to become self-sufficient.* Washington, D.C.: U.S. General Accounting Office, Report 5/31/94, GAO/HEHS-94-115.

Wilson, W. J. (1991). Studying inner-city social dislocations: The challenge of public agenda research. *American Sociological Review* 56(11): 1–14.

6. Early Childhood Programs and Success in School

Achenbach, T. M., & Edelbrock, C. S. (1983). *Manual for the child behavior checklist and revised behavior profile.* Burlington: University of Vermont, Department of Psychiatry.

Bates, J. E. (1987). Temperament in infancy. In J. D. Osofsky (Ed.), *Handbook of infant development,* 2nd ed. New York: Wiley, pp. 1101–49.

Bayley, N. (1969). *Bayley scales of infant development.* New York: Psychology Corporation.

Baumrind, D. (1993). The average expectable environment is not good enough: A response to Scarr. *Child Development* 64:1299–1317.

Becker, W. C., & Gersten, R. (1982). A follow-up of a follow through: The later effects of the direct instruction method on children in fifth and sixth grades. *American Educational Research Journal* 19:75–92.

Bloom, B. S. (1964). *Stability and change in human characteristics.* New York: Wiley.

Bradley, R. H., Caldwell, B. M., & Rock, S. L. (1988). Home environment and school performance. A ten-year follow-up and examination of three models of environmental action. *Child Development* 59:852–67.

Bradley, R. H., Caldwell, B. M., Rock, S. L., Barnard, K. E., Gray, C., Hammond, M. A., Mitchell, S., Siegel, L., Ramey, C. T., Gottfried, A.

W., & Johnson, D. L. (1989). Home environment and cognitive development in the first three years of life: A collaborative study involving six sites and three ethnic groups in North America. *Developmental Psychology* 25(2):217–35.

Bronfenbrenner, U. (1979). *The ecology of human development: Experiments by nature and design.* Cambridge, Mass.: Harvard University Press.

Caldwell, B. (n.d.). *Inventory of home stimulation (ages 3–6).* Little Rock: University of Arkansas at Little Rock, Center for Child Development and Education.

Caldwell, B. M., & Bradley, R. H. (1979). *Home observation for measurement of the environment.* Little Rock: University of Arkansas at Little Rock, Center for Child Development and Education.

Campbell, F. A., & Ramey, C. T. (1994). Effects of early intervention on intellectual and academic achievement: A follow-up study of children from low-income families. *Child Development* 65:684–98.

Campbell, F. A., & Ramey, C. T. (1995). Cognitive and school outcomes for high-risk African American students at middle adolescence: Positive effects of early intervention. *Research Journal* 32(9):743–72.

Cicirelli, V. G. (1966). *The impact of Head Start: An evaluation of the effects of Head Start on children's cognitive and affective development,* vol. 1. Athens: Ohio University and Westinghouse Learning Corporation.

Duncan, G. J., Brooks-Gunn, J., & Klebanov, P. K. (1994). Economic deprivation and early-childhood development. *Child Development* 65:296–318.

Dunn, L. M., & Markwardt, F. C., Jr. (1970). *Peabody Individual Achievement Test.* Circle Pines, Minn.: American Guidance Service.

Emmerich, W. (1969). The parental role: A functional cognitive approach. *Monographs of the Society for Research in Child Development* 34. Whole Number 8.

Farran, D. C. (1990). Effects of intervention with disadvantaged and disabled children: A decade review. In S. J. Meisels & J. P. Shonkoff (Eds.), *Handbook of early-childhood intervention* (pp. 501–39). New York: Cambridge University Press

Goodnow, J. J. (1988). Parents' ideas, actions, and feelings: Models and methods from developmental and social psychology. *Child Development* 59:286–320.

Hale-Benson, J. (1989). The school learning environment and academic success. In G. L. Berry & J. K. Asamen (Eds.), *Black students: Psychosocial issues and academic achievement.* Newbury Park, Calif.: Corwin Press, pp. 83–98.

Heath, S. B. (1983). *Ways with words.* Cambridge: Cambridge University Press.

Hunt, J. McV. (1961). *Intelligence and experience.* New York: Ronald Press.

Johnson, D. L., & Walker, T. (1991). A follow-up evaluation of the Houston Parent-Child Development Center: School performance. *Journal of Early Intervention* 15:226–36.

Kelly, J., Marisset, C. E., Barnard, K. E., & Patterson, D. L. (1996). Risky beginnings: Low maternal intelligence as a risk factor for children's intellectual development. *Infants and Young Children* 8(3):11–23.

McKey, R. H., Condelli, L., Ganson, H., Barrett, B. J., McConkey, C., & Plantz, M. C. (1985). *The impact of Head Start on children, families, and communities.* DHHS Publication No. (OHDS) 90–31193. Washington, D.C.: U.S. Government Printing Office.

Miller, S. A. (1988). Parents' beliefs about children's cognitive development. *Child Development* 59:259–85.

Moos, R. H., & Moos, B. S. (1981). *Family Environment Scale Manual.* Palo Alto, Calif.: Consulting Psychologists Press.

Palmer, F. H. (1983). The Harlem Study: Effects of type of training, age of training, and social class. In Consortium for Longitudinal Studies (Eds.), *As the twig is bent . . . lasting affects of preschool programs.* Hillsdale, N.J.: Erlbaum, pp. 201–36.

Ramey, C. T. (1992). High-risk children and IQ: Altering intergenerational patterns. *Intelligence* 16:239–56.

Ramey, C. T., & Campbell, F. A. (1976). Parental attitudes and poverty. *Journal of Genetic Psychology* 128:3–6.

Ramey, C. T., & Campbell, F. A. (1984). Preventive education for high-risk children: Cognitive consequences of the Carolina Abecedarian Project. *Special Issue: American Journal of Mental Deficiency* 88(5):515–23.

Ramey, C. T., & Campbell, F. A. (1987). The Carolina Abecedarian Project: An educational experiment concerning human malleability. In J. Gallagher & C. Ramey (Eds.), The malleability of children. Baltimore, Md.: Paul H. Brookes.

Ramey, C. T., & Campbell, F. A. (1991). Poverty, early-childhood education, and academic competence: The Abecedarian experiment. In A. Huston (Ed.), *Children reared in poverty.* New York: Cambridge University Press, pp. 190–221.

Ramey, C. T., Collier, A. M., Sparling, J. J., Loda, F. A., Campbell, F. A., Ingram, D. L., & Finkelstein, N. W. (1976). The Carolina Abecedarian Project: A longitudinal and multidisciplinary approach to the prevention of developmental retardation. In T. Tjossem (Ed.), *Intervention strategies for high-risk infants and young children.* Baltimore, Md.: University Park Press, pp. 629–65.

Ramey, C. T., & Haskins, R. (1981). The causes and treatment of school failure: Insights from the Carolina Abecedarian Project. In M. Begab, H. Garber, & H. C. Haywood (Eds.), *Causes and prevention of retarded development in psychologically disadvantaged children.* Baltimore, Md.: University Park Press, pp. 89–112.

Ramey, C. T., & Ramey, S. L. (1990). Intensive educational intervention for children of poverty. *Intelligence* 14:1–9.

Ramey, C. T., & Smith, B. (1977). Assessing the intellectual consequences of early intervention with high-risk infants. *American Journal of Mental Deficiency* 81:318–24.

Ramey, C. T., Yeates, K. O., & MacPhee, D. (1984). Risk for retarded development among disadvantaged families: A systems theory approach to preventive intervention. In B. Keogh (Ed.), *Advances in special education*, vol. 4. Greenwich, Conn.: JAI Press, pp. 249–72.

Reynolds, A. J. (1994). Effects of a preschool plus follow-on intervention for children at risk. *Developmental Psychology* 30:787–804.

Rist, R. C. (1970). Student social class and teacher expectations: The self-fulfilling prophecy in ghetto education. *Harvard Educational Review* 40(3):411–51.

Scarr, S. (1992). Developmental theories for the 1990s: Development and individual differences. *Child Development* 63:1–19.

Schaefer, E. S., & Bell, R. Q. (1958). Development of a parental attitude research instrument. *Child Development* 29:339–61.

Schaefer, E. S., & Campbell, F. A. (1996). Teachers' ratings of verbal intelligence as predictors of academic performance. Manuscript in preparation.

Schaefer, E. S., Edgerton, M. D., & Aaronson, M. (1977). Classroom behavior inventory. Unpublished. Available from E. S. Schaefer, Department of Maternal and Child Health, University of North Carolina at Chapel Hill, Chapel Hill, NC 27599.

Sietz, V., Apfel, N. H., Rosenbaum, L. K., & Zigler, E. (1983). Long-term effects of projects Head Start and Follow-Through: The New Haven Project. In Consortium for Longitudinal Studies (Eds.), *As the twig is bent . . . lasting effects of preschool programs*. Hillsdale, N.J.: Erlbaum, pp. 299–332.

Sparling, J. J. (n.d.). *Early intervention: Experiences in implementing the Partners and Learningames Curricula*. Photocopies available from the Frank Porter Graham Child Development Center, University of North Carolina at Chapel Hill, CB#8180, Chapel Hill, NC 27599-8180.

Sparling, J. J., & Lewis, I. (1978). Helping your baby learn faster. *Parents* 70–71 (September):108.

Sparling, J. J., & Lewis, I. (1979). *Learningames for the first three years: A guide to parent-child play*. New York: Walker.

Sparling, J. J., & Lewis, I. (1984). *Learningames for threes and fours: A guide to adult and child play*. New York: Walker.

Terman, L. M., & Merrill, M. A. (1972). *Stanford-Binet Intelligence Scale: Manual for the third revision, Form L-M*. Boston: Houghton-Mifflin.

Walker, H. M. (1983). *Walker Problem Behavior Identification Checklist.* Los Angeles: Western Psychological Services.

Wechsler, D. (1967). *Wechsler Preschool and Primary Scale of Intelligence.* New York: Psychological Corporation.

Wechsler, D. (1974). *Wechsler Intelligence Scale for Children—Revised.* New York: Psychological Corporation.

Woodcock, R. W., & Johnson, M. B. (1977). *Woodcock-Johnson Psychoeducational Battery, Part 2: Tests of Academic Achievement.* Boston: Teaching Resources.

7. How Preschool Education Influences Long-Term Cognitive Development and School Success

Allington, R. L., & Walmsley, S. A. (1995). *No quick fix: Rethinking literacy in America's Elementary Schools.* New York: Teachers College Press.

Barnes, H. V. (1989). Gender-related long-term outcome differences in the Perry Preschool Study. Unpublished master's thesis, University of Michigan, Ann Arbor.

Barnett, W. S. (1993). Benefit-cost analysis of preschool education: Findings from a twenty-five-year follow-up. *American Journal of Orthopsychiatry* 63(4):500–8.

Barnett, W. S. (1995). Long-term effects of early-childhood programs on cognitive and school outcomes. *The Future of Children* 5(3):25–50.

Barnett, W. S. (1996). Economics of school reform: Three promising models. In H. Ladd (Ed.), *Holding schools accountable.* Washington, D.C.: Brookings Institution, pp. 299–326.

Bronfenbrenner, U. (1989). Ecological systems theory. In R. Vasta (Ed.), *Annals of child development,* vol. 6. Greenwich, Conn.: JAI Press, pp. 187–251.

Brown, J., Collins, A., & Duguid, P. (1989). Situated cognition and the culture of learning. *Educational Researcher* 18:32–42.

Campbell, F. A. (1994). Unpublished analyses of Abecedarian data on IQ and achievement by group and gender. Chapel Hill: University of North Carolina.

De Corte, E. (1995). Fostering cognitive growth: A perspective from research on mathematics learning and instruction. *Educational Psychologist* 30(1):37–46.

Gramlich, E. (1986). Evaluation of education projects: The case of the Perry Preschool Program. *Economics of Education Review* 5:17–24.

Gray, S. W., Ramsey, B. K., & Klaus, R. A (1982). *From three to twenty: The early training project.* Baltimore, Md.: University Park Press.

Haskins, R. (1989). Beyond metaphor: The efficacy of early-childhood education. *American Psychologist* 44(2):274–82.

Herrnstein, R. J., & Murray, C. (1994). *The bell curve: Intelligence and class structure in American life*. New York: Free Press.

Lally, J. R., Mangione, P. L., & Honig, A. S. (1988). The Syracuse University Family Development Research Program: Long-range impact of an early intervention with low-income children and their families. In D. R. Powell (Ed.), *Parent education as early-childhood intervention: Emerging directions in theory, research and practice*. Norwood, N.J.: Ablex, pp. 79–104.

Lazar, I., Darlington, R., Murray, H., Royce, J., & Snipper, A. (1982). Lasting effects of early education: a report from the consortium for longitudinal studies. *Monographs of the Society for Research in Child Development* 47(2–3). Serial No. 195.

Locurto, C. (1991). Beyond IQ in preschool programs? *Intelligence* 15:295–312.

McKey, R. H., Condelli, L., Ganson, H. Barrett, B. J., McConkey, C., & Plantz, M. C. (1985). *The impact of Head Start on children, families, and communities*. Final report of the Head Start Evaluation Synthesis and Utilization Project. Washington, D.C.: CSR.

Natriello, G., McDill, E. L., & Pallas, A. M. (1990). *Schooling disadvantaged children: Racing against catastrophe*. New York: Teachers College Press.

Piaget, J. (1952). *The origins of intelligence in children*. New York: International Universities Press.

Resnick, L. B. (1987). Learning in school and out. *Educational Researcher* 16:13–20.

Reynolds, A. J., Mavrogenes, N. A., Bezruczko, N., & Hagemann, M. (1996). Cognitive and family-support mediators of preschool effectiveness: A confirmatory analysis. *Child Development* 67(3):1119–40.

Ross, S. M., Smith, L. J., Casey, J. & Slavin, R. E. (1995). Increasing the academic success of disadvantaged children: An examination of alternative early-intervention programs. *American Educational Research Journal* 32(4):773–800.

Schweinhart, L. J., Barnes, H. V., Weikart, D. P., Barnett, W. S., & Epstein, A. S. (1993). *Significant benefits: The High Scope/Perry Preschool Study through age twenty-seven*. Ypsilanti, Mich.: High/Scope Educational Research Foundation.

Schweinhart, L. J., & Weikart, D. P. (1980). *Young children grow up: The effects of the Perry Preschool Program on youths through age fifteen*. Ypsilanti, Mich.: High/Scope Press.

Seitz, V., Rosenbaum, L. K., & Apfel, N. H. (1985). Effects of family support intervention: A ten-year follow-up. *Child Development* 56:376–91.

Terman, L. M., & Merrill, M. A. (1960). *Stanford-Binet Intelligence Scale Form L-M: Manual for the third revision*. Boston: Houghton-Mifflin.

Tiegs, E. W., & Clark, W. W. (1963). *Manual: California Achievement Test, complete battery.* Monterey Park: California Test Bureau, McGraw Hill.

Vygotsky, L. S. (1978). *Mind in society: The development of higher psychological processes.* Cambridge, Mass.: Harvard University Press.

Wechsler, D. (1974). *Manual for the Wechsler Intelligence Scale for Children (revised).* New York: Psychological Corporation.

Weikart, D. P., Bond, J. T., & McNeil, J. T. 1978. *The Ypsilanti Perry Preschool Project: Preschool years and longitudinal results through fourth grade.* Ypsilanti, Mich.: High/Scope Press

Weinert, F. E., & Helmke, A. (1995). Interclassroom differences in instructional quality and interindividual differences in cognitive development. *Educational Psychologist* 30(1):15–20.

Woodhead, M. (1988). When psychology informs public policy: The case of early-childhood intervention. *American Pyschologist* 43(6):443–54.

Zigler, E., & Freedman, J. (1987). Early experience, malleability, and Head Start. In J. J. Gallagher & C. T. Ramey (Eds.), *The malleability of children.* Baltimore, Md.: Brookes, pp. 85–96.

8. Economic and Social Disadvantages of Young Children

Blankenhorn, D. (1995). *Fatherless America: Confronting our most urgent social problem.* New York: Basic Books.

Duncan, G., Brooks-Gunn, J. (1997). *Consequences of growing up poor.* New York: Russell Sage Foundation.

Conger, R. D., & Elder, G. H., Jr. (1994). *Families in troubled times: Adapting to change in rural America.* Hawthorne, N.Y.: Aldine de Gruyter.

Conger, R. D., Elder, G. H., Lorenz, F. O., Conger, K. J., Simons, R. L. Whitbeck, L. B., Huck, S., & Melby, J. N. (1990). Linking economic hardship and marital quality and instability. *Journal of Marriage and the Family* 52:643–56.

Elder, G. H. (1974). *Children of the Great Depression: Social change in life experience.* Chicago: University of Chicago Press.

Elder, G. H., Conger, R. D., Foster, E. M., & Ardelt, M. (1992). Families under economic pressure. *Journal of Family Issues* 13:5–37.

Harrison, R. J., & Bennett, C. E. (1995) Racial and Ethnic Diversity. In R. Farley (Ed.), *State of the union: America in the 1990s, Volume Two: Social trends.* New York: Russell Sage Foundation, pp. 141–210.

Hernandez, D. J. (1993a). *America's children: Resources from family, government, and the economy.* New York: Russell Sage Foundation.

Hernandez, D. J. (1993b). *We the American children.* U.S. Bureau of the Census, Series WE-10, Washington, D.C.: U.S. Government Printing Office.

Hernandez, D. J. (1994). Children's changing access to resources: A historical perspective. *Social Policy Report, Society for Research in Child Development* 7(1):1–23.

Hernandez, D. J. (1995). Changing demographics: Past and future demands for early-childhood program. *The Future of Children* 5(3):145–60.

Hernandez, D. J. (1996). The family environment of children. In *Trends in the well being of America's children and youth: 1996*. Washington, D.C.: Office of the Assistant Secretary for Planning and Evaluation, U.S. Department of Health and Human Service, pp. 231–342.

Hernandez, D. J. (1997). Child development and the social demography of childhood. *Child Development* 68(1):149–69.

Hobbs, F., & Lippman, L. (1990). Children's well being: An international comparison. *International Population Reports*, Series P-95, No. 80. Washington, D.C.: U.S. Government Printing Office.

Hofferth, S. L., Brayfield, A., Deich, S., & Holcomb, P. (1991). *National child-care survey, 1990*. Urban Institute Report 91-5, Washington, D.C.: Urban Institute Press.

Jensen, A. M. (1994). The feminization of childhood. In J. Qvortrup, M. Bardy, G. Sgritta, & H. Wintersberger (Eds.), *Childhood matters: Social theory, practice and politics*. Aldershot, England: Avebury, pp. 59–75.

Liker, J. K, & Elder, G. H. (1983). Economic hardship and marital relations in the 1930s. *American Sociological Review* 48:343–59.

McLanahan, S., & Sandefur, G. (1994). *Growing up with a single parent: What hurts, what helps.* Cambridge, Mass.: Harvard.

O'Connell, M., & Bachu, A. (1990). *Who's minding the kids? Child-care arrangements: Winter 1984–1985*. Current Population Reports, Series P-70, No. 9. Washington, D.C.: U.S. Government Printing Office.

Oppenheimer V. K. (1979). *The female labor force in the United States.* Population monograph Series, no. 5, Institute of International Studies. Berkeley: University of California Press.

Oppenheimer V. K. (1982). *Work and the family*. New York: Acdemic Press.

Phillips, D. A. (Eds.). (1995). *Child care for low-income families*. Washington, D.C.: National Academy Press.

Presser, H. B. (1989). Can we make time for children? The economic, work schedules, and child care. *Demography* 26: 523–43.

Presser, H. B., & Baldwin, W. (1980) Child care as a constraint on employment: Prevalence, correlates, and bearing on the work and fertility nexus. *American Journal of Sociology* 85:5 (March):1202–13.

Qvortrup, J. (1987). Introduction. In J. Qvortrup (Ed.), The sociology of childhood. Special issue of *International Journal of Sociology* 17(3):3–37.

Qvortrup, J. (1994). Childhood matters: An introduction. In J. Qvortrup, M. Bardy, G. Sgritta, & H. Wintersberger (Eds.), *Childhood matters:*

Social Theory, Practice and Politics Aldershot, England: Avebury, pp. 10–32.

Smeeding, T. M., & Torrey, B. B. (1996). Revisiting poor children in rich countries. Unpublished paper.

Sorrentino, C. (1990). The changing family in international perspective. *Monthly Labor Review* (March):41–58.

Sorensen, E. (1995) *Noncustodial fathers: Can they afford to pay more child support?* Washington, D.C.: Urban Institute.

Wilson, W. J. (1987). *The truly disadvantaged: The inner city, the underclass, and public policy.* Chicago: University of Chicago Press.

9. Equity-Efficiency Tradeoffs and Government Policy in the United States, the Netherlands, and Sweden

Altonji, J. G., Hayashi, F., & Kotlikoff, L. J. (1992). Is the extended family altruistically linked? Direst tests using micro data. *American Economic Review* 82 (5):1177–98.

Baker, P. C., Keck, C. K., Mott, F. L., & Quinlan, S. V. (1993). *NLSY Child Handbook* (revised edition). Columbus: Ohio State University, Center for Human Resources.

Barro, R. J., & Lee, J. W. (1993). *International comparisons of educational attainment.* Cambridge, Mass.: National Bureau of Economic Research.

Barnett, W. S. (1993). New wine in old bottles: Increasing the coherence of early-childhood care and education policy. *Early Childhood Research Quarterly* 8:519–58.

Becker, G. S. (1981). *A treatise on the family.* Cambridge, Mass.: Harvard University Press.

Blau, D. M. (1992). The child-care labor market. *Journal of Human Resources* 27(1):9–40.

Borg, W. R. (1980). Time and school learning. In C. Denhan & A. Lieberman (Eds.), *Time to Learn.* Washington D.C.: U.S. Department of Education, National Institute of Education.

Bound, J., & Johnson, G. E. (1992). Changes in the structure of wages in the 1980s: An evaluation of alternative explanations. *American Economic Review* 82 (3):371–92.

Brown, B. W., & Saks, D. H. (1975). The production and distribution of cognitive skills within schools. *Journal of Political Economy* 83(June):571–93.

Cigno, A. (1991). *Economics of the family.* Oxford: Clarendon.

Droogleever Fortuijn, J. (1993). *Een druk bestaan: Tijdsbesteding en ruimtegebrek van tweeverdieners met kinderen* (A busy life: Time and space use of two earner families with children). Dissertation, Sociaal Wetenschappelijke Studies, Amsterdam.

Eaton, D., & Kortrum, S. (1991). Engines of growth: Domestic and foreign sources of innovation. Paper presented at the Center for Japan-U.S. Business and Economic Studies, Stern School of Business, New York University.

Esping-Andersen, G. (1990). *The three worlds of welfare capitalism*. Princeton, N.J.: Princeton University Press.

Flood, L., & Klevmarken, A. (1992). Market work, household work and leisure. An analysis of time-use in Sweden. Memorandum no. 172, School of Economics and Legal Science, Gothenburg University.

Flood, L., & Gråsjö, U. (1995). Changes in time spent at work and leisure: The Swedish experience, 1984–1983. Paper at the Fifteenth Arne Ryde Symposium, Runstedgaard, Denmark.

Getis, V. L., & Vinovskis, M. A. (1992). History of child care in the United States before 1950. In Lamb, Sternberg, Hwang, and Broberg (Eds.), *Child care in context, cross-cultural perspectives*. Hillsdale, N.J.: Erlbaum.

Goldin, C., & Margo, R. A. (1992). The great compression: The wage structure in the United States at midcentury. *Quarterly Journal of Economics* (February):1–34.

Griliches, Z. (1979). Sibling models and data in economics: Beginnings of a survey. *Journal of Political Economy* 87(5, part 2):S-37–S-64.

Groot, W., & van den Brink, H. M. (1992). Labor supply, child care, and consumption. Research manuscript. Department of Economics, University of Amsterdam.

Gustafsson, S. (1990). The labor-force participation and earnings of lone parents: A Swedish case study with comparisons to Germany. In *Lone-parent families: The economic challenge*. Paris: OECD.

Gustafsson, S. (1994). Child care and types of welfare states. In D. Sainsbury (Ed.), *Gendering welfare states*. London: Sage.

Gustafsson, S., & Stafford, F. (1992). Child care subsidies and labor supply in Sweden. *Journal of Human Resources* 27(1):204–30.

Gustafsson, S., & Stafford, F. (1994). In R. Blank (Ed.), *Social protection vesus economic flexibility: Is there a trade-off?* Chicago: National Bureau of Economic Research and University of Chicago Press.

Gustafsson, B., & Klevmarken, A. N. (1993). Taxes and transfers in Sweden: Incentive effects on labour supply. In *Welfare and work incentives*. New York: Oxford University Press.

Hermanns, J., de Boer, M. A., & Kruidenier-Bron, O. (1993). Early intervention for children with developmental disabilities in the Netherlands. Mimeo. Maastricht.

Hermanns J., & Hol, A. (1992). Jeugdhulpverlening: van opvoedingsvervangend naar opvoedingsondersteunend. *Tijdschrift voor Jeugdhulpverlening en Jeugdwerk* 4(3):4–8.

Hill, R. C., & Stafford, F. P. (1985). Parental care of children: Time-diary estimates of quantity, predictability and variety. In F. T. Juster & F. P. Stafford (Eds.), *Time, goods and well-being*. Ann Arbor: University of Michigan, Institute for Social Research.

Hill, M. S., & Juster, F. T. (1985). Constraints and complementarities in time use. In F. T. Juster & F. P. Stafford (Eds.), *Time, goods and well-being*. Ann Arbor: University of Michigan, Institute for Social Research, pp. 439–70.

Hill, M. S., & Duncan, G. J. (1987). Parental family income and the socioeconomic attainment of childeren. *Social Science Research* 16(March):39–73.

Hirdman, Y. (1989). *Att lägga livet till rätta—studier i svensk folkhemspolitik*. Stockholm: Carlssons.

Hoem, B. (1994). Resultat av nagraintentitets regressioner for tredje barnets fodelse. University of Stockholm, Demography Unit.

Hoem, J. M. (1993). Public policy as the fuel of fertility: Effects of a policy reform on the pace of childrearing in Sweden in the 1980s. *Acta Sociologica* 36:19–31.

Hofferth, S., Brayfield, A., Deich, S., & Holcomb, P. (1991). National child-care survey, 1990. Urban Institute report 95. Washington, D.C.: Urban Institute Press.

Hofferth, S., & Wissoker, D. (1992). Price, quality and income in child-care choice. *Journal of Human Resources* 27(1):70–111.

Hofferth, S., & Stafford, F. P. (1995). A proposal to the National Science Foundation: The panel study of income dynamics, 1997–2001. Survey Research Center, University of Michigan, August.

Johnson, G. E., & Stafford, F. P. (1995). Occupational exclusion and the distribution of earnings. Paper presented at the fifteenth annual Arne Ryde Symposium, Rungstedgaard, Denmark, August.

Jones, et al. (1986). *Teenage fertility in industrialized countries*. Alan Guttmacher Institute. New Haven, Conn.: Yale University Press.

Juster, F. T., & Stafford, F. P. (1991). The allocation of time: Empirical findings, behavioral models, and problems of measurement. *Journal of Economic Literature* 29:471–522.

Knutsen, O. (1991). Offentlig barneomsorg i Norden. Õn komparativ studie av utviklingen i de nordiske land. INAS rapport 91:2, Oslo.

Knutsen, O. (1992). Utdanninger og personell i bareomsorgen. Õn komparativ studie av utviklingen i de nordiske land. INAS rapport 92:5, Oslo.

Lamb, M. E., Sternberg, K. J., & Ketterlinus, R. D. (1992). Child care in the United States: The modern era. In M. E. Lamb, K. J. Sternberg, C-P.

Hwang, & A. G. Broberg (Eds.), *Child care in context*. Hillsdale, N.J.: Erlbaum.

Leibowitz, A., Klerman, J. A., & Waite, L. J. (1992). Employment of new mothers and child-care choice. *Journal of Human Resources* 27(1):127.

Löfström, Å., & Gustafsson, S. (1991). Policy changes and women's wages in Sweden. In S. L. Willborn (Ed.), Stability and change in six industrialized countries. *International Review of Comparative Public Policy* 3.

Maassen van den Brink, H. (1994). *Female labor supply, child care and marital conflict*. Amsterdam: Amsterdam University Press.

Manser, M., & Brown, M. (1980). Marriage and household decision making: A bargaining analysis. *International Economic Review* 21(1, February):31–44.

Milgrom, P., & Roberts, J. (1992). *Economics, organization and management*. Englewood Cliffs, N.J.: Prentice-Hall.

Mincer, J., & Polachek, S. (1974). Family investment in human capital: The earnings of women. *Journal of Political Economy* 81(2):76–108.

Mott, F. L. (1993). Center for Human Resource Research, NLS Annotated Bibliography 1990–1993. Supplement. Columbus: Ohio State University.

Murphy, K., & Welch, F. (1993). Occupational change and the demand for skill: 1941–1990. *American Economic Review Papers and Proceedings* 83(2):122–26.

Myrdal, A., & Myrdal, G. (1934). *Kris i befolkningsfrågan*. Stockholm.

Natali, D. E. (1976). A methodological and developmental study of maternal time use and cognitive abilities in preschool and early elementary school children. Ph.D. dissertation, Department of Psychology, University of Michigan.

OECD. (1994). *Economic Growth* 56(December).

Olah, L. S. (1995). The impact of public policies on the second birth rates in Sweden. Dissertation research,. University of Stockholm, Demography Unit.

Olsen, R. J. (1994). Fertility and the size of the U.S. labor force. *Journal of Economic Literature* 32(1, March):6–100.

Ott, N. (1992). Intrafamily bargaining and household decisions. Berlin: Springer Verlag.

Pen, J., & Tinbergen, J. (1977). *Naar Een Rechtvaardiger Inkomens-Verdeling*. Amsterdam/Brussels: Elsevier.

Pott-Buter, H. A. (1995). *Veranderingen in de levensloop van vrouwen. Ontwikkeling van vrouwenarbeid in zes landen*. Amsterdam: Nationaal Vakbondsmuseum, Welboom.

Ribar, D. C. (1992). Child care and the labor supply of married women: Reduced form evidence. *Journal of Human Resources* 27(1):134–66.

Rijswijk-Clerkx, L. van (1981). *Moeders, kinderen en kinderopvang. Veranderingen in de kinderopvang in Nederland.* Nijmegen: Social-istische Uitgeverij.

Romer, P. M. (1990). Human capital and growth: Theory and evidence. *Carnegie-Rochester Series on Public Policy* 32(Spring):251–86.

Rosen, S. (1995). Public employment and the welfare state in Sweden: NBER/SNS Project. Reforming the Welfare State. Occasional paper no. 61.

Schultz, P. T. (1981). *Economics of population.* Reading, Mass.: Addison-Wesley.

Singer, E. (1990). Geeft de overheid thuis? *Jeugd en samenleving* 4(April):271–79.

Singer, E. (1992). Family policy and preschool programs in the Netherlands. In G. A. Woodhill, J. Bernhard, & L. Prochner (Eds.), *International handbook of early-childhood education.* New York and London: Garland.

Solon, G. (1992). Intergenerational income mobility in the United States. *American Economic Review* 82(3, June):393–408.

SOU. (1991). Handikapp välfärd rättvisa (Handicap, well being, justice), Swedish government report. Stockholm: Allmänna Förlaget, 46.

Stafford, F. P. (1987). Women's work, sibling competion, and children's school performance. *American Economic Review* (December):972–80.

Stafford, F. P. (1991). Early education of children by families and schools. Manuscript. Department of Economics, University of Michigan.

Stafford, F. P., & Robinson, M. (1990). Industrial growth and social institutions. In J. E. Jackson (Ed.), *Institutions in American Society.* Ann Arbor: University of Michigan Press.

Statistics Sweden. (1989). Barns levnadsvillkor. Living conditions report no. 62, Stockholm.

Stephan, P. E. (1996). The economics of science. *Journal of Economic Literature* 34(3, September):1199–1235.

Stevenson, H. W., Lee, S-Y., & Stigler, J. W. (1992). Mathematic acheivement of Chinese, Japanese and American Children. *Science* 23(1986):693–99.

Stuurman, S. (1993). *Verzuiling, kapitalisme en patriarchaat. Aspecten van de ontwikkeling van de moderne staat in Nederland.* Doctoral dissertation, Socialistiese Uitgeverij Nijmegen, Nijmegen.

Sundström, M. (1994). Do family leave benfits reduce the gender wage gap? Evidence on wage effects of usage of family leave benefits among female and male employees in the Swedish telephone company. Working paper. Demography Unit, Stockholm University.

Sundström, M., & Stafford, F. (1992). Parental leave and female labor-force participation and public policy in Sweden. *European Journal of Population* 8:199–215.

Therborn, G. (1989). Pillarization and popular movements. Two variants of welfare state capitalism: The Netherlands and Sweden. In F. Castles (Ed.), *The comparative history of public policy*. Cambridge: Polity Press.

Tijdens, K., & Lieon, S. (Eds.). (1993). *Kinderopvang in Nederland, Organisatie en financiering*. Utrecht: Jan van Arkel.

Tinbergen, J. (1975). *Income Distribution: Analysis and Policies*. Amsterdam: North-Holland.

Varian, H. (1990). Redistributive taxation as social insurance. *Journal of Public Economics* 14(1980):49-68.

Walker, J. R. (1995). The effect of public policies on recent Swedish fertility behavior. *Journal of Population Economics* 8, 3:223–51.

WRR. (1991). Een werkend perspectief: Arbeidsparticipatie in de jaren 90, Den Haag.

10. Culture Clash

Bailar, J. C., III. (1995). How statisticians can help the news media do a better job. *Chance* 8(1):24–29.

Byrk, A. S., Strenio, J. F., & Weisberg, H. I. (1980). A method for estimating treatment effects when individuals are growing. *Journal of Educational Statistics* 5:5–34.

Cook, T. D., & Campbell, D. T. (1979). *Quasi-experimentation: Design and analysis issues for field settings*. Chicago: Rand McNally.

De Lone, R. H. (1990). *Replication: A strategy to improve the delivery of education and job-training programs*. Philadelphia: Public/Private Ventures.

Foster, R., Mandolang, N., Ellzey, M., Weller, R., & Terrie, W. (1991). *Florida's cost-implementation study for Public Law 99-457, Part H, infants and toddlers: Prevalence utilization study: Summary of activities, findings and policy implications*. Tallahassee: Florida State University and Florida Department of Education.

Glass, G. V., McGaw, B., & Smith, M. L. (1981). *Meta-analysis in social research*. Beverly Hills, Calif.: Sage.

Hall, J., Stone, L., Walsh, M., Wager, D., Zervigon-Hakes, A., & Graham. M. (1993). Predicting the cost of early intervention. In D. M. Bryant and M. A. Graham (Eds.), *Implementing early intervention: From research to practice* (chapter 13). New York: Guilford Press, pp. 288–312.

Hall, J., Walsh, M., & Walby, K. (1991). *Florida's cost-implementation study for Public Law 99-457, Part H, infants and toddlers: Cost and funding for early intervention services to infants and toddlers in Florida*. Tallahassee: Florida State University, Florida Taxwatch, and Florida Department of Education.

King, F., Rohani, F., & Cappellini, C. (1993). *Third-party evaluation report : A four-year longitudinal study of the Florida prekindergarten early-intervention program*. Tallahassee: Florida State University and Florida Department of Education.

Lally, J. R., Mangione, P. L., & Honig, A. S. (1988). The Syracuse University family-development research program: Long-range impact of an early intervention with low-income children and their families. In D. R. Powell (Ed.), *Parent Education as Early Childhood Intervention: Emerging Directions in Theory, Research and Practice*. Norwood, N.J.: Ablex.

Lazar, I., Darlington, R., Murray, H., Royce, J., & Snipper, A. (1982). Lasting effects of early-childhood education: A report from the Consortium for Longitudinal Studies. *Monographs of the Society for Research in Child Development* (195).

Renz, L., & Lawrence, S. (1994). *Foundation giving: Yearbook of facts and figures on private, corporate, and community foundations*. New York: Foundation Center,

Schweinhart, L. J., & Weikart, D. P. (1982). Perry preschool effects nine years later: What do they mean? Paper presented at the NICHD conference on Prevention of Retarded Development in Psychosocially Disadvantaged Children, University of Wisconsin.

Stone, L., Graham, M., Duwa, S., Strousse, C., & Fanin, J. (1991). *Florida's cost implementation study for Public Law 99-457, Part H, infants and toddlers: Service delivery and design study: Recommendations for an early intervention service delivery system under P.L. 99-457, Part H*. Tallahassee: Florida State University and Florida Department of Education.

Tallmadge, G. K. (1997). *The joint dissemination review panel ideabook*. Washington D.C.: U.S. Department of Health, Education, and Welfare.

U.S. Department of Commerce. (1994). *Statistical abstract of the United States: 1994*. 114th ed. Washington, D.C.

Zervigon-Hakes, A. (1991). *Florida's cost-implementation study for Public Law 99-457, Part H, infants and toddlers: Executive summary*. Tallahassee: Florida State University and Florida Department of Education.

Zervigon-Hakes, A., Graham, M., & Hall, J. (1993). *Handbook of resources for forecasting early-intervention services and costs*. Tallahassee: Florida State University, Center for Prevention and Early Intervention Policy, Institute for Science and Public Affairs.

Zervigon-Hakes A., & Lochenbach, R. (1991). *Florida's children: Their future is in our hands. Preventing and minimizing disabilities: A focus on the first sixty months of life*. Tallahassee: Task Force for Prevention of Developmental Handicaps. (Rewrite of author's previous publication [1989] on the status of early intervention in Florida. The report incorporated the early-intervention study findings and other research studies.)

Zervigon-Hakes, A., Nabors, J., & Harris, D. (1991). *Give Florida's children a healthy start and a healthy tomorrow: Recommendations from Florida's prevention and early-intervention forums* (Executive Summary). Tallahassee: Florida State University, Center for Prevention and Early Intervention Policy, Institute for Science and Public Affairs.

Contributors

W. Steven Barnett is professor at the Rutgers University Graduate School of Education, where he specializes in the economics of education, evaluation of preschool programs, and research on the well-being and development of children and their families. He is well known for his economic research on the costs and outcomes of preschool programs, home visiting programs, and other innovative programs and interventions for young children and their families. Dr. Barnett's most recent research on the long-term economic returns to preschool education was published as *Lives in the Balance: Age-27 Benefit-cost Analysis of the High / Scope Perry Preschool Program*. His current research includes a longitudinal study of the cost, quality, and outcomes of early intervention for infants and toddlers with disabilities.

Sarane Spence Boocock is professor of sociology at Rutgers University, currently in the Graduate School of Education, formerly in the Department of Sociology. Before coming to Rutgers, she was a staff sociologist at the Russell Sage Foundation, and has also taught at Yale University, the University of Southern California, Johns Hopkins University, and the Hebrew University of Jerusalem, Israel. She is the author of *An Introduction to the Sociology of Learning, Simulation Games in Learning, Turning Points: Historical and Sociological Essays on the Family,* and *International Comparison of Childrearing: Children, Parents and Society*. Dr. Boocock is currently engaged in a study comparing childrearing values and practices in Japan, China, France, and the United States, and a study comparing the education of minority children in Japan and the United States.

J. LAWRENCE ABER is associate professor, Department of Psychology, Barnard College and Graduate Faculties, Columbia University, where he also serves as director, Barnard Center for Toddler Development, and director, National Center for Children in Poverty, Columbia University School of Public Health. He is widely published and has received numerous grants and fellowships for his research on toddlers and their parents, maltreated and disadvantaged preschool and school-aged children, and high-risk adolescents.

HELEN V. BARNES, a specialist in developmental and clinical psychology and education, is an associate in the Education and Child Development Department at Abt Associates, Inc. Dr. Barnes co-authored *The High/Scope Perry Preschool Study Through Age 27*, and she recently participated in the revision and validation of the Child Observation Record, an instrument for measuring children's progress in preschool settings.

JEANNE BROOKS-GUNN is Virginia and Leonard Marx professor of child development at Teachers College, Columbia University, where she also directs the Center for Children and Families and the Adolescent Study Program. Formerly, she was a senior research scientist at the Educational Testing Service and a visiting scholar at the Russell Sage Foundation. She is the author of eight books and more than 250 articles focusing upon family and community influences on child and adolescent development, sources of risk and resilience, and interventions aimed at ameliorating the developmental problems associated with childhood poverty.

FRANCES A. CAMPBELL, a clinical psychologist, has been associated with the Abecedarian Project since its beginning in 1972. She is a fellow at the Frank Porter Graham Child Development Center, University of North Carolina, where she is principal investigator for the Abecedarian Project, for which she is currently directing an age-21 follow-up of the study participants, and co-principal investigator for the evaluation of a Head Start Transition Demonstration study.

ELLEN FREDE, a developmental psychologist who specializes in early childhood care and education, is associate professor at the College of

New Jersey. She has taught in Head Start and other early childhood programs, and has trained teachers and other trainers in diverse settings throughout the United States and abroad. Dr. Frede currently is project co-director of the New Jersey Early Intervention System Study and is working with the World Bank to develop a system of quality preschool education in Indonesia.

SIV S. GUSTAFSSON is professor of economics at the University of Amsterdam. She has been a fellow or research associate at Columbia University and the National Opinion Research Center, University of Chicago, as well as at the Institute for Economic and Social Research and the Centre for Work Studies in Stockholm, Wissenschaftszentrum in Berlin, and the Centre for Economic Policy Research in London. Her recent research includes studies of the effects of child care subsidies, taxation, and other public policies on women's labor force participation and wages.

RONALD HELMS is professor, Department of Biostatistics, University of North Carolina, Chapel Hill. He has served on the board of directors of the American Statistical Association and the Society for Clinical Trials, and on the editorial boards of the *Journal of Statistical Computing and Simulation* and other scholarly journals. Dr. Helms has published more than 100 papers on research design, methodology, and statistical analysis, as well as research on pediatric pulmonology and a wide range of public health issues.

DONALD J. HERNANDEZ, formerly chief, Marriage and Family Statistics Branch, U.S. Bureau of the Census, currently serves as study director, Board on Children, Youth, and Families, National Academy of Sciences, and as senior subject matter expert with the Survey of Program Dynamics at the Bureau of the Census. He is the author of numerous publications on population policy and the impact of family planning programs, and on the implications of demographic trends in family formation on children's living arrangements and well-being.

MARY LARNER is a policy analyst and editor at the Center for the Future of Children, The David and Lucile Packard Foundation, where she develops and edits issues for the center's journal, *The Future of Children*, which summarizes knowledge relating to the well-being of children for policy makers. She was previously at the National Center for Children in Poverty, Columbia University, and the High/Scope Educational Research Foundation. Recent publications include *Linking Family Support and Early Childhood Programs* (1995), and *In the Neighborhood: Programs that Strengthen Family Day Care for Low-income Families* (1994).

JEAN I. LAYZER is a senior associate at Abt Associates, Inc. She is directing the National Evaluation of Family Support Programs for the U.S. Department of Health and Human Services, and is also currently involved in studies of the Head Start Family Services Centers and the Comprehensive Child Development Program. In recent years, she directed a national observational study of early childhood programs and an evaluation of Project Giant Step, an innovative program for four-year-olds and their families in New York City.

REBECCA A. MAYNARD is trustee professor of education, social policy and communication at the University of Pennsylvania, and senior fellow at Mathematica Policy Research, Inc., of which she was formerly a senior vice president. She has directed several evaluations of large-scale social experiments and has published on topics ranging from employment and training policy, to welfare policy, child care, and teenage pregnancy.

CRAIG T. RAMEY is director of the Civitan International Research Center and professor of psychology, pediatrics, public health science and sociology at the University of Alabama-Birmingham. Dr. Ramey has been a founder and principal investigator of some of the most important American intervention studies, including Project Abecedarian, Project CARE, and the Infant Health and Development Project.

ROBERT ST. PIERRE is a vice president at Abt Associates, Inc., where for the past 19 years he has been principal investigator for research, evaluation, and policy analysis projects in the areas of child development, compensatory education, curricular interventions, child nutrition, and school health education. He has published widely in evaluation and educational research journals and currently directs national evaluations of the Even Start Literacy Program.

LARRY J. SCHWEINHART chairs the research division at High/Scope Educational Foundation, where he has, since 1975, conducted research and written about High/Scope's Perry Preschool Project, Preschool Curriculum Comparison study, and other early childhood projects and studies. He has taught fourth and seventh grades, has taught early childhood courses at High/Scope, the University of Missouri at Columbia, and the University of Indiana at Bloomington, and serves as a consultant to policy makers throughout the United States.

JOSEPH J. SPARLING is a former elementary school teacher and principal who shifted careers when he decided that "very important things happen to children before they reach school." Since receiving his Ph.D. in child development and educational psychology, Dr. Sparling has worked intensively on the interventions for the Abecedarian Project, Project CARE, and the Infant Health and Development Program. He is the author of the curricula used in *Learningames for the First Three Years* and *Partners for Learning*.

FRANK P. STAFFORD is professor of economics and faculty associate, Survey Research Center, at the University of Michigan. He was project director and principal investigator for a study, based on a large-scale national probability sample, of household time allocation, which resulted in a book, *Time Goods and Well-Being* (co-edited with Tom Juster). Other recent publications include papers and reports on women's work, sibling relationships, and children's school performance.

JOHN W. YOUNG is associate professor of educational statistics and measurement in the Department of Educational Psychology, Rutgers Graduate School of Education. Before coming to Rutgers, he was a statistical consultant and researcher at the Educational Testing Service and at Stanford University, where he received his Ph.D. in 1989. A principle area of research is the validity of the Scholastic Aptitude Test (SAT) for different populations of examinees.

ANITA ZERVIGON-HAKES is associate professor for research at the University of South Florida, Lawton and Rhea Chiles Center for Healthy Mothers and Babies, and serves state government as interagency coordinator for maternal and child health. She founded and directed the Center for Prevention and Early Intervention Policy, a center dedicated to interdisciplinary research, training, and technical assistance on public policies that reduce adverse outcomes for young children and their families.

Author Index

Page numbers in *italics* refer to diagrams, figures, or tables.

321

Subject Index